The Lost Theatres
of
Dublin

By Philip B. Ryan

The Badger Press, Westbury, Wiltshire

1998

The Queen's Theatre, Pearse Street, Dublin. Assistant Manager Bill Bailey and Chief Usher Jack Cassells supervise the matinee line for "Dick Whittington and His Cat".

The Lost Theatres
of
Dublin

By Philip B. Ryan

The Badger Press, Westbury, Wiltshire

1998

THANKS FOR THE MEMORY

Dedicated to the memory of my father,
PHILIP RYAN
(1891–1962)
who was a devoted music hall and theatregoer during their great heydays of
his youth and who became my first enthusiastic mentor

By the same author:

George Formby — A Catalogue of his Work
Jimmy O'Dea — The Pride Of The Coombe (Poolbeg Press, 1990)
Noel Purcell — A Biography (Poolbeg Press, 1992)

Published in Westbury, Wiltshire by
The Badger Press

Copyright © 1998 Christine Ryan
Foreword © 1998 Philip Chevron
Afterword © 1998 Noel Sheridan
Cover design: ABA, Dublin

ISBN 0 9526076 1 1

Printed in Great Britain

Acknowledgements

The author wishes to thank the following important sources:

Majella Breen, Sound Archivist at RTÉ; Paddy Bailey, son of the Queen's Theatre Assistant Manager, who gave access to his father's Archives; Seamus de Burca; Mrs. Joan Cruise, widow of the late Jack Cruise; Val Fitzpatrick; The Gilbert Library, Pearse Street; Tony Kenny, Senior; George McFall, late Stage Manager at the Gaiety Theatre; John J. Finegan, retired theatre correspondent of the *Evening Herald*; Sean Mooney, the last survivor of the regular Theatre Royal company; The National Library; Mrs Thelma Nolan, widow of the late Mike Nolan; Noel Sheridan, son of the great Cecil Sheridan.

The author acknowledges the rights of the following in the reproduction of performers' dialogue:

Mrs Ruth Harris (Max Miller); Mrs Margaret Galletly (Billy Bennett); Mr James Casey (Jimmy James), and the literary executors of Max Wall; Lucan & McShane; Clapham & Dwyer; Naughton & Gold; Tom Payne and Vera Hilliard; Cecil Sheridan; Jack Cruise, Harry Bailey; and any others who may, inadvertently, have been overlooked.

The author's estate wishes to thank Mr Nicholas Charlesworth of The Badger Press, Westbury for his help in the editing and production of this book.

Contents

PHILIP B. RYAN 1927–1997

The author in 1948, aged 20

Foreword
A Note about the author, Philip B. Ryan (1927-1997)
By Philip Chevron

There is a photograph on my desk of a handsome young man. He is 20, although on the rear of this standard theatrical agency shot, where he has, in his immaculate handwriting, listed his experience as an actor and writer of sketches and revues, he has added three years to his age. Perhaps the fib carries within it the hope that the otherwise truthful resumé is less likely to be considered a work of fiction by a prospective casting director.

Already, with the Rocklin Players alone, he has done three O'Caseys (both Davoren and Grigson in *The Shadow Of A Gunman*, Jerry Devine in *Juno*, and Jack Clitheroe in *The Plough and the Stars*), Lennox Robinson's *Drama At Inish*, and three other plays, as well as "revues, one act plays, excerpts from Shakespeare etc". He also lists his first credit as a Producer – of the Yeats play *Cathleen Ní Houlihan* – and the fact that he has written comedy material for Cecil Sheridan at the Olympia Theatre.

I happen to know, from the young man's scrapbooks, that before his twenty-first birthday, the Theatre and Cinema Players (comprising behind-scenes staff of Dublin theatres like the Royal) will present the revue *It's The Business*, for which the young man will receive the credit "Devised, Written and Produced by.....", and that his next show, *See Dublin First*, will contain ambitious original material, making intriguing use of specially prerecorded gramophone records to create atmospheric and evocative scenas.

Before the year (1948) is out, he will be back in Pigott's recording studio in Dublin to lend his bass-baritone voice, richer and much older than its owner's chronological years, to Kern and Hammerstein's "Ol' Man River"; the "b" side of the record will contain a piano-medley of some of the young man's own compositions.

*The author, Philip B. Ryan,
as Jack Clitheroe in
"The Plough and The Stars", 1948*

I gaze at the photograph, not really sure what it is I'm expecting to find there. I suppose I'd like to have known the guy, but I was not born until a decade after the picture was taken; by then he was my father and, as is often the way of such things, he became, for many years, unknowable. Until, in fact, I also was twenty and taking my own first impatient adult steps into the Show Business, at which point we discovered in each other the deepest of kindred spirits and the most supportive and lifelong of friendships.

It was only the ache of hindsight which allowed me to see just how great a part he had already played in helping to form his son's own passions. When I was a young boy, he had no vocabulary with which to discuss the relative merits of Charlie George and Georgie Best, but he could, and did, trace a line between Boucicault and O'Casey, or from Bernard Shaw to Alan Jay Lerner. He could, and did, take me on unforgettable trips to Dublin's theatres.

He would tell, with some pride, the story of how I had thrown a massive tantrum and refused, aged three, to leave the Gaiety after my first Jimmy O'Dea pantomime. I was already a veteran of *Show Boat* the previous year. By the time I was nine, he considered me ripe for the Abbey's famous revival of Boucicault's *The Shaughraun*, starring Cyril Cusack, and we spent my eleventh birthday at the Dublin Grand Opera Society's *Rigoletto* in the Gaiety. These were rites of passage, almost like secular bar mitzvahs: his way of acknowledging that the "Sonny Boy" he once reduced to tears – of terror – with his full-blackface Al Jolson impersonation, was growing up.

It must have disappointed him a little in later years that I spent so much of my own career trying to reconcile theatre with rock music but, if it did, he never actually said so: he merely reserved his greater enthusiasm for my theatrical ventures, as when he and my mother spontaneously hopped onto the Dun Laoghaire boat-train to present themselves in the stalls of the West End's Ambassadors Theatre during my fleeting run in a show there.

Yet I never introduced him to a contemporary musician who wasn't utterly charmed by him, by his articulate wit and hearty appreciation of life's absurdities. Elvis Costello, Christy Moore, Shane MacGowan. . . . . he was just as much at ease with these guys as with a Ken Dodd or a Cecil Sheridan. Perhaps he saw them all as just old troupers, but as I witnessed each new encounter, my own admiration of him grew ever deeper. With his awkward grasp of conventional bonding skills, he may have been an unlikely father/hero, but that's what he assuredly was, nonetheless.

❦

Not long after the death of my father in May 1997, his boyhood friend Jack Byrne, a playwright whose earliest work, such as *The Man On Platform Two*, was directed by Dad when both men were in their early twenties, sent me an affectionate letter. Jack (these days better known as the Tony Award winning Hugh Leonard) wrote that Dad was "a remarkable man, the more so because he had no adolescence. . . . . He was boyish and an adult, both at once, with a chasm in the middle."

This is the young man I see in the photograph, a kid so eager to escape the low expectations life held for a working class Dubliner from Ballybough, that at the earliest opportunities, he found footholds in as many different aspects of the theatre as his talents allowed; and all this concurrent with the pursuit of the "respectable" trade demanded of him by his station in life. While his own grandmother had been an opera singer, it is a measure of how highly-rated that noble profession was within our family that, even today, there exists no record of her career.

Catering was considered a fitting vocation for my father and, while he proved incapable of being anything less than distinguished in it, rising swiftly through the management ranks of the Odeon (Ireland) Group in their cinemas, theatres, ballrooms and restaurants in Ireland, the profession became his prison for much of his life. There were respites, as when he became Irish tour manager for Harry Gold and his Pieces of Eight, but he was unmistakably drifting further away from his ambitions. At the same time, he began a lifelong enchantment with a beautiful Liberties' girl of Huguenot stock, Christine LaGrue. When marriage and children – myself and my sister Deborah – followed, Dad did what work was necessary to support his family obligations. Even then, it is possible

vi

that he may have found a way back into the theatre, as a writer, but the odds were perhaps stacked against him.

Critically, he had severe health problems for most of his adult life, beginning with a near-fatal bout of pneumonia, and while he dutifully and efficiently executed his tasks as catering manager for a Dublin hospital for many years, the job taxed his reserves of energy to the limit.

The great irony of my father's later life was that it was his bad health which finally liberated him, and almost certainly added several years to his life span. Forced to take early retirement when the hothouse atmosphere of the hospital kitchen threatened to exacerbate his newly-diagnosed emphysema, Brendan [although the name is not in his birth lines, he was known as Brendan to absolutely everyone except his doctors and nurses and, paradoxically, his readers, all of whom called him Philip] at last dedicated himself full-time to the book he had quite recently begun to write.

❧

For some years, Philip Brendan Ryan had been accumulating archive materials, press cuttings, theatre programmes, playbills, photographs, films and so on, relating to Irish variety theatre and music hall and, in particular, Dublin's great comic entertainers. His subsequent and well-founded reputation as a meticulous and thorough researcher and archivist has its roots in the painstakingly detailed notebooks he filled in as the material grew.

Now, liberated from concerns about the dietary needs of hundreds of hospital patients, he set to making use of this research work. It had become obvious to him that, while many scholarly books exist about Irish theatre, there were almost none available about the great popular performers who had made contributions of at least equal validity, whose work perhaps more accurately reflected a period of Irish social history than did that of many loftier artists. While Dad was careful not to do these entertainers a disfavour by making such immodest claims on their behalf, the context in which he placed their lives and their work tended to speak for itself. He rather felt that his books, if sought out at all, would be found by kindred spirits who already accorded the greatest respect to their subjects.

His first project was a biography of Dublin's own comic genius, the great Jimmy O'Dea. Despite his variable health, Dad conducted hours of personal interviews with family members and peers of the comedian, building their trust and gaining access to their private photo files and memorabilia. Everywhere he went, my mother went too, acting as assistant, photographer, secretary and nurse and, whenever necessary, diplomat; they were quite an act.

The O'Dea book was an Irish bestseller and Dad launched into a follow up on the comic and film character actor Noel Purcell. Even as his health weakened, he still showed up at his temperamental typewriter almost daily, hammering away sometimes to the point of exhaustion; a word-processor might have helped, but I think he felt he would be wasting valuable time acquiring the necessary new skills. There were frequent bouts in the hospital, but each time, he pulled through, in large part thanks to the unfinished work which required his attention back home in his study.

During his final illness, when even he had to accept that he was dying, he no longer had this life-prolonging motivation. "The Lost Theatres of Dublin" was with his publisher and he was awaiting early proofs. He died, on May 30, 1997, secure in the knowledge that he could rely on his son, to whom he had passed on a lifelong passion for live theatre, to take care of all the proofing and editing. One of his final acts was the dedication of the book to his own father, about whom he rarely spoke but whose own theatregoing habits must in turn have had a similarly profound effect on him.

As I was writing this Foreword, I had a letter from Professor Noel Sheridan; Dad had been delighted to receive from Noel the terrific and illuminating contribution on his own father Cecil Sheridan (who in many ways tops the bill in "The Lost Theatres of Dublin") which closes the book. "This is the fate of sons", Noel wrote, "it is only time that shows us how alike we sons are to fathers who, when we were younger, we thought incomprehensible in many ways".

⁘

This is the human engine which drives "The Lost Theatres of Dublin". The book is not so much about bricks and mortar (though certainly considerations of real estate play their part in designating theatres as "lost"), as the characters and personalities who help to define the preoccupations and engagements of an era, be it Peg Woffington dragging herself out of the Dublin slums to sparkle in the West End; Seán O'Casey's troubled relationship with the old Abbey; the homegrown comics who kept the Theatre Royal lighted during "the Emergency", as Dubliners understood the Second World War; or the righteous triumph of veteran performers who saved the Olympia Theatre from the developers.

With vigilance, we may conclude that the worst of the demolition fever has passed: one only has to walk down New York's 42nd Street today to see how so many old theatres can survive in even this most real estate-crazed of cities. There, restored to its former glory, stands the New Amsterdam, alongside imaginative landmarking of such treasures as the Lyric, the Apollo, the Republic and the Selwyn. At the time of writing, there have been ominous rumblings that the Liberty, where Irish-American George M. Cohan first gave the world "Give My Regards To Broadway", may lend its facade only to something called – the Gods of Comedy and Tragedy help us – a Virtual Reality arcade, but generally, there can be no better indication that our playhouses are becoming safe for future generations to enjoy an experience that can not be had from cinema, television or even Virtual Reality.

⁘

But this is a book about the lost theatres of Dublin, a city my father loved unconditionally and from which he never strayed for long. One final enduring image of him remains. Towards the end of his life, it became my custom, in some small measure of gratitude, to send him theatre tickets for birthdays and anniversaries. His very last outing was to Peter Ustinov's one-man show at the Gaiety. Afterwards, Dad took what would be his final walk along his cherished Grafton Street, encountering along the way the motor car taking Mr Ustinov away from the theatre. They had never met, but exchanged friendly waves nevertheless, perhaps recognising in each other some kindred impulse. I have this mental picture of Brendan, in the end, as a man at ease with himself, with his heroes and with his beloved native city.

P. Chevron. Nottingham, June 1998

Introduction

The fact that since the 17th century about 40 theatres in Dublin, large and small, commercial and experimental, have disappeared is a matter of no concern to its citizens. Nor should it be. It is not a local phenomenon as all over Britain and Ireland since the time of Shakespeare's Globe Theatre, theatres have recorded a high casualty rate; they have been built and demolished and rebuilt on the same sites, they have been built and demolished and re-sited a few yards from their original sites, and some have been demolished never to rise again. The ever changing names of some of these theatres would require a separate volume.

Seven important theatres have disappeared within living memory, but the original location of even the last to be demolished is unknown to most younger Dubliners. Why should they care, they never sat in them, never enjoyed an evening's entertainment in one and most certainly were never exposed to the magnetic personalities who filled their stages.

The first to go in this century was the Tivoli Variety Theatre (1252 seats) in 1928. Next to go was the nearly 4000-seater Theatre Royal (the third theatre on the same site in Hawkins St.). The owners, the Corporation and the Government, were accused of vandalism when it was demolished, but now it has faded from the public memory. The Queen's Theatre (1233 seats) was demolished in 1969. The Capitol Theatre (1900 seats) although it had operated as a cinema for years, closed its doors in 1972. The Torch Theatre had a short life of six years, ending in 1941. One other Dublin theatre of which few are aware was destroyed during the Easter Rising, 1916; this was the Coliseum which had opened only a year before in April, 1915, in Henry Street.

With hindsight, it is impossible to argue that any of these theatres might have been saved. If the public withdraws its support in significant numbers it cannot be expected that they will be preserved for their architectural or decorative value, assuming that they have any. Other commercial factors are considered, such as the value of the site for redevelopment against the prospect of strong, and eventually overwhelming, competition from new forms of entertainment. Before the closure of the Tivoli, the old style music hall was dead and replaced by variety or cinevariety which was itself threatened by radio, the silent movies and the talkies. In the fifties even the talkies were threatened by television and thousands of cinemas closed. All over the world beautiful old theatres and interesting cinemas in the art deco style were demolished.

It is pointless to bemoan the disappearance of these buildings, all of which were a part of Dublin in 'the rare old times'. What we really regret is the passing of our own youth, and we are aware that much of it was spent in those old buildings and we can pinpoint fleeting memories of it in a seat in the Royal or the Queen's, but it disappeared with them without warning, and now even the dust and rubble has been cleared away.

But these theatres musn't be forgotten. They must be celebrated, and for a little time awaken nostalgic memories for those who remember them. More importantly this may serve as a record for the curious theatregoer of the future.

Apart from their eventual demolition the most outstanding crises faced by the Dublin theatres was their isolation during the Second World War, when it was impossible for the usual visiting artists to visit this country. A handful of local artists developed the professional talents and drawing power to keep the theatres open. This feat was accomplished mainly by the comedians. But when a comedian dies he leaves nothing behind. A few brief clips on a video from a TV archive or even a film are only shadows of the man who offered himself, his personality and warmth in a live performance. Audiences didn't go the theatres expressly to hear the jokes, they went to experience the warmth, love, absurdity, honest vulgarity, vulnerability and rapport when these men gave themselves. Their material and techniques can be analysed, but their performances cannot be described, they had to be experienced.

-P.B.R. 1996

The First
Theatre Royal

Exterior of the Smock Alley Theatre (1662–1787)

Interior of Crow Street Theatre (1758–1819)

THE FIRST THEATRE ROYAL
(January 1821 – February 1880)

In Goldsmith's *She Stoops To Conquer*, Mr. Hardcastle remarks: "I love everything that is old, old friends, old times, old manners, old books, old wines" to which the older theatre lover would undoubtedly add, old performers and old theatres.

In the early 1900s there were in London, apart from the 'legitimate' West End theatres, over 60 beautifully designed Music Halls strategically placed in highly populated outlying areas. The ever changing names of some of these theatres would require a separate volume.

Seven important theatres have disappeared in Dublin within living memory, but the original location of even the last to be demolished is unknown to most younger Dubliners.

The first Dublin theatre, designed as such, was situated in Werburgh Street. Built in 1637 by John Ogilby it was known as the New Theatre, but it didn't survive for long as it was closed by the Puritans in 1641. Following the restoration of the monarchy, Mr Ogilby opened his second theatre in 1662. Known as the Smock Alley Theatre it won the distinction of becoming the Theatre Royal by special patent. It was built on the eventual site of the church of Saints Michael and John on Essex Quay. It was rebuilt in 1735, but it closed in 1787, and became a grain store prior to the building of the church in 1815. The theatre historian, Seamus de Burca wrote to the *Sunday Independent* in April, 1991:

> "I am saddened and shocked to notice that Dublin's SS. Michael and John's Church is to be sold. May I remind the reader that the church is built on the actual site of Smock Alley Theatre, possibly the first permanent theatre in Dublin. I loved the church where the crypt was built on the theatre pit and in the balcony the acoustics were so perfect I was reminded of a theatre".

At one period Smock Alley was controlled by Thomas Sheridan, father of Richard Brinsley Sheridan, and he presented David Garrick as Hamlet with the urchin from the Dublin slums, Peg Woffington as Ophelia, in August, 1742. So great was the demand for admission that the street outside was crowded, and it was said that every word from the stage could be clearly heard by the hushed audience outside. Smock Alley had very close associations with both the Theatre Royal, Drury Lane and Covent Garden as the stars from the London theatres appeared fairly regularly at the Dublin theatre. Thomas Sheridan himself, notwithstanding a coolness between himself and Garrick, appeared at Drury Lane with considerable success, and there is no doubt that he aroused Garrick's jealousy. Sometimes when Sheridan and Garrick appeared together they packed the theatre. Sheridan's son, Richard Brinsley, wrote his first three plays, *The Rivals*, *St. Patrick's Day* and *The Duenna* for Covent Garden, but when he became Patentee of Theatre Royal, Drury Lane, he wrote his greatest masterpiece for that theatre, *The School For Scandal*.

Theatregoing in those days was not always as sedate as the courtly manners of the time might suggest. Sir Jonah Barrington (1760-1834) in his *Personal Sketches* describes the high-jinks at Dublin theatres which were similar to the frequent outbursts at Drury Lane, Covent Garden and the unlicenced Haymarket Theatre. The theatres were then lighted with tallow candles, stuck into tin holders hanging from the centre of the stage, and in Dublin, two soldiers, with fixed bayonets always stood like statues on each side of the stage, close to the boxes, to keep the audience in order. This was in contrast to Drury Lane where a sergeant and 12 men patrolled the theatre where the audience sometimes participated as vigorously as the actors in the action of the drama. Barrington wrote that such exploits were by no means uncommon when the young gentlemen of the University forced themselves in, to revenge some insult to a member of their body: on which occasions, all the ladies, well-dressed men, and other peaceable people, decamped forthwith, and the young gentlemen proceeded to beat or turn out the residue of the audience, and to break everything that came within their reach.

In 1758 an actor called Spranger Barry, who was reputed to be one of the finest Othellos to appear at Drury Lane, opened, in partnership with Henry Woodward a fellow Lane actor, the Crow Street Theatre (off Dame Street) on the site of a concert hall that had opened in 1731. The aim of the partners was to build a stage as big as that of Drury Lane, and it was Dublin's Largest theatre until the first Theatre Royal was built in Hawkins Street. Crow Street cost £22,000 – a huge sum in those days, and the Royal Patent was transferred from Smock Alley to Crow Street which entitled it to be officially recognised as the Theatre Royal.

At one period, as often happens in theatres which open with high ideals, a change of policy dictated that pony races should be featured on a specially constructed oval shaped runway raised over the Pit as a counter attraction to Astley's Amphitheatre on the corner of Bride Street. The Crow Street Theatre closed in 1819 following a serious disturbance which practically wrecked the theatre. There can be no doubt as to the tragic outcome, but conflicting reasons for the mayhem have been recorded. Known as "The Crow Street Riots", an unacceptable political play was given as one reason, and in another version blame was apportioned to the theatre manager, 'Buck' Jones who had unwisely, apparently, cancelled the engagement of a Miss Byrne, who was a very popular performer.

The Royal Patent was transferred, apparently, to the Rotunda Concert Rooms which had opened in 1767 as part of the Rotunda Hospital. This must have facilitated those who rented the Rotunda facilities for gain as otherwise the law stated that "Any person performing in an unauthorised place is liable to a £300 fine, except in the Rotunda, *for the benefit of the hospital*" (Act of George III – 1786).

PEG WOFFINGTON AND DAVID GARRICK AT THE THEATRE ROYAL, SMOCK ALLEY.

Peg Woffington, a child of the Dublin streets, began her stage career in a most extraordinary way and she developed into a most striking personality and probably the greatest actress to emerge from the Irish theatre. She was born Margaret Woffington on October 18th, 1720.

(The following account is freely adapted from the works of W. Macqueen Pope, official historian of the Theatre Royal, Drury Lane, and 'The Life And Adventures of Peg Woffington' by J. Fitzgerald Molloy; (2 Volumes) published by Hurst and Blackett, London, 1884).

On an evening in October, 1727, an urchin of about seven years old tottered along Ormond Quay, Dublin supporting a heavy pitcher of water on her head. The night was dark and bleak and soon there was drenching rain soaking her thin frock and inadequate shawl. A coach or two rattled over the uneven road and a few passers by with heads bowed low and cloaks and coats drawn tightly round them as protection against the bitter wind and rain hastened to and fro ignoring the child in her scarcely covered limbs shivering in her wet rags and seeking temporary shelter in a doorway, weeping in her misery. Unaware that she had been followed for some distance by a lady who now sought the protection of the doorway, the stranger said, "You are cold, my child". The little girl raised her eyes in surprise to the stranger and replied simply, "Yes, ma'am". Even now in her damp rags the child looked beautiful. Her dark damp, unkempt hair curled naturally round a

Peg Woffington
Painting by John Lewis
(By courtesy of The National Gallery of Ireland)

well shaped head and about a wide low forehead; her eyes large and expressive seemed almost black under the shadow of her long lashes; her cheeks were pale and beautifully oval; her lips were red and her dimpled chin gave a piquant look which contradicted the gravity of her eyes.

"And what is your name, my leetle child?" asked the lady in a soft foreign accent. "Me name is Peg, ma'am" said the urchin, "Peg Woffington". Encouraged by the mysterious lady Peg told her story. She lived in George's Court with her mother who was a widow who took in washing and since this was washing day she had been helping her mother by carrying jugs of water all day. "This is the last one", she said with relief, "and I must be goin' now ma'am for me mother will be wonderin' what's keepin' me". "And I shall go with you" said the lady, "I am Madame Violante. You perhaps have heard my name?" "You are Madame 'Lante that dances on the rope in the lovely booth in Fownes Court?" said Peg in amazement. "The same" said the French woman, smiling, "Would you like to dance also on the rope?"

Peg could see herself balanced on a tight-rope and skipping upon a slack-wire above the heads of the applauding crowds and wear such beautiful dresses with spangles and a brilliant silver star on her forehead.

"Would you like to dance on the rope?"

"Oh! ma'am I would be delighted"

"Very well, I will teach you if you learn quickly and well, but first we must ask your mother and hear what she has to say. Now tell me about yourself as we walk" said Madame Violante.

Peg lifted the earthenware pitcher and placed it upon her shapely head. She told her new friend that she and her mother and her baby sister, Polly, were as poor as church mice, since the doctor killed her father a couple of years ago when he had the faver. An me mother, she continued, takes in washin' an' works hard all day, and at night she sells oranges outside the Theatre Royal [as the theatre in Aungier Street was then known – the right to use this name was later transferred to Smock Alley-Author] and sometimes I sell oranges too, and the young gentlemen in Trinity College behave dacent to me, and often give me a penny for nothing at all, only because I talk to them, and make them laugh, an' it's many a time I popped their clothes for them, comin' to the end of the month, y'know. Ah! they're real good hearted an' they like me well. This evidence seems to point to the fact that this seven year old was an experienced young street arab.

Peg directed Madame to a hovel in a dimly lit unsavoury court where her mother welcomed the stranger in the mistaken belief that this was an additional customer to the wash tub, but her daughter explained that this was Madame 'Lante, the lady that dances on the rope. Madame went on to explain that she had been struck by the beauty of Peg's face and by her natural grace. She offered to take her as an apprentice and teach her the art of a tightrope dancer. "It will be well for leetle Peg; she will earn good salaries in a short time and I will dress and support her in the meantime."

The low esteem in which theatre folk were held at that time was reflected in the answer from the penniless and careworn Mrs Woffington. "Well ma'am, none of my blood has ever been play actors, and for the matter of that, me mother's people never disgraced themselves by earning a penny piece, but lived upon their own 'states like the highest in the land, and 'twas often told that the head of the family was one of the rale kings of Ireland himself. But now with me good man taken from me with little warning, it's a miserable world we live in".

This family history may be taken at face value, but it could apply equally to a tribe of tinkers. The poverty stricken woman had no option but to consider her position and the offer of financial reward for her daughter; so it was agreed that Peg was to become one of Madame's pupils, and she learned to dance and skip about on the stage and eventually to sing songs – for all of which she was greatly admired by the frequenters of the booth who flung her showers of pennies which she duly gave to her mother.

But public taste is notoriously fickle and although Madame Violante's heart-stopping performances on the tight rope had never been seen in Dublin before, they became monotonous and by degrees the gay booth in Fownes Court, with its sconces of tallow lights, its fiddles and drums and its merry dances, became deserted. Now Madame Violante was an enterprising woman, and she became aware of a recent London production which had caused extraordinary excitement. This was *The Beggars' Opera* by the poet John Gay. It had been produced by John Rich, the manager of the Lincoln's Inn Field Theatre for an extraordinary sixty two consecutive nights, which it was claimed by the wits in the coffee shops – "made Rich gay and Gay rich".

Madame Violante formed a company of children and cast them in the parts of the opera which she presented in a new more commodious booth in George's Court. The principal role of Polly Peachum was given to Peg Woffington to the delight of the crowded booth on the first performance. Peg's old friends and admirers from Trinity College who, when this lovely girl with the blue black hair and the liquid eyes came forward, received her with an ovation that sent her nervousness to flight. Amongst those who most warmly congratulated Peg and her patroness was Mr. Charles Coffey, composer of a ballad opera, *The Beggar's Wedding* which had met with some success in London where it had been performed at Covent Garden, the little theatre in the Haymarket and Drury Lane. He offered to instruct Peg in the role of Nell in his ballad farce to the delight of Peg and her mistress, and when the piece was performed in Madame Violante's canvas covered booth Peg was looked upon as a prodigy destined for real fame in the future, and was sought after by the noble and polite circles of the town, and from frequent contact with such high society she, being very impressionable and clever, quickly learned their mode of speech and gracious manners just as she had rapidly learned singing from Coffey and French from Violante. For some time thereafter Peg acted small speaking parts, sang ballads and danced under Madame's management, but fate proved unkind to that lady and she was obliged to let her booth.

Peg's reputation as a clever and accomplished performer did not escape the attention of Elrington, then manager of the Theatre Royal (Aungier Street) where he engaged her to sing in operas, act in farces and dance with great charm between the acts. In February, 1737 she was given her first important role at the Royal purely by accident. The play was *Hamlet* and two days before the performance was announced the lady cast in the role of Ophelia fell ill. Despite Elrington's doubts about Peg's offer to play the role she persuaded him to give her an audition with the result that she was announced in the playbills to play the part of the tragic heroine.

Peg had long been a favourite with the Dublin public and on the evening of 17th February, 1737 the Aungier Street playhouse was packed from pit to gallery to witness her performance; and at length when Ophelia came forward she held her audience as by a spell, and it was felt that she had secured a triumph which gave promise of great achievements in the future. From this date she no longer danced between the acts or sang ballads in small parts. Her next important role was that of Phyllis in Sir Richard Steele's *Conscious Lovers*. For two seasons she played leading parts, the most outstanding of which was "the breeches part" (a girl dressed as a man, which must have had some bearing upon the evolution of the pantomime principal boy), of Sir Harry Wildair in Farquhar's comedy *The Constant Couple*. She played the well-bred rake of quality, who lightly trips across the stage, singing a blithe song with no trace of the woman in her performance. Her playing was truly nature and not art.

At this point in her career she fell in love with the son of a needy Irish peer named Taaffe. She loved him not wisely but too well, trusting him with the precious treasure of her honour and expected him to make her his lawful wife. At his request she left the stage at a time when a great career shone before her and left Dublin to accompany him to London. Peg and her lover arrived in London in early Summer and took up residence in York Street, Covent Garden. All went well with them for a few brief months in which they enjoyed the attractions, novelties and personalities of the capital. But slowly Taaffe grew increasingly cold in his ardour and disappeared for days and even weeks at a time. Finally, he announced that his affairs obliged him to return to Ireland for three weeks in connection with his property. He had gone scarcely a week when Peg learned that he had been unfaithful to her and had been wooing a young lady of quality and fortune named Miss Dallaway, and that they planned to marry when he returned to town.

It was natural that a woman of Peg's temperament should feel indignant, heartbroken, humiliated and all of the other pangs of rejectment in between, and the strongest of these to emerge were hatred and contempt. She was determined to have vengeance. She resolved to meet the lady and reveal to her that Taaffe was the lover and cohabited with

5

an Irish actress. She knew that Miss Dallaway frequented the fashionable Vauxhall Gardens with her friends, but that she herself would not be admitted unaccompanied as a single female. Remembering how successfully she had played the part of Sir Harry Wildair on the stage she now resolved to act the part of a young man of fashion in real life.

Attired in silken hose and satin breeches with broidered waistcoat and wide flapped coat, powdered, painted and bewigged she met her rival discreetly and informed her that Taaffe made love to her from purely mercenary motives while he was conducting an affair with an actress whom he had brought to town from Ireland. The letters she produced, some of recent date, bearing Taaffe's seal and addressed to Mrs. Peg Woffington, spoke of love and faithfulness for the actress. The horrified Miss Dallaway terminated her association with her deceitful lover, and Peg, a woman scorned, had her revenge in a fantastically unusual way.

Peg Woffington was not a woman to sit down idly and break her heart because of a lover's betrayal. John Rich, who had eight years previously built Covent Garden Theatre was a notorious eccentric and when Peg visited his home in Bloomsbury Square seeking an interview she was refused because she would not send in her name. After a subsequent nineteen visits she eventually told the servant to announce Miss Woffington, whereupon she was received immediately because the fame of her achievements had crossed the Channel, and in the event encouraged Rich to entertain her proposal of appearing at his theatre. Peg's first meeting with Rich never ceased to amuse her; entering his room she found the manager lounging on a sofa, a book in one hand, a china cup from which he occasionally sipped tea in the other, whilst around him were twenty seven cats engaged in the various occupations of staring fixedly at him, licking his tea cup, eating toast from his mouth, and walking and frisking round his shoulders and about his person.

He offered her a salary of nine pounds a week and a contract was entered into which stipulated that she should make her first appearance before the English public in the following November as Sylvia in George Farquhar's comedy *The Recruiting Officer* and when it was presented at Covent Garden on the evening of 6th November 1740, by command of His Royal Highness the Prince of Wales the part of Sylvia was by Mrs Peg Woffington (Being the first time of her performing on that stage). Whatever their marital state actresses at that time were billed as Mrs. or Madame – the title Miss had other connotations. During the course of the play, when the beautiful and charming Peg came on stage at one point in the apparel of a pretty young gentleman about town, with a red coat, a sword, a marital twist in his cravat, a hat and a fierce knot in his periwig with a cane hanging from his button, the effect was sensational. Her air was at once graceful and rakish, her delivery pert and pointed, and the witchery of her glances were pronounced inimitable. Her acting was the talk of the coffee houses and the play was repeated for three consecutive nights; a not inconsiderate compliment to the actress's powers when, in those days, a fresh play was as an unbreakable rule performed nightly.

Later in the season she appeared as Lady Sadlife in *The Double Gallant*. Subsequently, she played Aura in *The Country Lasses* and inevitably, on the 21st November, she appeared for the first time in London (apart from her appearance in Vauxhall Gardens) as Sir Harry Wildair in *The Constant Couple* by Farquhar. 'Sir Harry' was even more popular than her first success as Sylvia although both had that dash and brilliancy which suited the complexion of the times. "So infinitely did she surpass expectations" wrote Tate Wilkinson in his memoirs, "that the applause she received was beyond any at that time ever known" So crowded were the houses she drew that the play was repeated for twenty consecutive nights. She followed with other roles: Elvira in the *Spanish Fryar*; Violante in the *Double Falsehood*; Laetitia in Congreve's *Old Bachelor*; Amanda in Colley Cibber's *Loves Last Shift* and Phillis in Sir Richard Steele's *Conscious Lovers*.

She took great pains in all that concerned her profession; made-up with great care and judgement suitable to the part; committed her lines to memory (a practice that did not always obtain in her day) and strove to realise the author's intentions in the characters she assumed. She was a favourite with the public during her bright brief career. The poets wrote sonnets to her, and the print sellers sold her portraits, and as Conway wrote to Walpole "All the town is in love with her". In May, 1741 Peg had a disagreement with John Rich at Covent Garden, and four months later she was appearing as Sylvia at Drury Lane of which Fleetwood was then manager of the theatre which was described by a later Patentee, Alfred Bunn, as the greatest theatre in the Empire. Quite an achievement for Peggy, the washer-woman's daughter from Dublin.

The Irish were always well represented at Drury Lane, as actors and actresses, dramatists, managers and patentees, musical directors and even composers – William Balfe's *The Bohemian Girl* was first produced at Drury Lane on 27th November, 1843 – and very often these Irish artists in company with their fellow English performers took up engagements at Dublin's Theatre Royal, Smock Alley. When Peg first went to the Lane there was an Irishman called Delane in the company. The son of an Irish gentleman who had hoped that his son would be destined for the Church opted instead for the stage. He remembered Peg when as a student at Trinity College she sold oranges and watercress to the boys and entertained them with her wit. Now at Drury Lane he paid her particular attention.

During her first season a frequent visitor to the Green Room was a very sprightly, shortish but neatly made young man named David Garrick. Night after night young Garrick who was, at the insistence of his respectable family, a reluctant wine merchant in Covent Garden, was to be found amongst the crowds which flocked to see Peg, although he had in addition a great passion for the theatre in general. But Peg was an actress after his own heart and appealed to his critical sense. She neither reduced comedy to burlesque nor tragedy to rant and declamation, but who was at one with nature. This bright young man with ambitions for a stage career told Peg all that he thought of her as an actress, and much that he felt for her as a woman, This was a happy time for both of them as they sat in a corner of the Green Room in the evenings after the play, his hand touching hers, her eyes flashing on him in the full radiance of her love. Another admirer of Peg's at this time was Sir Charles Hanbury Williams who composed poems addressed to her, one of which, "Lovely Peggy" was greatly admired and published in an edition of his works in 1776. Garrick meantime, risking the wrath of his family, went secretly to Ipswich to test his talents with a strolling theatrical company. Back in London he obliged an actor friend by standing in for him in a Harlequinade at an unlicenced theatre in Goodman's Fields in the East End of London. The management of this flea pit cast him in the role of "Richard the Third" billing him as "A gentleman who never appeared on any stage". Garrick was a sensation in what was virtually the first demonstration of natural, realistic acting which was in complete contrast to the strutting, ranting style of his time. Even at its most subdued this style was no more than oratorical. Crowds flooded to see him in the unsavoury district in which he was appearing to the detriment of the box offices at Covent Garden and Drury Lane, the only two London theatres, incidentally, with official Royal Patents to present drama. Other managements resorted to various nefarious devices to overcome their illegitimacy. In April, 1742 Garrick made his first appearance at Drury Lane in a Benefit performance, and in the course of conversation with Fleetwood he contracted to play a season at the theatre in the coming Autumn.

Before the end of this most successful season his fame had spread so far that DuVal, the manager of the Smock Alley Theatre in Dublin, arranged for Garrick and Peg Woffington to play in that fair city for the three months June-August.

The announcement that Peg Woffington, the Dublin waif, who had thirteen years before danced in a canvas booth in George's Court was to appear at the Theatre Royal, Smock Alley, threw the proud citizens of Dublin into a fever of delight. This was heightened by the news that the new genius David Garrick would appear at the same time. They must have been comparable to the Olivier and Leigh of their time. Four days after their triumphal arrival, the season commenced when Peg appeared as Sir Harry Wildair. The audience remembered her beauty and stories of her wit and repartee were still recounted at Trinity College. Cheer upon cheer greeted her entrance in response to which, with tears in her eyes she bowed again and again.

Garrick was not playing that night, but he stood in the wings to witness her reception, and when she came off the stage he whispered, "Ah! Peggy you are the queen of all hearts". She looked sadly at the animated face before her and replied "Aye, queen of all hearts, yet not legal mistress of one". *The Dublin Mercury* of 6th July reported that "oats is very near being reaped, and if the weather continues favourable we will have some in our own market next Saturday, which is something extraordinary, oats being the latest grain". Despite this stifling heat Smock Alley was filled to capacity, and the result of this unusually warm weather, and the crowded houses at the theatre, in a less than hygienic age, was that a fever broke out in the city which affected many, and carried away numbers from the playhouse to the grave.

The combination of two such famous players playing in the same theatre, and on the same bills, made the town stage mad. There were occasional distressing scenes when women shrieked at Richard's death, sobbed aloud at poor Ophelia's madness, and went into hysterics over the sorrows of Lear. It was during this engagement that Garrick first attempted the part of Hamlet, which he had long and carefully studied. He gave his Dublin admirers of Shakespeare unbounded satisfaction; never had they witnessed such acting which riveted their attention. Nothing could be more graceful, more pathetic, more beautiful, than Woffington as Ophelia; her love and sorrow were inexpressively tender, and her madness filled the house with awe and brought tears to many eyes. This brief but remarkable season ended on 19th August, 1742, and the stars went back to London to prepare for their season in September at old Drury Lane.

The lines of carriages blocked up Drury Lane and the adjoining streets night after night and nothing could exceed the delight and applause when the two reigning favourites appeared in the one piece.

The two lovers set up house together at 6 Bow Street; another tenant was Garrick's friend, an important Irish actor called Charles Macklin. Macklin always insisted that no other Macklin existed because it was a name he had invented 'to get rid of that damned Irish name, McLoughlin. Peg and David agreed between them that they should alternately defray the monthly expenses. Garrick was extraordinarily mean, and it soon became a standing joke among their friends that a more hospitable board was always spread before them when it was Peg's turn to pay the bills. Unfortunately, their personal alliance did not last more than a couple of years (until about 1745). They really had nothing in common save that art in which they both held superior rank. Peg was impetuous and extravagant, whereas Garrick was cold, cautious and mean. Peg was convinced that Garrick would marry her, and her friend Arthur Murphy heard her tell on different occasions that Garrick went so far as to try the wedding ring on her finger whilst Bowden claimed that "it was supposed that Garrick had indeed married her". She loved him with all the strength of her passionate nature, but despite his entreaties and false promises she left the house leaving for him a parcel containing all the presents he had given her, and a written request that he might return those that she had given to him. This he did with the exception of a fine pair of silver shoe buckles which were never returned. Soon after her departure from Bow Street, Peg took up residence in Teddington and sent for her sister Polly, for whose education she was paying in a French convent. When in 1747 Garrick became joint Patentee with Lacy of Drury Lane the situation was objectionable to Peg. She did not want to work for Garrick, but she had an outstanding contract with Lacy which she honoured; immediately afterwards she returned to Covent Garden, but she left there too, feeling slighted by John Rich. She went over to Dublin where the new manager of Smock Alley, Thomas Sheridan engaged her for the season of 1751 at a salary of four hundred pounds. She resided in Capel Street in a house opposite the Gunning family. Peg opened her season on 5th October, as Lady Townley in *The Provoked Husband* and the crowded house gave her a rousing welcome. Night after night she appeared to densely crowded houses playing alternately as Andromache and Hermione in *The Distressed Mother*, Sylvia in *The Recruiting Officer*, Calista in *The Fair Penitent* and, of course, Sir Harry Wildair in *The Constant Couple* and never failed to meet with the most enthusiastic applause. Presently, she rehearsed for an appearance as Maria in Colley Cibber's *The Nonjuror* to be followed by a series of appearances with Thomas Sheridan in six plays by Shakespeare. Sheridan was a great actor, and it was even said that Garrick was wary of him, and to see Peg Woffington and Thomas Sheridan in Shakespearean plays was a treat which the stage loving people of Dublin could not resist, and places were quickly taken. The bills announced: "The manager of the Theatre Royal (Smock Alley) proposes to perform the six following plays of Shakespeare as soon as the boxes are engaged, viz. , "Richard"; "Hamlet"; "Macbeth"; "King John"; "The Merchant Of Venice" and "As You Like It". The house will be illuminated with wax lights". Woffington had been praised before, but now she was lauded, and was the pride and glory of the stage. In the following season, 1752, Sheridan engaged her at a salary of eight hundred pounds and on the night of 8th October, Peg appeared as Lady Betty Modish, followed a week later as Belvidera in *Venus Preserved*. Later on, according to the bills, she played in *Julius Caesar*, in *Ulysses*, writ by Mr Rowe, and in various Congreve comedies.

Who could have visualised her standing drenched to the skin in sheets of rain with an earthenware jug of water on her head?

Hitchcock testifies to her bearing in private life:

> "To her honour, be it ever remembered that, whilst in the zenith of her glory, courted and caressed by all ranks and degrees, it made no alteration in her behaviour; she remained the same gay, affable, obliging, good natured Woffington to everyone around her"

It is a mystery that her dreadful childhood did not appear to affect her adulthood to the slightest degree.

It was noted that during the season of 1756-57 her appearance was not so regular as in days of yore; now her health began to give way. This indisposition was not, however, regarded by her as in any way serious, but rather as the result of overwork which rest would no doubt quickly remedy. But this was the last season in which she was destined to play. On the night of the 17th May, 1757, she appeared as Rosalind, in a Benefit performance for two minor actors. The boxes were filled with beautiful women; the pit overflowing with its usual complement of coffee house critics, elegant dilletanti, and men about town. For the first four acts of the play all went well, though it was obvious to those backstage that Peg Woffington was unwell. During the fifth act, she complained of serious indisposition; her dark eyes wore a haggard look; her cheeks were blanched under the rouge. When, in the last scene she left the stage to change her dress, she spoke again of being unwell, but managed to go on to finish her part. Speaking the epilogue her voice faltered; she clasped her hands to her side, and cried out in a voice of pain and terror, "O God! O God!" tottered to the wings where she was caught to break her fall. She lived for almost three years after that terrible night, though the playhouses were now in the past. "When" she said "I can no longer bound on the boards with elastic step, and when the enthusiasm of the public begins to show symptoms of change, that night will be the last appearance of Margaret Woffington". She now kept her word, residing quietly at Teddington. During that three years many of Peg's old friends and fellow performers died or retired. When Peg lay dying (apparently from a tumour) attended by her sister whom she had rocked in the garret in George's Court, and whom she had married to a scion of the nobility she willed the sum of five thousand pounds and her valuable jewellery. To her mother she had long allowed thirty pounds a year, and she was remembered as a respectable old lady, in her short, black velvet cloak, with deep, rich fringe, a diamond ring, and a small agate snuff box, going the rounds of the Catholic churches and visiting her neighbours.

Peg died on 28th March, 1760. Her remains were laid in a vault beneath Teddington Church, in which a tablet records the following inscription:

> "Near this monument lies the body of Margaret Woffington, spinster, born Oct. 18th, 1720 who departed this life March 28th, 1760 aged 39 years".

Theatre Royal, Hawkins Street, 1821.

The First Theatre Royal (1821–1880)

The site in Hawkins Street (now Hawkins House) on which three theatres and a concert hall would be built was originally a meat market, and in 1796 the Royal Dublin Society built their headquarters there before moving to Leinster House in 1818 when the Mendicity was housed in their vacated premises.

In 1820, Henry Harris, London, purchased the site, and in January 1821 the first theatre there, designed by the English architect, Samuel Beasley, at a cost of £50,000, was opened to the public. The theatre which seated 2,000 was known first as the Albany New Theatre, but in August of the opening year King George IV, who had landed at Howth, attended a performance of Sheridan's *St. Patrick's Day* as a result of which the theatre received the Lord Chancellor's Patent, and with it the right to name the theatre the Theatre Royal. This was the first of three on the site so named.

The building was far from finished on the opening night, which was not an unusual circumstance, and although the auditorium could be said to be nearly completed, the staircases and lobbies presented such a dangerous appearance that many of the invited audience were alarmed for their safety. It could be said, in more senses than one, that there was an overflowing audience, for those seeking entry by the Pit doors found themselves practically up to their ankles in water. All the doors had not been fitted to the Pit entrance, which resulted in a freezing draught which swept through the Stalls. It seemed to be vital also that Mr. Harris should dispose of the piles of builder's rubble and rubbish that was scattered about the house, and over which the elegant ladies and their gentlemen gingerly made anxious progress.

The auditorium was designed in the shape of a Grecian lyre, complete with two tiers of boxes supported by fluted columns. The King's Arms were painted rather indifferently over the proscenium arch, and hovering over them were two cherubs holding between them a wreath of tatty appearance bearing the motto – "To hold, as 'twere, the mirror up to nature" which was held to be pretentious by contemporary critics, but it was really no worse than other examples in English theatres "All the World's A Stage" or "The Drama's laws the Drama's patrons give and we who live to please, must please to live". It is no reflection on Mr Harris to state that his immediate aim was to recover his big investment of £50,000. It was reported that he issued fifty debentures of £200, and also mortgaged it to a Mr. Bicknell.

The centre of the ceiling, which was divided into compartments, was ornamented by a large plaster harp, the real purpose of which was to conceal the ventilator, although it is not clear how this ventilator worked. The green stage curtain didn't rise until 9 o'clock on the first night when a Mr. Farren, a member of the resident stock company came forward to deliver the opening address. We rely, for this account, on one of the several little papers which were distributed daily at that time. It was the custom in the early 1800s for theatres to change their bills nightly. A production of Shakespeare might be followed on the next evening by opera, then a comedy, burlesque or melodrama on the following nights. There might even be a melange of several types of entertainment on the same bill, but details were seldom announced till the close of the previous night's performance which resulted, in Dublin, in a series of little theatrical daily papers giving a full and critical account of the previous evenings' performances, and details of productions currently on offer. These were delivered to the wealthier citizens at one penny per copy early each morning. *The Theatrical Observer* and *The Dramatic Argus* were just two of these valuable little publications.

According to the former, Mr Farren's opening address came from the pen of a Mr. George Coliman, from which the following is an extract:

> Hail, generous natives of green Erin's Isle,
> Welcome, kind patrons, to our new-rais'd pile,
> Three fleeting months have scarcely slipped away
> Since a mere waste this scene of action lay;
> Not long the block was laid, which all must own
> Damps eagerness – the slow foundation stone
> Ere expectation kept no more aloof,
> The architect was hope-crowned with the roof!
> Brisk went the work – exertion still increasing,
> Hods, trowels, hammers, chisels never ceasing;
> Labour was wing'd on expectations plan,
> And every labourer – an Irishman.

This piece of doggerel was received with contempt by at least one contemporary commentator, who questioned its originality, and claimed to have read something similar which had been delivered by the manager of a strolling company in England who had pitched his tent over a slaughter-house at Bury St. Edmunds.

The cast list of the opening production which was *The Comedy Of Errors* does not include the name of any player of distinction, and the critic in the *Theatrical Observer* wrote:

> "In the state in which it is now represented, the play is made the vehicle of some good music, adapted to Shakespeare's poetry, which has alone rendered its revival successful. Certainly, a worse play to exhibit the talents of the company, of which it ought to have been the policy of the Patentee to give a favourable impression, could not have been selected"

Commenting on the farce that followed, *Youth, Love and Folly*, translated from the French, the critic noted that....

> "Mrs. Humby sported her figure to great advantage in a pair of leather inexpressibles" !!!

On the second night the critic was no happier with a production of *Romeo and Juliet*:

> "A young lady (Miss Kelly) made a most successful debut at this theatre last night in the role of Juliet. She is about middle size, with rather an elegantly proportioned figure, and possessing a countenance of great sweetness and flexibility; perhaps it may be objected to by some, that there is in her face too much of roundness – too much of health, but we are not amongst those who consider a long chin and a high nose as absolute essentials for a 'tragedy actress.'"

But Mr. Warde did not please as Romeo, and Mr. William Farren, (who had delivered the opening address on the previous night) presented Mercutio not as the gay, gallant and high-spirited gentleman that the author intended, but on the contrary as a swaggering, face-making buffoon. It was a relief when the sword of Tybalt dismissed Mr. Farren.

Audiences were sparse at first as Dubliners seemed to retain an unconscious loyalty to the city's first Royal theatre at Smock Alley, and the later theatre at Crow Street. After a production of *The Beggars' Opera* it was noted that the house was well attended, but it was apparent that completion of the interior decoration was proceeding slowly. Apparently the space above the upper side boxes, which it had been thought was intended for the slips (side seats), were boarded up.

A patron in the Circle reported receipt of an invitation from another patron in the 'gods' to visit him in the upper regions, but he had no ambition to soar so high, particularly as the ascent was rendered very difficult by the want of light. The conduct of some of the denizens of the 'gods' gave rise to frequent complaints. *The Dramatic Argus* reported in 1824:

> "There is no matter in the whole course of our theatrical experience which has given us so much pain as the truly disgraceful conduct of a portion of our Dublin audience, and the still more shameful apathy of that part of it which should act as a corrective. Why, we ask, does our audience (we mean the better educated part of it) permit a nightly display of the grossest and most indecorous and often very ruffianly conduct? We were not a little surprised on perceiving by a morning paper of Saturday, that the person who threw an orange on Thursday evening at one of the female performers was discharged by the magistrate of College *without any punishment whatever*. Now, really this is most lamentable in the extreme".

Conduct, even in the exclusive boxes, did not escape attention. Criticism was expressed, in deference to the ladies who occasionally grace the theatre by their presence, and the custom of mixing whiskey punch in the lobby at the back of the boxes was deplored. If gentlemen could not enjoy a dramatic feast without washing it down with hot whiskies they were advised to repair, for that purpose, to a neighbourhood tavern kept by a veteran actor, Tom Lee. Henry Harris also had his critics and it was claimed that he had no interest in improving public taste by his insistence in presenting incomplete versions of operas, and transforming the works of Shakespeare into musical trifles by the mal-introduction of songs and glees, thus reducing the role of the theatre manager to a mere mercantile speculator. In fairness, it must be recorded that the managers were not the only offenders. Highly respected tragedians had been known to sing sea shanties and dance a hornpipe as a divertissement following one of the more harrowing scenes in a Shakespearean tragedy. In 1828 Mr. Luke Plunket, upon receiving an encore for his death scene in *Richard III* responded with a lively rendition of "Scots Wha Hae!"

When Charles Keen was playing *Richard III* his fearful grimaces in character, much to his amusement, almost paralysed some of the other actors with fright. On one occasion a new man was called upon to take the role of the sentinel who awoke Richard. When asked, Who is there? he had to say: "'Tis I my lord; the early village cock hath twice done salutation to the morn". But Keen was making such fearful grimaces, and scowling at him, that the poor fellow lost his head, and could only stammer, "'Tis I my lord; 'tis I my lord; the – village cock!" By this time there were amused titters all over the theatre, which were followed by roars of laughter when Keen growled "Then why the hell don't you crow?"

In about the year 1740 Thomas Sheridan had written a farce called *Captain O'Blunder* which presented the stage Irish Paddy in an unexpectedly favourable light and its central figure inspired Macklin to write his famous comedy *Love a la Mode*. But this was not sufficient to rid the stage completely of the stage Irishman, and he was slipped into many a production at the Theatre Royal. Playbills of the period record such forgotten blockbusters as: Dalby's *Leah the Forsaken* (1866); *Belphegor, the Mountebank* was offered in 1867 and in November 1869 a bumper bill included: A three-act comedy, *Home* followed by the farce, *That Blessed Baby*; another farce, *The Quiet Family* was followed by an extravaganza, *Lord Dundreary Married and Settled*. Shortly afterwards the "eminent tragedian" Mr T.C. King doubled in the roles of *The Corsican Brothers*. In 1871 the excitement continued with *The Prisoner Of Zenda* and *Rupert Of Hentzau*. These dramatic pieces were lightened by short farces such as *Cool As A Cucumber* and *Who's Who or All In A Fog*. There was a literary genre known as comediettas which included works like *A Cup Of Tea* and *Nine Points Of The Law*.

These productions are listed as much to give the reader an insight into the atmosphere of the theatre of that time, with all its affectations and exaggerations, as to welcome, in retrospect, the arrival of Henrik Ibsen upon the European stage.

There were, of course, some fine first rate performers engaged at the Theatre Royal. The violinist, Paganini appeared in a concert in 1831. Jenny Lind, Grisi, Titens, Albani and their male counterparts, Mario, Braham, Sanley, Sims Reeves and Foli sang there. Famous comedy actors included Mathews, Tyrone Power, the Farrers and Sothern while the heavyweights of tragedy could not he surpassed; the erratic, turbulent and undisciplined genius, Edmund Kean and, later his son, Charles Kean; Charles Kemble, Sheridan Knowles, William Charles Macready, and Barry Sullivan, who had been a draper's assistant in Cork and lived to be described by *The Times* of London as the greatest actor on the English stage – a sentiment with which George Bernard Shaw concurred. Sullivan is buried in Glasnevin cemetery and his grave is surmounted by a statue of himself as Hamlet.

By 1830 Mr. Henry Harris had had enough and Mr. Calcraft became the lessee of the Royal at a rent of £2, 000 and £250 to keep the rival Adelphi Theatre, Brunswick Street, closed. In August 1831 the Adelphi, now re-named the Queen's Royal Theatre, was re-opened by consent of Mr. Calcraft.

By 1851 the Royal was in financial difficulties and the theatre was noticeably shabby. John Harris, who had skilfully managed the Queen's, took over the Royal with a time limit of three weeks to pay £12,000 in outstanding rent and expend in excess of £3,000 in refurbishing the house. He re-opened in December, 1851 with Dion Boucicault's play *Love In A Maze*, and a pantomime, *Bluff King Hal*, which is, in fact, better described as a Harlequinade, an entertainment of its time peopled by the characters from the Commedia del Arte, and completely different to pantomime as we knew it until fairly recently, in which a girl who plays a boy, who is the son of a man who plays a woman, wins another girl's affection often with the help of someone playing an animal dressed as a cat or a goose. The managements of the Queen's and the Royal united in 1857 in order to block the granting of a Licence for a third theatre in the city, and it was not until 1871 that a third Patent was granted to the brothers John and Michael Gunn in respect of the Gaiety Theatre. Mr. and Mrs. Dion Boucicault made their first personal appearances in Dublin at the Theatre Royal, on April 1, 1861 in *The Colleen Bawn*. It ran for four weeks and would undoubtedly have run longer but for other engagements. They returned in November, 1864 to present for the first time on any stage, *Arrah-na-Pogue* with the playwright himself as Sean-the-Post and his wife as Arrah. The play was much too long which made it tedious in parts, but it was successful, nevertheless, and was performed on 25th November by command of the Lord Lieutenant and Lady Wodenhouse. When

Boucicault revived the play at the Royal four years later, it was "Judiciously curtailed and altered".

A Herr Bandmann played Hamlet at this period and it's possible that he may have been related to Mrs Bandmann-Palmer who was herself attracted to the role of the moody Dane and is mentioned in Joyce's *Ulysees*, though in kinder terms, than those employed by a theatre critic who described her as " a Principal Boy in deep mourning"! In 1823, two years after the opening night, gas was first introduced at the theatre, superseding the old oil lamps, and it was the gas which caused the destruction of the theatre in February, 1880, by which time ownership had passed to Michael Gunn who also owned the Gaiety Theatre in South King Street.

A boy with a taper was lighting the gas jets in preparation for a matinee performance of the pantomime *Ali Baba*, when suddenly there was a loud explosion and the red plush curtains of the Viceregal box were enveloped in flames. A careless plumber had unscrewed a gas bracket and omitted to close the pipe. Francis Egerton, the business manager, tried to bring a fire-hose in the stage area into operation but it was out of order, and as efforts were made to adjust it, the fire attacked the stage. There was no concept of fire proofing or fire safety curtains in those days. In spite of pleas by other members of the staff to abandon his dangerous efforts, Egerton stuck to his post heroically, and was never seen again. Egerton is another example of theatre folk who regard their theatre as something special to them, a second home, an extension of themselves, and to very many the theatre was regarded as holy ground.

The 9th February, 1880 was a cold, miserable, wet day, but thousands of Dubliners assembled to watch "the dear old Royal", which they had grown to love, being reduced to a heap of smouldering damp, black ashes. At about 4. 30 in the afternoon the 7th Duke of Marlborough, then Viceroy of Ireland, arrived accompanied by Lord Muskerry and were shown the tragic results of the fire by Captain Ingram of the Fire Brigade. The matinee performance to be given on that afternoon was to be in aid of Dublin charities, and one young patron preparing to attend up in the Little Lodge, near the Vice Regal Lodge, was a lad called Winston Churchill.

The theatre library, as with everything else, was destroyed; it had contained valuable old manuscripts of plays, material relating to the history of the theatre, artists' salary book, and a collection of autographed pictures of the famous artists who had appeared at the Royal over many years.

One item which survived was the bell of the old Carmelite Abbey, formerly St. Mary's Abbey, off Capel Street, the tones of which were often heard from the stage calling mourners to the grave of fair Ophelia. The bell was recast and taken to the Gaiety Theatre, where it may still rest, unrecognised perhaps, in a dusty corner of some property room. A few years ago the manager of the Gaiety, the late Joe Kearns, assured the present author that he was ignorant of the history of this bell or its present whereabouts.

All that remained of the first Theatre Royal was the statue of Hibernia which from 1876 had stood in a niche over the front entrance and was afterwards placed over the entrance to the Grand Enclosure in the showyard of the RDS (Royal Dublin Society) at Ballsbridge.

An advertising throwaway for the First Theatre Royal dated 1848 promising "To perform every evening The Pantomime" on behalf of the Manager and Director of the Bank of Fun

The Leinster Hall

The Leinster Hall (1886–1895)

THE LEINSTER HALL
(November 1886 – 1895)

When the first Theatre Royal was destroyed Michael Gunn did not seek to renew his Patent, and instead employed C.J. Phipps, the London architect who had designed the Gaiety Theatre for him, to plan a new music hall on the site of the old theatre. The term 'music hall' is a misnomer frequently in use at that time, and a more appropriate description would have been a concert hall. The Leinster Hall opened on November 2, 1886, and seems to have been used exclusively for musical recitals, and operas. The Rousbey Opera Company regularly attracted full houses for their six week seasons.

Dame Nellie Melba, amongst other celebrities, gave two concerts in 1893, and a contemporary critic wrote:

> "Those who attended her two concerts cannot forget the pleasurable sensation they experienced in listening to her. Her rendering of Tosti's "Good-bye" was one of the most divinely dramatic things I ever listened to, and the higher she sings the sweeter. and more bird-like her voice becomes. Her 'costume recital' of the 'mad scene' from *Lucia de Lammermoor* with its wealth of florid passages was a vocal treat to rave about".

The Leinster Hall was probably in competition with the Round Room of the Rotunda, but it closed finally in 1895 when it was sold to a syndicate.

It is possible that Michael Gunn needed the cash to invest in the Gaiety which he closed for a short period in 1896 for some necessary reconstruction and re-decoration in preparation for its Silver Jubilee.

There is evidence that apart from the addition of a new pillared portico the facade of the Leinster Hall remained unchanged when it became the second Theatre Royal. The interior was undoubtedly demolished and redesigned and decorated.

The Second
Theatre Royal

Photo by GLOVER, Dublin

THEATRE ROYAL, DUBLIN

The Second Theatre Royal designed by Frank Matcham

THE SECOND THEATRE ROYAL
(December 13, 1897 – March, 1934)

Frederick Mouillot, a thirty year old actor-manager, the son of a Dublin hotel proprietor, bought the Leinster Hall with the help of his partner, H. H. Morell, a Dublin accountant David Telford, and the four sons of David Allen, the great theatrical printer whose huge colour posters could be seen on hoardings all over the city. They aimed at the very highest quality, and appointed the great Frank Matcham to design the new theatre for them. Matcham was the most prolific and successful theatre architect of all time. He was born In Newton Abbot, Devonshire in 1854, and died of blood poisoning in 1920. During the course of his career he is credited with the design of over 150 theatres – Empires, Palaces and Hippodromes, most of which have been demolished to make room for shopping centres and office blocks. John Earl, a Director of The Theatres Trust wrote of Matcham:

"Say the words "theatre architect" and a surprising number of people claiming no particular knowledge of art history will respond immediately with "Frank Matcham". He is still seen as the Master for the best of all reasons. In present day terms his theatres are thoroughly efficient and they generate an atmosphere and excitement which few designers have ever equalled and none have excelled. In every one of his theatres, Matcham demonstrated his complete mastery of the art of providing every member of the audience with a good view of the stage and excellent audibility for the performance. He also created an astonishing diversity of interior decorations to seduce the eye and generate expectation. His magical interiors delight audiences as much today as when they were built."

A few outstanding examples of his work may still be seen today; the Lyric Hammersmith, the Victoria Palace, the Hackney Empire, the London Coliseum, the London Palladium (described in 1910 as "the latest thing in music halls"); The Grand theatre in Blackpool (1894) is credited as being one of his finest creations and is now a Grade II listed building. Nearer home, the Grand Opera House, Belfast, which he designed in 1895 is reputed to be the best surviving example in the UK of the Oriental style of theatre architecture. When Matcham's Theatre Royal was replaced in 1935 Dubliners spoke nostalgically for decades of "the old Theatre Royal".

The second Theatre Royal opened on December 13, 1897. It had 2,011 seats and an outstanding feature was its much admired marble staircase. The Directors, Messrs. Mouillot, Telford, David and S.C. Allen, and the resident manager, Arthur Armstrong introduced a system of queuing for seats, which had recently been tried successfully in London, came as a welcome innovation to Dublin audiences who were accustomed to an undignified and uncontrolled melee when the doors opened at the Dublin theatres. The facade of the building bore the inscriptions – Theatre Royal and Opera House, but later on when variety shows were introduced it was also known as the Theatre Royal Hippodrome. There was also a Winter Gardens beside the main building.

Initially, the theatre was described as being not nearly so suitable for light musical pieces as the Gaiety. It was felt that the catchy, thinly orchestrated music, and the small,

THEATRE ROYAL, DUBLIN.

FRIDAY EVENING, JANUARY 4th, 1907, at 8.

— THE —

MOODY-MANNERS

OPERA COMPANY Ltd.

FROM COVENT GARDEN, DRURY LANE, and LYRIC THEATRES, LONDON.

Grand Opera in English.

THE LARGEST ENGLISH OPERA COMPANY THAT HAS EVER TOURED GREAT BRITAIN.

MASCAGNI'S

CAVALLERIA RUSTICANA.

TURRIDU	- MR. JOHN CHILD
ALFIO	- MR. LEWYS JAMES
LUCIA	MISS ARNOLD
LOLA	MISS GARLAND
SANTUZZA	- MADAME DE VERE

The Action is laid in Sicily.   Time, Easter Morning.

To be followed by LEONCAVALLO'S

PAGLIACCI.

CANIO	MR. JOSEPH O'MARA
TONIO	MR. WILLIAM DEVER
BEPPE	- Mr. V. BRODO
SILVIO	- MR. LEWYS JAMES
NEDDA	MISS KATE ANDERSON

The Scene is laid in Calabria, near Montalto, on the Feast of the Assumption.   Period, between 1865 and 1870.

Managing Director		Mr. CHARLES MANNERS
Treasurer	For the	Mr. Percy Crawford
Adv. Representative	Moody-Manners Opera	Mr. Horace Terry
Stage Manager	Companies.	Mr. T. C. Fairbairn
General Manager		Mr. W. M. Chapman Huston

Conductor   -   -   Signor Romualdo Sapio.

Great favourites in Dublin, The Moody-Manners Opera Company

sweet voices of the vocalists were quite lost, and seemed poverty-stricken in such a big house. Grand opera, Shakespearean plays and serious drama would be more suited to the Royal stage. This reaction was prompted by the first production at the theatre –*The Geisha* with music by Sidney Jones. The criticism was ignored by the management who continued to present similar works, and even successfully revived their opening production some years later.

The resulting competition for pre-eminence between the two theatres encouraged Frederick Mouillot to attract all the greatest theatrical stars and companies to the Royal and met with a great measure of success. These included the Frank R. Benson Shakespearean and Old Comedy Company; Charles Wyndham appeared in *Cyrano de Bergerac* although it was felt that his interpretation was inferior to that of the French actor M. Coquelin who had appeared in the role at the Gaiety. The ever-popular Moody-Manners Opera Company ran into disconcerting language difficulties on one occasion with a production of *Faust*. A programme note informed: "Owing to Miss Margaret MacIntyre being engaged at such short notice, it was impossible for her to learn the English version of the opera, she will, therefore, sing it in Italian". The audience, on hearing the others sing in English, strained their ears to hear the words which fell from Marguerite's lips with the disappointing result that they didn't understand a word! The Moody-Manners Company always attracted a very knowledgeable and vocal type of opera buff to the lofty heights of the 'gods' where the enthusiasts sat on long running bench-like seating arranged in tiers like steps of stairs with the result that patrons were conscious of the boots of the person seated directly behind digging into the small of his back. During the intervals certain members of this regular closely knit clientele rose from their uncomfortable seats and regaled their fellows with arias from the opera being performed on that evening in a feast of communal enjoyment.

The gods were notorious for registering their displeasure with performers on the stage. "Who did you sleep with last night?" roared an interested party to a well known soprano. The foolish diva gazed scornfully up at the top of the theatre – "Manners, you oaf!" she hissed in an unfortunate choice of words. At one stage there appears to have been a locally imposed censorship so as not to upset the sensibilities of Irish theatregoers. In Britain the Lord Chamberlain vetted all scripts intended for public performance, but his powers did not extend to Ireland. When a production of *La Poupee*, a French comic opera with music by Audran and an English libretto was announced, a big crowd sought admission to the Royal to see the show about which much, apparently, was known in advance from those who had seen the London production, and as any theatre manager will agree, word-of-mouth is the best form of publicity. A Dublin critic wrote:

> "There was a record house at the Royal on Friday night eager to see the comic opera, *La Poupee* (The Doll) performed in English. The little work came with a great reputation, but it has been considered risky to produce it here in its original form, as monks were freely introduced. However, the management got over this difficulty by changing the monks into a Huguenot brotherhood vowed to celibacy, but it weakened the "argument" considerably, nevertheless. The plot need not be repeated; suffice it is to say that the youth who thinks he has married a mechanical doll finds out that he has got wed to a charming young girl instead. Of course, much of the fun of bringing the supposed doll-wife into the monastery is lost in the Dublin version, and those who came expecting dangerous situations were sadly disappointed".

It appeared, also, that some actresses, by their actions, drew attention to that which they might be expected to conceal as the following snippet reveals:

> "The gestures indulged in by Miss Irene Vanbrugh as Sophy Fullgarney at the end of Act 1 in *The Gay Lord Quex* which puzzled many, to judge by their remarks, were simply intended to see if her garters were all right".

Miss Vanbrugh's investigations of her person would not have been approved of by the *Irish Playgoer* critic whose contribution from the high moral ground read:

> "Some productions cannot be commended to every class of theatre-goer. Our playhouses are public buildings. Thirty years ago denunciations were hurled at the head of Dion Boucicault for putting a courtesan on the stage. Our stomachs have grown stronger since then. Board school education has made children more precocious. The rapid advance of female labour; the contact of women with men in the commercial jostle of the world; the increased freedom of tone and manner in the discussion of general topics have, it would appear, made the young folk of, today less sensitive than formerly. Old fashioned parents will adhere to the belief, honoured in many centuries of practice, that the knowledge of wickedness must obtrude itself upon children quite soon enough. There is no necessity to go half-way to meet it, or to go to the theatre to search for it. But to say these things is only to echo the voice of one crying in the wilderness.
>
> Theatrical managers, though it is their custom to air a few feeble platitudes about art, are, in the main, traders seeking monetary success. Their "noble sentiments" vanish before the chink of the treasury returns. Spiced and seasoned to the appetite, *The Gay Lord Quex*, and *The Degenerates*, and other writings of the same class found that fortune awaited them......."

It is very doubtful if children could find easy access to the Theatre Royal much less find the price of admission, but it is abundantly clear that the minds of the innocents were used, as they are today, to bolster the insular, narrow-minded, arguments of moral watchdogs as long ago as 1900.

The musical appreciation of Dubliners was questioned when the Dublin Orchestral Society's afternoon concert at the Royal was badly attended. The concert itself was a great artistic success, but the ever-improving fine orchestra deserved better support, and that a few people on the front row of the gallery, a fair upper circle, and an empty parterre did no credit to the "musical taste" and judgement of Dublin. Dubliners seemed to prefer concert artists of the calibre of Nellie Melba or Enrico Caruso, but they were not adverse to giving a sympathetic hearing to one of their own like John McCormack or Margaret Burke Sheridan. A very nervous, eighteen year old Miss Sheridan was very well received when she appeared in the Thomas Moore Memorial Concert in the Theatre Royal in 1908, and there was an over-flow audience a year later when a benefit concert was organised in the Royal on her behalf in order to finance her training at the Royal Academy of Music in London. Such was her popularity that the audience gave her a standing ovation.

On Thursday, April 28, 1904 there was a state performance at the Royal by command of His Majesty King Edward VII which he attended with Her Majesty Queen Alexandra.

COPYRIGHT.

MR. MARTIN HARVEY.
IN 'THE ONLY WAY.'

ELLIS & WALERY
51, BAKER ST. W.

John Martin Harvey in "The Only Way". A typical big name visitor to the Royal

The specially arranged programme included excerpts from *King Richard II*; *The Last Of The Dandies*, and *Trilby* – all starring Beerbohm Tree, owner of His Majesty's Theatre, Haymarket, London. He was supported by his regular company, Oscar Asche, J.H. Irving, H.B. Warner, Lionel Brough and Constance Collier. Such an occasion today when a Royal Variety Performance may be seen at the touch of a television switch means practically nothing, but at that time it was regarded as a momentous affair. The celestial inhabitants of the 'gods' looked down on their betters in the more salubrious parts of the theatre who after the performance would go on to a fashionable soiree or salon and other forms of extravagant and costly entertainments and dining. Royal visits, did not, of course, meet with universal acclaim in Dublin; even less acceptable to some was the introduction of what was known as "Jingoism" into stage productions. "Jingo" songs were first introduced into the music halls in 1877 by a performer known as The Great MacDermott (G.H. Farrell) in an effort to arouse public opposition to the Russians in the Near East:

> "We don't want to fight, but by Jingo if we do,
> We've got the ships, we've got the men, and got the money too,
> We've fought the bear before, and while we're Britons true,
> The Russians shall not have Constantinople".

There were riots, and mobs sang "By Jingo if we do".

In Dublin, such songs were received with divided loyalties expressed in cheers and hisses according to the hearers loyal, rebel or party sentiments. When a Mrs Charles Sugden announced that she would recite two specially desired war poems, "The Women Of Britain" and "Fighting Bobs" which had nothing whatever to do with the play in which she was appearing, the audience was noticeably thin, as playgoers probably were scared away for fear of a recurrence of disturbances in the theatre, such as had occurred in the past over the same sort of thing.

It is not known if the word 'Girl' then possessed titillating properties likely to boost the box office takings, but the numbers of musical comedies incorporating the word in their titles in the early part of the century was extraordinary. Perhaps there was an element of repeating a successful gimmick such as is done today in the movies. The Theatre Royal presented the following musicals, among others, within the space of a few years:

My Girl; *The Shop Girl*; *The Runaway Girl*; *The Country Girl*; *The Earl And The Girl*; *The Circus Girl*; *The School Girl*; *The Girl From Kay's*; *The Gipsy Girl*; *The Golden Girl*; *The Girl From Biarritz*.

These shows were produced by Frederick Mouillot with music by well-known composers like Lionel Moncton and Leslie Stuart. There were others with slight variations in the titles like: *An Artist's Model*; *The Dairy Maids*; *The Belle of Mayfair*; and the most enduring of them all, *The Belle Of New York*. There was one attempt to balance matters with a production of the show *Our Boys*, – a title which seemed to have been appropriated by the Christian Brothers for their schools magazine.

In 1907 Charles Frohman presented J.M. Barrie's *Peter Pan* from the Duke of York's Theatre, London. It was produced under the direction of Dion Boucicault with the delightful Pauline Chase in the leading role, flying gracefully with Kirby's Flying Ballet. The role of Michael Darling was played by a curly-haired young lad called Alfred Willmore who was destined, years later, to become famous as Micheál MacLíammóir.

A year later Granville Barker appeared in a season of Shaw plays including *Man And Superman* and *Arms And The Man*.

The Safety Curtain or "the iron" as it is known in the profession, used as an advertising medium, and a useful source of income, seems to have raised the ire of at least one misguidedly highminded patron around this time:

> "On visiting the Royal on Tuesday I was disgusted to find a glaring, vulgar advertising curtain filling the place of the rich curtains that usually shut off the stage from the auditorium, and to me it was anything but a fit preparation for the delightful old world comedy which occupies the stage this week [Mr. Auguste Van Biene in *The Broken Melody* – Author]. It was bad enough to have to gaze on this wretched inartistic monstrosity previous to the play, but when it intruded its offensive presence on the audience again after Act 2, it offended me and many others around "to the soul" to see how all idea of artistic taste was slain by the thoughtlessness of the management in making their theatre a mere advertising hoarding to be shunned by all people of artistic taste. Until the Royal came into existence most people thought the advertising curtain was sacred to pantomime time, and as so much offended the artistic sense within us at such a season, one shock more or less mattered little; but when the same thing occurs before and during the progress of a comedy, it is quite a different matter, and should not be tolerated for an instant".

It must have been some comedy, worthy of immediate resurrection if it drew a laugh from that pompous, egotistical ass with the 'artistic sense'! The colourful innovation which always added to the atmosphere in a theatre must have appealed to the business sense of at least two of the theatres directors, the Allens, who had a vested interest in advertising which was the family business.

In 1909 discussions took place between the managements of the Royal and the Gaiety which was now being run by Michael Gunn's widow, with the result that the Royal directors formed the Gaiety Theatre (Dublin) Co. Ltd with Frederick Mouillot as managing director and David Telford as chairman. Mouillot died suddenly at Brighton in 1911, and David Telford took control.

A bronze bust of Frederick Mouillot was erected in the vestibule of the Theatre Royal, and was later removed to the foyer of the Gaiety. Mouillot had been the creative influence at the Royal where he had been responsible for the production and direction of many successful musicals and pantomimes. The directors were now faced with the problem of booking quality productions for the Royal and the Gaiety, each in opposition to the other. George Edwardes, the London impresario who was related to the Gunn family, released from any long-standing obligations of loyalty to the Gaiety, transferred his companies to the Royal, but Richard D'Oyly Carte, who was also related to Edwardes, refused to break the connection, and continued to make his periodic and hugely successful visits to the Gaiety, and his company never played in any other Dublin theatre. A prominent member of the D'Oyly Carte Company, Sir Henry Lytton, said of Dublin audiences:

MONDAY, JULY 2nd.   MATINEE SATURDAY (2.30).

---

1. **OVERTURE**..."La Couronne d'Or..............*Hermann*

---

2. **LA TOSTIA**
   Instrumentalist.

Great Starring Engagement and First Appearance of

3. **MICHAEL BRAHAM**
   AND HIS EDUCATED BULL TERRIER, "MICKY,"
   From the Palace Theatre, London, in his latest and greatest
   Comedy Success— "A QUIET REHEARSAL."
   "Micky" is not a Trick Dog, but the nearest approach to
   humanity ever attained by an animal.

---

4. **ROYAL PICTURES**
   Portraying all the Latest and most Interesting Events.

---

5. **EIGHT LANCASHIRE LADS**
   The Smartest Combination of Singers and Dancers extant.

---

6. **ALICE BLANFORD**
   A Charming Ballad Vocalist.

---

7. **BROWN AND KELLY COMBINATION**
   "THE BUTLER KNOWS." The Funniest Sketch in Existence.
   Scene   ...   . Love Bird Villa

   CHARACTERS.
   Mrs. Lovebird   ...   .   Miss Blanche Holt
   Mr. Lovebird   ...   .   Mr. Jack Foster
   The Butler   ...   .   Mr. Edwin Brown

---

8. **INTERVAL.**

   SELECTION........."La Cigale".....................*Audran*

---

9. **A-BA-BE PICTURE POST CARD ALBUM**
   An Artistic Novelty—The Living Picture Postcards.

---

10. **EVELYN TAYLOR**
    Comedienne.

Special Engagement of the Masterpiece of the Century—

11. **DRONZA**
    THE MARVELLOUS MECHANICAL TALKING HEAD—
    The Greatest Sensation of the Age. Scientists, Electricians, and
    all the great men of the present day have failed to solve the mystery
    of this wonderful invention. The most ingenious and startling act
    ever placed before the public. From the Hippodrome, London.

---

12. **HARRY BROWN**
    America's Greatest Coloured Comedian and Dancer,
    who is the author of all his own songs.
    "IS EVERYBODY HAPPY?"

---

13. **PAUL CONCHAS**
    EXTRAORDINARY ATHLETE.

---

*A Royal Variety bill (1906) featuring the Eight Lancashire Lads which included
the youthful Charles Chaplin*

"Nowhere are there truer lovers of Gilbert and Sullivan.
Maybe Gilbert's fantastic wit is the wit they understand, and maybe too
their hearts are warmed by the plaintive song of their fellow countryman,
Sullivan. Whatever the cause we had no better reception anywhere".

Musical comedy was losing favour, and the Royal increasingly featured music hall bills. Scores of mediocre and quickly forgotten acts appeared there as elsewhere, but the names of a few survive in the history of music hall for reasons other than their artistic abilities. At the Royal, in July 1906, for instance there was a supporting act called "The 8 Lancashire Lads" (actually one of them was a girl, the daughter of the man who ran the act), but what is of interest is the fact that the young Charlie Chaplin was a member of the troupe, and he left it in 1906 to take a juvenile role in *Sherlock Holmes*, and it follows that if he left the 'Lancashire Lads' after July 1906 it is possible that Chaplin played the second Theatre Royal. There was a notable appearance by one of the earliest great names in the art of ventriloquism, Fred Russell, affectionately known in the profession as "Uncle Fred". He was a great stalwart of the exclusive show-business club, The Grand Order Of Water Rats. One of his sons became Val Parnell, the famous former boss of Moss' Empires which controlled the London Palladium. Fred's dummy, Coster Joe, was a crude replica of a pearly king covered with pearl buttons; it wasn't a work of art, but he used it effectively, and it was a novelty in its time. After Fred's death, Bud Flanagan had a slot made in its head, and used it as a collecting box for charity propped up in his dressing room at the Victoria Palace during the runs of the Crazy Gang shows.*

Many famous performers appeared at the Theatre Royal – they were the equivalent of film stars and pop idols of their time, with magnetic personalities and songs which still live on in folk memory. Unfortunately, it is now a matter of the song, and not the singer. There are many enthusiastic students of the old music hall, which disappeared after the first world war to be replaced by a faster moving entertainment called Variety, and these collectors of memorabilia such as old posters, programmes, sheet music and early gramophone records can unfailingly match the singer to the song. Otherwise all that is remembered is the song and the general public rarely recognise the once famous name associated with it.

The song "Daisy Bell" known even now to school children made a fortune for Katie Lawrence in England the US and Europe. Charles Coburn bought "The Man Who Broke The Bank At Monte Carlo" outright for £10, but the song was unsuccessful at first, and Coburn is credited with being the first 'song-plugger' as he repeatedly sang chorus after chorus when he launched the song at the Oxford Music Hall, until the audience finally took to it. Although he was described as being "Dublin's Favourite Comedian" on the posters when he appeared at the Royal, he certainly wasn't top of the bill on that occasion. Neither the performer, J.W. Rickaby or his song "Silk Hat Tony" are remembered now:

"I said to the King once at tea,
They built you a Palace,
I bear you no malice,
They built Piccadilly for me".

This song has the stamp of William Hargreaves upon it for it, was he who wrote "Burlington Bertie From Bow" for his American born wife, Ella Shields. Although the characters in the songs, Tony and Bertie, are down on their luck their thoughts are on the opulent life of pre world war London – the majestic sweep of Regent Street into Piccadilly Circus past the Café Royale on to the notorious promenade at the Empire, and ending at the fashionable Romano's in the Strand.

It must not be assumed that all of these old timers were irreproachably above criticism. Albert Chevalier with his "My Old Dutch" was very popular in his day, but now it comes across as nauseous unadulterated, cloying sentimentality, but it was true to life in its time. Performers were not conscious of creating a sort of living folklore; songs were composed and sung for their greatest commercial value, and if the subjects of some of them displayed vividly the vitality of the working classes and their refusal to be defeated by grim housing conditions and mean streets, it was merely a reflection of the only life they knew. Dublin audiences went to the Royal, the Empire Palace (later the Olympia) and the Lyric (later the Tivoli) and sang the songs they heard around the piano in the parlour at home on Sunday evenings. A few of these songs are half remembered today:

> "I Belong To Glasgow" (Will Fyffe)
> "Has Anybody Here Seen Kelly"; "Down At The Old Bull And Bush" (Florrie Forde)
> "Don't Dilly Dally On The Way" (Marie Lloyd) "Nellie Dean" (Gertie Gitana)
> "The Lily Of Laguna" (G.H. Elliott and originally Eugene Stratton)
> "Waiting At The Church" (Vesta Victoria)
> "I Do Like To Be Beside The Seaside" (Mark Sheridan)
> "Boiled Beef And Carrots"; "Any Old Iron" (Harry Champion)
> "If You Were The Only Girl In The World" (George Robey)

When Madame Fanny Moody was appearing at the Royal some of her arias from *The Lily Of Killarney*, *Maritana* or *The Bohemian Girl* were sure to be included in the Sunday sing-song, and no doubt some of the gentlemen fancied themselves as Valentine in *Faust*.

The reader may add his or her song title of another age, but it is perhaps doubtful if the original singer will spring readily to mind.

The First World War proved to be a difficult period for the Dublin theatres. Apart from the fact that many performers had been called-up for war duty, travelling was difficult and many acts contracted to appear didn't honour their engagements, and this was further exacerbated by the events of the Easter Rising in 1916. With the exception of a few native performers of the calibre of Mike Nono from Ennis, Co. Clare, who had the comedy gimmick of wearing a tea-cosy on his head as he sang his still popular number, "McNamara's Band", Irish artists could not fill the breach. The management at the Royal succeeded under difficult circumstances in keeping the theatre open, ever mindful that come revolution or World War 'the show must go on!'.

Later on during the tragic and bitter Civil War, the Irish baritone, Walter McNally, invited Margaret Burke Sheridan, who was by now a star at Covent Garden and La Scala, Milan, to join him in a concert at the Theatre Royal, Dublin, and she appeared there in November, 1922, accompanied by her former teacher, Dr. Vincent O'Brien, and filled the theatre with an appreciative audience, and her popularity was such that an additional concert was arranged to facilitate the crowds of music lovers. Apart from such gala occasions the attractions took the form of a new concept known as Variety which was a fast moving version of the old style music hall. Artists were given less time on the bill and sketches and cross-talk comedians were introduced. Previously comedy had been provided by individual comedians, but it was Dan Leno's interpolation of amusing dialogue between the verses of his comic songs that led eventually to incomparable character comedians like Gus Elen ("It's A Great Big Shame" and "If It Wasn't For The Houses In Between"), and the eventual creation of the 'stand-up-comic' and the genius of Max Miller.

The Royal attracted its share of eccentric performers, chief of whom was a very popular comic called Wilkie Bard who sang a tongue-twister – "She sells sea shells on the sea shore" and "I Want To Sing In Opera". His true name was Billy Smith, but he called himself Bard because he cherished a deep admiration for William Shakespeare, The Bard of Avon; so much so that he affected to look like Shakespeare by wearing a wig with a bald pate and locks dangling over his ears.

> "I want to sing in opera,
> I've got that kind of voice.
> I'd only sing in opera
> If I could have my choice.
> Signor Caruso
> Told me I ought to do so,
> That's why I want to sing in op'ra
> Sing in op-pop-pop-popera! Hurrah!"

These artists invariably gave a light hearted view of a life which wasn't by any means light hearted for the majority of people. An evening at the music hall or Variety theatre was an invitation to laugh at adversity and thumb one's nose at authority.

> "So let theatres and music halls 'increase and multiply',
> To cheer and gladden weary ones, whose lives are made awry,
> By hard and cruel customs, which grind poor workers down
> To barest wages, longest hours, and the dreariest homes in town.
> So give them funny jokes and songs, with jollity and mirth,
> And make them laugh both long and loud, these tired ones of the earth."
> – *Hettie Nesga. January, 1905.*

The music hall was a comment on life, and several eminent writers have written that it was the only genuine comment, but it could not be mistaken for life itself. Back outside the plate glass doors lay reality, and this was especially true for many of the very performers who entertained nightly with their fantastic concepts of mankind, and a clear-sighted sense of the ridiculous. Many, who earned fortunes and the adulation of the public during the course of their careers, died in poverty.

Leo Dryden, who was known as The Kipling Of The Halls, and was famous for songs like "Good-bye Dolly", "The Dublin Fusiliers" and especially, "The Miner's Dream Of Home"

"The bells were ringing the old year out, and the New Year in"

fell completely out of favour after World War I, and was reduced to singing his most celebrated song on the streets until he died old and forgotten in 1939. Some aspects of Dryden's life may be detected in Chaplin's film *Limelight*, and the entire Chaplin family were no strangers themselves to adversity in their lives on the halls. Mention must be given to the illusionist Lafayette, who lost his life in a fire which destroyed the Edinburgh Empire in 1911. The lives of some performers ended tragically and bore no possible comparison to their happy-go-lucky appearances on the boards.

T.E. Dunville was a top-liner in the twenties, but his popularity waned with a fickle public, and when he couldn't secure engagements he walked into the river Thames and drowned himself at Reading. Mark Sheridan ("Beside the Seaside") shot himself in 1918 in a fit of depression.

Harry Fragson – The Entente Cordiale, was a big star at the Folies Bergere in Paris, and topped the bill at the Royal seated as usual at the piano singing "Hullo! hullo! Who's Your Lady Friend" in a rather cheeky manner. He was shot dead by his own father who was insanely jealous of his son's great success.

But occasionally, apart from the ephemeral glow of good-fellowship emanating from the general atmosphere, some tangible good which influenced the life of some poor soul came like a revelation over the footlights.

Bransby Williams, a Londoner whose mother (maiden name, Giles) came from Dublin, was famous for his sketches of characters from the works of Dickens, and he recorded a heartwarming story. Williams was playing the Tivoli, London and one of his Dickens characterisations was of old "Dan'l Peggotty" the fisherman, at the moment when he is afflicted by the news of the flight of "Little Em'ly". On one particular night he somehow became Dan'l Peggotty and actually felt the loss of Em'ly, and the tears streamed down his face. He was not only acting the part, but seemed to be watching the effect on others. Towards the end of his monologue, at the words "God guide her footsteps that she may come back", there was a long-drawn sob and a moan, and a woman made her way out of the theatre. Next day he received a letter which he presumed to be from the same poor soul who had left the theatre so abruptly –

> To Mr. Bransby Williams
>
> Sir,
>
> I have no doubt you never think of yourself as a preacher. I was at the Tivoli on Wednesday evening – since then I have decided to go home to my uncle; he also is a fisherman, and I was brought up by him. I left home as a lot of others do, but I am going back, and by the time you get this I shall be with him. He is good, and you must be good to act the way you do. I shall try now I am going back to him to be a comfort and help to him, and shall always remember and pray for you, and if the prayers of a fallen one will help you, you should be helped to great things.
>
> Yours gratefully,

After reading the letter, and realizing its full meaning, Williams reflected on the good that it was possible for the stage to create – and the much abused music-hall stage too. People had their troubles on both sides of the footlights.

Pantomimes were not neglected at the Royal, and very often included names that would later become outstanding, like Paul Cinquevalli, whom nobody has heard of now, but he became the acknowledged king of jugglers at the Folies Bergere. It was said of him that he turned Juggling into poetry, and that he could play billiards better on his back than the normal player could on a table. He was really an Englishman, and he appeared at the Royal in *Puss In Boots* by J. Hickory Wood who had written pantos for Dan Leno at Drury Lane, and wrote Leno's biography. Dorothy Ward, (the Queen/Prince of the Principal Boys) who was married to the Dublin dame comedian, Shaun Glenville – whose mother ran the old Mechanics Theatre where the Abbey Theatre now stands – appeared with George Lashwood ("In the Twi-twi-twilight") in another Hickory Wood panto, *Jack and Jill*. Wee Georgie Wood, the Jimmy Clitheroe of his day, a tiny man with an unbroken childish voice who worked with his "stage mother", Dolly Harmer, appeared in *Aladdin* at the Royal. Gracie Fields appeared in a solo act when she was a fourteen year old, and returned years later in her own revues – *It's A Bargain* and her best remembered one that

MONDAY, JANUARY 25th, 1909, at 7.45.

(FOR FIVE WEEKS).

ELABORATE PRODUCTION OF THE GORGEOUS

ELEVENTH ANNUAL PANTOMIME

JACK AND JILL.

Written by J. HICKORY WOOD   Locals by F. P. BYRNE.

Jack, Eldest Son of the Widow Cobble	Dorothy Ward
Jill, the lost Princess	Edith Fink
Baron Bounce, of the Old School	J. A. Warden
The Widow Cobble, who lived in a Shoe	George Miller
Margery, the Widow's Youngest Daughter	Stella de Marney
Jack Straw	
A Bull — who develops	Fred Conquest
A Bear	
Gleam, a Fairy	May Rawlinson
Glum, a Demon	Harry Trevanion
Mr. Chatter, the Baron's Solicitor	J. G. McMahon
First Witch	Gwendoline Francis
Zoe, Queen of Happy Land	Kitty Baughton
Prince Opulent, in search of his Fiancee	George Lashwood

Florence Manners, Ella Hoyle, Gloria Egmont, Violet Chester, Flo Keely, Ethel Ramsey, Lily Hamilton, &c. Thomas Hill, Joseph Speed, R. Beaumont, H. Edwards, Theodore Jones, E. A. Foster, &c.

"TILLER'S" SUPERBA QUARTETTE OF DANCERS.

SYNOPSIS OF SCENERY.

SCENE 1	THE ENTRANCE TO THE MAGIC WELL
SCENE 2	THE BARON'S CORNFIELD
SCENE 3	THE OFFICE OF THE BARON'S SOLICITOR
SCENE 4	HOME OF THE WIDOW COBBLE
SCENE 5	INTERIOR OF THE SHOE
SCENE 6	THE MAGIC HILL
SCENE 7	HAPPY LAND
SCENE 8	THE FAIRY MOUNTAINS
SCENE 9	THE RIVAL WELLS
SCENE 10	EXTERIOR OF PRINCE'S PALACE
SCENE 11	THE PALACE OF JEWELS

Produced Specially for Dublin by Mr. Frederick Mouillot.

Pantomime "Jack and Jill" (1909) starring Dorothy Ward and George Lashwood

brought her real fame, *Mr. Tower Of London*. Gracie, of course, gave one of her many farewell performances in the third and last Theatre Royal. A fellow Lancastrian, fighting his way to the top which he achieved as a film star, was George Formby Junior, who, as many old timers would tell you if there were any still alive, wasn't a patch on his father, Formby Senior. Formby Pere had a genuine hacking cough due to a weak chest and made it a part of his act, ("I'm coughing well to-night") and sang songs like "Standing At The Corner of the Street" and "John Willie, Come On". George Junior appeared with his banjo-ukulele in Thomas Convery revues – *Formby Seeing Life* and *A Chip Off The Old Block*.

In July, 1933 the then twenty year old Jack Doyle was disqualified and fined after the second round of his fight with Jack Peterson at White City and he devoted most of his six month suspension to appearances on the halls. When he appeared at the Theatre Royal he was greeted as a hero and the Irish demonstrated their view of the decision of the British Boxing Board of Control by packing the Royal for four weeks. Jack was on a percentage of the receipts and his cut averaged about £600 per week. He opened his act by singing some songs that he had just recorded for Decca, "Mother Machree", "My Irish Song Of Songs", "Little Town In The Old County Down" and "Where The River Shannon Flows". He left the stage and changed from evening dress into boxing strip while a boxing ring was hastily assembled on stage to which he returned to display his massive physique and perform a series of exercises and shadow boxing. In his excellent biography of Doyle, "Fighting For Love", the author, Michael Taub gives the impression that this appearance was in the much larger third Theatre Royal, but since the latter did not open until September 1935 at which time Doyle was in America, Mr. Taub must have confused the two theatres. Jack did eventually appear in the new theatre with his wife Movita in 1944.

The second Theatre Royal was sold to the Theatre Royal Co. Ltd, of which J.E. Pearse was chairman and managing director. The old theatre closed on Saturday, March 3, 1934 with the showing of the Jean Harlow film, *Dinner At Eight*. It was demolished soon afterwards. On Sunday, May 6, 1934 a Benefit Concert for the staff of the old Theatre Royal was given at the Gaiety Theatre. The artists included the Carl Rosa Opera Co; Cora Goffin, a London soubrette and Principal Boy who later married the impresario, Emile Littler; F.J. McCormick of the Abbey Theatre; P.J. Henry appeared as a puny figure with false bravado in his recitation 'The Night I Fought Carnera', and at the top of the bill was Jimmy O'Dea whose only appearances at the old Royal that can be traced were on December 10, 1922 in a complimentary benefit concert to the singer, Florence Ryan (Hewson), and a Sunday concert on November 4, 1923 billed as James A. O'Dea-Humorist.

All that survived from the second Theatre Royal was a part of Frank Matcham's famous old grand marble staircase, which until recently led to the lower ground floor of the original premises of Messrs. Brown Thomas & Co. Ltd., the Grafton Street speciality department store. In the 1996 conversion of the store into a Dublin branch of Marks & Spencer, the staircase was given even greater prominence, between the ground and first floors, and it still looks truly graceful.

One other example of Matcham's work, most of which has been demolished in Britain, survives in Ireland. This is the splendid Grand Opera House in Belfast which opened on December 23, 1895 with seating for 1,050 and was described as "... a gilded pleasure dome with the ornate facade, facing out over Great Victoria Street adding to the sense of intrigue: Cirque and Grand Opera House, it reads, the circus reference taken up in the famous elephants in the auditorium". In 1974, it became the first building in

Belfast to be listed as being of historical and architectural importance, and its future was assured. Matcham knew how to package any stage production in an atmosphere of beauty and warmth, thus making his creations a part of the theatrical experience.

There is no need to wonder why Dubliners lamented the passing of 'the old Theatre Royal', as they called it, for many years after its demolition.

---

* In a recent interview with the present author, John Adrian, Secretary of the Water Rats denied Bud Flanagan's claim, and entering the inner sanctum of the Order removed a velvet covering from a figure which occupied a place of honour at the long polished table – it was the legendary "Coster Joe", and Mr. Adrian explained that Fred Russell's true name was Parnell, but it wasn't a popular name to use in the political atmosphere of the time when he was starting his career. His son, Val Parnell, reverted to the family name in more recent times.

The Third
Theatre Royal

Exterior of The Third Theatre Royal

THE THIRD THEATRE ROYAL

(23 September, 1935 – 30 June, 1962)

Hawkins Street in Dublin extends from Burgh Quay to College Street. At one time it had the distinction of having a public monument sited at each end. At the Burgh Quay end an unremarkable memorial records the bravery of Constable Patrick Sheahan of the Dublin Metropolitan Police, who, on 5th May, 1905 rescued two workers who had been overcome by sewer gas down a manhole at that spot before he himself was overcome and lost his life. At the other end at the corner of College Street stood the Crampton Memorial erected in honour of Sir Philip Crampton MD (1777-1858), who was surgeon in ordinary to Queen Victoria and a founder member of the Royal Zoological Society. The elaborate monument included a bust of Crampton surrounded by lion masks emitting water into shell shape basins which sparkled in the light of the three lamp posts at the edge of the memorial. It is doubtful if many patrons hastening towards the Theatre Royal ever paused to examine these structures or were aware of their purpose. Certainly nobody seemed to notice when the Crampton Memorial collapsed in 1959 and was removed.

At the corner of Burgh Quay and Hawkins Street stood the Scotch House, one of the city's most celebrated watering holes. It was a listening post for the humorous and acerbic, as the fancy took him, columnist Myles na Gopaleen (Flann O'Brien) who referred to the place as "my office" in his column in the *Irish Times*. Further down the street was the back entrance to one of Dublin's most famous restaurants, the Red Bank which specialised in fine drinks and oysters. The disappearance of Dublin's theatres may be equated with the demolition of its best restaurants. Opposite stood the Theatre Royal, and the stage door was down at the side of the building in Poolbeg Street almost directly opposite Mulligan's pub which is part of the setting for James Joyce's story 'Counterparts' in *Dubliners*. It was in Mulligan's that Farrington arm-wrestled with Weathers, an acrobat and knockabout artiste from the Tivoli music-hall just around the corner. It was, of course, the local for all the performers at the Royal.

The third Theatre Royal was designed by Leslie C. Norton of London, and the executant architects were Messrs. Scott and Good of Dublin. The facade and that of the adjoining Regal Rooms Restaurant which stood on the site of the old Winter Gardens, where coffees, snacks and afternoon teas had been the main bill of fare, was in the art-deco style, and the decoration managed to convey the dual purpose of the building as a theatre and cinema. Sculptured figures carved by the Irish sculptor, Laurence Campbell, representing Eire as the centre piece with a Celtic Warrior on her left, and on her right the Celtic Muse of Imagination decorated the facade. Up at roof level, large letters picked out in neon proclaimed that this was the THEATRE ROYAL, and underneath were four huge masks representing Comedy, Tragedy, Drama, and Burlesque. Four double glass doors at the top of a short flight of marble steps were protected by a long canopy at each end of which there was a smaller canopy sited lower than the main one. The facade was floodlit at night, and the huge marble foyer with a staircase at each side, an elevator on the left hand side as one entered beside the cloakroom, the glass cash box in the centre (in which Bob Geldof's mother presided in the early years) were

Interior of the nearly 4,000-seater theatre

The Comics' Dressing Room: From Left to Right:
Cecil Nash, Bill 'Magso' Brady, Cecil Sheridan, Mickser Reid, Jimmy Harvey, Dolly Sparkes,
Val Fitzpatrick, Patty Ryan and Mick Eustace

brightly lit producing a very welcoming atmosphere. It was claimed that a lavish Moorish influence based on authentic details from the Alhambra at Granada was adopted for the decoration of the auditorium, and that there were some concessions to sentiment when some of the balustrading of Matcham's old Grand Stairway was incorporated on both sides of the proscenium ends of the Royal Circle. The place was so vast that none of this was immediately apparent to the casual patron. There were seven designated areas in the auditorium – The Stalls, Orchestra Stalls, Royal Circle, Grand Circle, Centre Circle, Upper Circle, and three Boxes on each side each seating four, and situated at the sides of the Royal Circle far back from the stage. The theatre accommodated, including standing room, four thousand people. There was little intimacy between audience and performers, and the design of the building didn't help. Traditionally in a Variety theatre the audience was seated almost in a circle around the performer; the stage boxes filled each side of the stage so that an artist played into a cosy cup or horseshoe-shaped assembly.

The designers of the Royal were more concerned with sight-lines appropriate to a cinema with the result that the front of the Royal Circle was in a straight line and deliberately made no effort to embrace anything that was happening on the stage. But money was never spared on the latest stage lighting, as it was developed, in order to enhance the effect of intimacy.*

Figures on the stage appeared so doll-like to patrons seated in the Centre and Upper Circles that the West End and Gate Theatre actor, Liam Gaffney, suggested that small opera glasses should be attached to each seat, and be made available for a nominal fee payable by means of a cash slot which would release the glasses. His idea, which still operates in some West End theatres, was never adopted.

Spaciousness was the keynote of the third Theatre Royal. Situated under the Orchestra Stalls there was a long bar filling the width of the building and known to revellers, particularly on holiday occasions such as Christmas Eve, Easter, St. Patrick's Day and Rugby matches (especially the Welsh ones) as the submarine bar. Upstairs, behind the Royal Circle, there was a more restrained clientele which would have frowned at any feeble effort to start a sing-song. The Circle bar was indeed that – a large bar in the form of a circle surrounded by comfortable tables and chairs and the occasional upholstered red leather sofa. At one end, between the two glass entrance doors there was a cocktail bar which was presided over in the early days by Charles Farrar and Arthur Gordon who shook and mixed cocktails of the conventional kind or to their own recipes for the more jaded palates. Part of the decorative design of the Circle bar was carried out in variform glass bricks, and when the theatre was demolished the wrecking crew carefully removed these bricks, and they now adorn the living rooms in various suburban semis. The bar at the upper circle did not merit decoration in veneered Australian Walnut and Black Beam timbering like the snootier locations downstairs.

There was, at the Gaiety Theatre at the turn of the century, a young Dublin stage electrician, Philip Sheridan, who attracted the attention of the D'Oyly Carte management who invited him to supervise the lighting effects at their own theatre, the Savoy Theatre in London's Strand. Sheridan accepted and wasn't long in London before he established a stage-lighting service which in time grew to be one of the most important organisations of its kind in the world, known predictably as Strand Electric. Now Philip Sheridan, Managing Director of Strand Electric supervised the installation of the Stage Switchboard and Dimmer Regulator controlling Footlights, Battens, and Auditorium circuits in addition to a multiplicity of mobile lighting units and twelve 1,000 watt Spotlights directed from the Spot Chamber in the Ceiling, and a Spot Box on each side of the auditorium close to the proscenium arch.

The orchestra pit was built on a special electric lift so that it and the musicians could ascend to stage level at the touch of a button. The orchestra pit was also surrounded by a wide topped barrier which enabled performers to walk out round the band and close to patrons in the front rows; this occurred mainly in ensemble scenes or grand finales.

The remarkable Compton Theatre Organ had an extraordinary range and was equipped with the Electrone – the most, advanced device in musical scientific research. This attachment did not rely upon pipes, bells or, any kind of musical device previously used – it was purely electrical, and the sounds were such that they blended with the familiar theatre organ tone. Besides the carillons, chimes and other special effects, the organ included almost every kind of musical sound known to the ear. As the beautiful instrument rose from its pit, patrons were aware of a gigantic specially designed organ, beautifully decorated with illuminated glass covered console, which had four manuals or keyboards from which the tones were obtained from electrical connections to the organ chambers, of which there were two over the stage.

Upstairs there was a small preview cinema seating ten or twelve people which was used to assess the quality of forthcoming productions and one end of this room opened on to a small iron-railed balcony which overlooked Poolbeg Street at the side of the theatre, and particular favourites amongst the visiting Hollywood stars would appear to their fans on this balcony and sign autographs on every conceivable scrap of paper from pawn tickets to holy pictures. But as even the greatest performers know the momentary insanity of the mob in pursuit of close contact with their idols soon fades into forget-fulness.

Backstage the wardrobe department and the dancing troupes' dressing rooms were on the left hand side. The other dressing rooms were on the right hand side. Most of the comedy teams used No 1 as a communal dressing room, each performer storing his costumes in a large ship's trunk. When a really big name came to top the bill, No 1 dressing room became his or hers exclusively and was probably redecorated with new carpeting and furniture. The normal inhabitants were banished to other rooms further upstairs.

The Regal Rooms Restaurant which, it was claimed, was the smartest and most cosmopolitan rendezvous in Ireland with an atmosphere of quiet luxury and an excellent cellar, was the first part of the new complex to open. It had been claimed that the Regal Rooms was the first night club in Ireland, but the presence of the Regal Rooms Restaurant under the management of a Donegal man, Hugh Margey, did not impress discerning Dublin diners despite the fact that the Regal Tipica Orchestra under the direction of Jimmy Campbell, fulfilling his first resident engagement in Dublin, was a feature of the establishment which was not in the end a financial success, and was later converted into the Regal Rooms Cinema.

It has been reported that John Count McCormack visited the as yet uncompleted Theatre Royal shortly before it was due to open, and was invited to try out the acoustics, and sang unaccompanied "Believe Me If All Those Endearing Young Charms", much to the alleged delight of the workmen. Tony Kenny Senior (the comedian not the young singer) claims that he has it on the authority of one of the same workmen that McCormack did indeed call to see the almost completed theatre, and was prevailed upon to sing

Harry Bailey and Musical Director, Jimmy Campbell

a few scales. When one of the workers asked him to sing a song his reply was – "Scales you can have for nothing, but songs must be paid for". Of such conflicting stories theatrical myths are made! John Count McCormack, did, however, sing "Bless This House" on the occasion of the Gala Opening of the Theatre Royal, on September 23, 1935, when as a guest of honour with Sean Lemass, then Minister for Industry and Commerce, and the Rt. Hon. Alfred Byrne T.D. Lord Mayor of Dublin, they performed the opening ceremony.

Francis A. Mangan presented *The New Royal Revue* with scenery and costumes imported from Paris. Mangan brought his own troupe of 24 dancers from London, and these were augmented by a Corps de Ballet, the 10 Irish Beauties, and the St. Helier Sisters. The No. 1 Army Band conducted by Colonel Fritz Brase contributed, and the principal singer was an Irish-American tenor, Danny Malone. A performer described as 'the famous American Political Comedian' a so-called 'Senator' Murphy provided the comedy. Alphonse Berg and Company provided a speciality act in Lightning Fashion Creations. Others included Joe Jackson, the clown eccentric, Darroll Richards, Iris Kirkwhite and Keith Lester; The Five Cleavers, and The Three Diamond Brothers. Dances were arranged by Betty Ann Hagler. There were two short film intervals – Mickey Mouse in a prize winning cartoon *The Band Concert*, and a short film called *Irish Melodies* which had been produced in Ireland, and about which nothing can be traced. The Compton organ console was played by H. Alban Chambers from Leeds, who was to be the first of many to fill that role.

The twenty five piece Theatre Royal Orchestra was conducted by Jimmy Campbell (who had recently vacated the Regal Rooms). He was musical director for most of the theatre's history except for a period between 1946 and 1951 following a disagreement with the management he went as M.D. to the Prince Of Wales Theatre, London for some Sid Field shows and worked later at Blackpool in addition to broadcasting for the BBC.

JIMMY CAMPBELL: was born in South Shields, Co. Durham, and was taught music by his father. He started his musical career at the age of 18 at the Scala Cinema, South Shields, and later broadcast from the BBC for three years as a solo violinist from Newcastle. Engagements in Sunderland (where he introduced Stage Presentations) and Preston followed. By this time he had formed his own orchestra and had developed a talent for orchestration and original musical arrangements which brought him finally to London and the Prince's Theatre, Shaftesbury Avenue. His faculty in selecting musicians who have the material for good team work in an orchestra made him an obvious choice to form the Regal Rooms Orchestra and later the Theatre Royal Orchestra. He became a well-known and loved character in Dublin; his love of and loyalty to the Royal were legendary, and he was genuinely missed during his five year self-exile, although he was replaced by fine musicians like George Rothwell, Alan Beale and the suave Roy Fox. Jimmy did not very long survive the eventual demolition of his beloved Theatre Royal. In October 1963 he suffered a heart attack and died on 1st November in the Adelaide Hospital aged 58.

The Resident Manager was Roscommon born Mr. Jack McGrath, who had been manager of the Savoy Cinemas in Dublin and Cork which with the Savoy, Limerick which was then nearing completion, were the creations of the Chairman and Managing Director, Mr. J.E. Pearce, an accountant of Ayesha Castle, Killiney, Co. Dublin. Jack McGrath later attained the rank of Colonel in the Second World War with the Allied armies.

The theatre was dedicated to "the entertainment of the people of the Irish Free State, and to Visitors from all countries. The New Theatre Royal would present to theatregoers Grand Opera, Musical, Comedy, Drama and Variety under conditions which had never before obtained in the Irish Free State, and, in fact, are not excelled elsewhere. Every encouragement would be given to local Artistes".

The Royal with a capacity of almost 4,000 (3,700 plus standing room), was often claimed as the biggest theatre in Europe, but there was, in fact, a 5,000-seater in Germany. Admission prices ranged from 1/- (5p) to 3/- (15p), and strangely, the prices were considerably cheaper on Sundays. Shows were twice nightly at 6.30 and 8.50 with one performance at 8.30 on Sundays. There were in 1930 at least eight first run cinemas in the city centre all of which featured the phenomenon of the new talking pictures which were a novel and irresistible attraction, and in addition the Royal had the added competition of live shows from the Gaiety, the Queens, and the Olympia, but oddly, the Capitol Theatre, which had been known as "The Mecca Of Entertainment in Dublin" and was famous for its troupe of Tiller Girls, dropped its stage show in 1934 at a time when the second Theatre Royal was being demolished, in favour of a full time programme of films.

The new Royal made every effort to keep faith with the public by adhering to its stated aims. There was an International Celebrity Season (1935/36) of Subscription Concerts at 2.30 on selected Saturday afternoons: John Count McCormack appeared on 12 October; on November 2, Richard Tauber was the celebrity; Fritz Kreisler, the violin virtuoso, came on 18 January, followed on 1 February by Paul Robeson, and Sir Thomas Beecham conducted the London Philharmonic Orchestra on 15 February. Prices were from 75p to £3.

The second of the regular weekly shows was called *Radio New York* with the American comedian Will Mahony at the top of the bill. The 12 Tiller Girls were also featured and it is possible that they had transferred from the Capitol. This was followed by a London revue *Stop Press*. The Carl Rosa Opera Company with a repertoire of six works arrived in October, and were succeeded by Alfredo and his Gypsy Band. The C.B. Cochran, London revue *Streamline* by A.P. Herbert and Ronald Jeans with music by Vivian Ellis followed. James Agate had written of its London production:

> "......But I am not sure that all these wonders and marvels do not pale before the acting of Miss Florence Desmond, who not only has a white-hot sense of the ridiculous but can present it in a dozen different disguises. A dozen times in the evening Miss Desmond nails the grotesque truth to the board; she is a whole show in herself"

Tom Arnold (by arrangement with Sir Oswald Stoll) brought *Waltzes From Vienna* with music by Johann Strauss (Father & Son) and the cast list included a George Arnett who was **very** likely the same performer who joined the Jimmy O'Dea Company in 1947. A revue called *Leicester Square Looks Round* was announced for production in 1935, but it appears to have been staged at the Gaiety. It was notable for the appearance of that magnificent comedian, Sid Field who was, before his untimely death, the widely acknowledged funniest man in England. Fortunately, many of his routines are preserved in the otherwise undistinguished film *London Town* in which Field starred with Kay Kendall.

There was a change of policy when Cine-Variety was offered with Edward G. Robinson in the film *The Man With Two Faces* and the supporting stage show under the direction of the resident stage manager, James S. Charters, formerly of the London

George Formby

Charcoal drawing of Gracie Fields

Harry Bailey

Palladium, was uninspired with its offering of 'All-Star Variety'. The first year ended with a presentation of the old reliable *Peter Pan*.

The population of Dublin at that time was not sufficient to keep a theatre of the size of the Royal economically viable. From the beginning the general opinion was "they'll never fill it" and was given the pessimistic description of "a white elephant". The truth of this became all too apparent to the Dublin Theatre Co. directors who were disappointed when attendances fell far below expectations. J.E. Pearse appointed Hugh Margey, the erstwhile catering manager of the by now defunct Regal Rooms Restaurant, general manager of the Royal. A very stout, imposing man with a persuasive voice, Margey could best be described as a charlatan, and the London agents and stage stars had little difficulty in exploiting his complete lack of knowledge of show business. Whether selling meals or theatre seats Margey's curious axiom was – "it's just like selling bars of chocolate"! His plan of action appeared to involve the booking of top rank stars guaranteed to fill the Royal with the result that the public would develop the habit of patronising the theatre on a regular basis regardless of the quality of bill. This stratagem was doomed to failure. When Gracie Fields was booked to top the bill in July, 1936 she negotiated a fee so high that it left a potentially small profit for the theatre. But the wily lass from Rochdale wasn't finished with Margey yet; she insisted that a short film she had backed financially, Synge's *Riders To The Sea* (Ire 1935 b/w) directed by Brian Desmond Hurst with Ria Mooney, Denis Johnston, Kevin Gutherie, Sara Allgood and Shelagh Richards in the cast, should be shown during the week she was making her stage appearance.

Before Hugh Margey opened the doors of the Royal that week he had already established a financial loss. Years later, during the Second World War, the last great impresario at the Royal, Louis Elliman, opened negotiations with the phenomenally popular Irish ballad singer, Delia Murphy, known mainly for her radio broadcasts and gramophone records, to appear for a week at the Royal. Miss Murphy (who was the wife of Dr. Thomas Kiernan – Irish Ambassador to the Vatican) wasn't short of a few bob, but she agreed to accept the booking on condition that she was paid exactly what Gracie Fields had received. The horror stricken "Mr. Louis" hastily withdrew his offer. Other top-liners who appeared in 1936 were Arthur Tracy, billed as "The Street Singer" although he had never done so in his life; his most popular song was "Marta". The previously outstandingly popular Jack Doyle was billed to appear with his first wife, Judith Allen in a routine dubbed "Punch & Judy" but their booking was cancelled due to public outcry; to Catholic Ireland the idea of their former hero marrying a divorcee was anathema to them, and the Church and laity regarded him as "living in sin".

Ramon Novarro, a popular film star and his sister Carmen came in April. Billy Kelly, the last stage manager at the Royal, claimed that one night six women tried to kidnap Navarro. This has all the hallmarks of a publicity stunt devised by the theatre publicist, Jack Lyons. The Broadway and West End star Elizabeth Welch made an appearance and was followed by Bebe Daniels and her husband Ben Lyon. Bebe Daniels had appeared in the 1929 version of the movie *Rio Rita*, and Ben Lyon was a leading man in films, including the 1930 Howard Hughes epic *Hell's Angels* with Jean Harlow, until he became a studio executive who was credited with having discovered Marilyn Monroe by insisting that she be given a screen test. Bebe and Ben remembered their week at the Royal with great affection as it was the first tryout of their new stage act, and they were genuinely grateful to the theatre manager, Jack McGrath, for his patience, help and above all his invaluable advice. They resided in Britain during the war and starred in a very successful

Max Miller –
The Pure Gold of the Music Hall

Arthur Tracy –
The Street Singer

Max Wall –
Prof. Wallofsky

Jimmy James and 'Hutton Conyers' –
"Are you putting it about that I'm barmy?"

BBC radio series called *Hi Gang* with their children, Barbara and Richard and Vic Oliver in support.

Another visitor was the incorrigible and irrepressible Max Miller, known variously as 'The Cheeky Chappie' and 'The Pure Gold Of The Music Hall'. Women adored him, and he would tell them – "Miller's the name, lady. There'll never be another"! And there wasn't. The basis of his act was innuendo, and his great skill was to allow his audience to complete his jokes by making the connections themselves:

> "I like the girls who do; I like the girls who don't
> I hate the girl who says she will, and then she says she won't
> But the girl that I like best of all
> And I think you'll say I'm right
> Is the one who says she never has
> But looks as though she.......
> No, 'ere, listen....."

Maxie related many true stories about his early struggles, and a tour of Ireland in 1921.

> "We played at Limerick during the Catholic retreat when no good Catholic must go to any sort of amusement. A priest stood at the door of the hall, taking down the names of any of his parishioners who dared to enter so we ended up with just a handful of people.
> We all had to dress in a room beneath the stage. We had to go down some rickety stairs to get to it, and two of them were missing. This left a big gap and if you fell through it you landed in the cellar.
> I complained to a sort of general dogsbody, who called himself the manager, that the girls didn't want to dress with the boys in the same room. He seemed perplexed.
> "Why? Have you had a row?"
> In the end we rigged up a curtain to cut the place in half. The boys had to go through the girls' part to get to the stage. With the sights they saw and the conversations they heard they were men by the end of the week.
> At another town in Ireland six of us stayed in one house, paying ten bob each. The landlady was determined to teach me the Irish jig. In the end I got board and lodging, dancing lessons and a spot of company for half a quid – not a bad bargain, eh? The hall at Cavan was lit by candles. When the dance routines got under way the movement made by the artists blew out the candles and the stage manager had to keep a box of matches handy – the audience seemed to take it all for granted".

Miller's routine involved the use of two books – his White book (with all his clean jokes), and his Blue book (with all the others). When he asked the audience which one they wanted, everyone roared "The Blue Book!" Max wasn't noted for nuance as, for example, when he peeled a banana counting the skins as he did so – "One skin, Two skin, Three skin... 'ere lady – like a bite?"

Compared with the present day so-called 'alternative comedy' with its foul-language and scatalogical references dear old Max was decidedly saintly.

Jimmy (Schnozzle) Durante, on his way to making a film in England called *Land Without Music* with Richard Tauber, stopped off to do a week at the Royal. His act included all his now familiar material – 'Umbriago', 'The Lost Chord' and

'Ink-a-dink-a-doo'; at the end of the latter he threw his hat at the band who responded by flinging dozens of hats at him. Audiences were unaware of the significance of the line with which he finished his act at every performance – "Goodnight, Mrs Kalabash, wherever you are". Mrs Kalabash was reputed to be the first landlady who showed him any kindness when he started his long career in tatty burlesque and vaudeville houses, and Jimmy remembered her after every performance until the day he died. Despite trips on a side car down Moore Street where he compared the length of the bananas with that of his nose for the benefit of the newspaper photographers, even he could not fill the Royal, but he rejoiced in quiet strolls around Greystones after the show, thinking about the sounds that could be produced by language. The word "redundant", for instance, sounded to Jimmy like someone banging on a bass drum.

Another performer who appeared in that year had a surrealistic way with words; this was the Glasgow born, Billy Bennett, who had been brought up in Liverpool. James Agate said of him in the *Sunday Times*:

> "Bennett will live in the annals of the music-hall. Nobody who ever saw him is likely to forget that rubicund, unaesthetic countenance, that black, plastered quiff, that sergeant-major's moustache, that dreadful dinner jacket, that well-used dickey and seedy collar, the too-short trousers, the hobnailed boots, the continual perspiration which was the outward and visible sign of a mind struggling for expression – these things will not be forgotten... Let it be said of Billy Bennett that he raised every night in the week to the level of Saturday night. Bennett's grossness had that gusto about it which is like a high wind blowing over a noisome place. He never meant more or worse than he raucously proclaimed...and never uttered a word at which sensible people could take offence".

"My Mother Doesn't Know I'm On The Stage" by Billy Bennett

I'm cherishing a secret in my bosom
About this dreadful stage-life that I lead,
I've heard it said that pros are decent people,
But according to the papers that I read
Both actresses and actors are dead wrong 'uns
Whether from the Palace or the Hippodrome.
The chaps I meet outside know I'm an actor,
But I never breathe a word of it at home.
So my mother doesn't know I'm on the stage,
It would break her poor old heart if she found out,
She knows I'm a deserter from the Scottish Fusiliers,
She knows I stole a blind man's can – that got me seven years
She knows I've been connected with a gang of West End thugs,
And the police have had me twice inside the cage,
And she knows I mix with ladies that have got a shady past,
But my mother doesn't know I'm on the stage.
Sometimes she sees the powder on my clothing,
And this is such a nuisance to explain,
If she thought it was powder she'd go crazy,
Of course I had to tell her its cocaine.

The day she met me out with Gladys Cooper
She started screaming murder and police,
And would have caused a dreadful scene in public
So I told her that the girl was Crippen's niece.
'Cause my mother doesn't know I'm on the stage,
And then I draw six hundred pounds each week,
If she knew where it came from she'd shoot me like a dog,
So I said I stole the money box from an Irish synagogue,
She can think that I'm a murderer before she knows the truth
I had to have respect for her old age,
She knows that I'm a bigamist, a blackguard and a crook,
But thank Heaven she don't know I'm on the stage.

There was an appearance by the spectacular tap-dancing duo, the Nicholas Brothers, who appeared later in the forties in Hollywood musicals like *Down Argentine Way*, *Stormy Weather* and *The Pirate*, in which they danced the 'Be A Clown' routine with Gene Kelly.

The Mills Brothers and Donald Peers were popular singing acts. In 1913 Arthur Lucan created an Irish washerwoman character called Mrs Kelly, which was a variation of a pantomime dame, and with his wife Kitty McShane, whom he had met in panto, at the Queen's Royal Theatre, they presented their mother and daughter routine for the first time at the Tivoli theatre, Dublin in a sketch called 'The Come Over'. By 1934 they were on the bill for the Royal Variety Performance in a new routine called 'Bridget's Night Out' which they performed at the Theatre Royal in 1936. In the following year, after making their first of 15 films, their act was known as "Old Mother Riley and her Daughter Kitty". Arthur Lucan was a master at invective, and could at times be a superb comedian, but he was hampered in his personal and professional life by the unattractive Kitty McShane.

Kitty: Hello Mother. (To audience) Hello, boys!
Riley: 'Hello boys'! How dare you be so familiar.
Kitty: That's not being familiar, saying 'Hello' to the boys.
Riley: I think it's familiar. You don't know them, do you?
Kitty: No, but I will before the night's out.
Riley: (Outraged, aggressive, and jumping about with arms weaving) Oh, did you hear that, Mrs Girochie? S.O.S.! Me daughter's at it again! Oh, give me patience, give me a crowbar, give me a gun to play with, I've got a 'Target for Tonight'. Let me see you talking to a boy tonight and I won't be responsible for my actions. I don't object to you speaking to your boyfriends. It's what you're speaking *about* to them that worries me.
Kitty: I only speak about the same things that you spoke about when you were courting.
Riley: Oh, you ought to be ashamed of yourself! How did you know? Were you listening? I mean, who told you? I deny it!

Jack Hylton and his band featured a firm Dublin favourite from the old La Scala Theatre (The Capitol) days, Peggy Dell, as his principal vocalist. A poll taken in Britain at that time of favourite vocalists, of which there were scores working on radio, the stage, cabaret and with orchestras, listed Peggy in a very respectable fourth place.

In the summer of that year the Elliman family took over control of the Theatre Royal (and the Gaiety), and honoured all existing contracts. Maurice Elliman, the father of the family was chairman and for a short time directed the stage shows; his son Louis was managing director, and later took responsibility for the shows; another son Abe was general manager responsible for booking the films, and Maxie who managed the Corinthian cinema for a time became house manager of the Royal.

Hugh Margey was given a take it or leave it offer of the management of the Savoy Cinema restaurant which he accepted. His theatrical activity would henceforth be confined to making up the salaries of the Madam Van Aalst trio, formerly of the Plaza Restaurant in Abbey Street, and which now provided music during lunches and suppers at the Savoy.

THE ELLIMAN FAMILY

Maurice Elliman arrived in Dublin as a refugee from the Tsarist persecutions in Russia with very little money. Like many other Dublin-Jewish men he was a resourceful and tireless worker. Initially, he engaged in various small ventures like replacing the broken panes of glass in neighbourhoods opulent enough to boast a green house in the garden. Then he set up a greengrocery business, but it was the film business, then in its infancy that caught his imagination. He took his projector and silent films around the village halls and barns or anywhere else where the locals could be amazed by the new invention of moving pictures. And he hit upon the idea of filling out his film shows with a concert featuring local amateur acts – the fore-runner to what was to be known professionally years later as Cine-variety. He prospered and his next project was to build a cinema in Camden Street after an unsuccessful trial period in O'Connell Street. His new

On right, Louis Elliman (T.R. Royle) with the former President of Ireland, Mr. Sean T. O'Kelly

cinema was called the Theatre de Luxe, and it still stands today. During its construction, his son Louis ran in to his father one morning and informed him breathlessly that the builders were erecting his cinema on the wrong site. A hasty investigation revealed that they were indeed building the cinema on the site of what would later become the Star Furnishing Company. Louis had earned his place in the business, but Maurice had other plans for his son.

Louis Elliman was born in 1906 and before his death at the age of 59 in November 1965, his advice or services were called upon to further any type of entertainment in the legitimate and variety theatre, films, radio and television. He was the greatest impresario Ireland ever produced, and in his own lifetime he was referred to as Mr. Show-Business. He was managing director of Odeon (Ireland) Ltd and of the Gaiety Theatre. He was chairman of Amalgamated Cinemas (Ireland) Ltd and vice-chairman of Irish Cinemas Ltd. His influence extended to Dublin, Cork, Limerick, Bray, Dun Laoihaire, and various other locations round the country. With Emmet Dalton he brought to fruition the idea of an Irish film industry when they founded Ardmore Studios in Bray, Co. Wicklow which was opened in May, 1958 by Sean Lemass.

He was a graduate of the National University, and his father had planned for him a career as a chemist to which end he was apprenticed to a chemist in South Richmond Street where he worked for very little money for eight years. Frustrated, he went to London and secured the Irish agency for First National Pictures and began his career in the entertainment business.

In 1936 on Louis's advice his father bought the Gaiety Theatre, and control of the Theatre Royal followed, thus launching the family in the theatre business as well, in which they featured the most famous names of stage and screen from Britain, Hollywood and France. Once asked for his opinion on the greatest performers he had managed in his career Louis replied "Jimmy O'Dea and Micheál MacLíammóir".

An astute business man who rarely took holidays except for the occasional busman's trip to Hollywood his most inspired and productive period was during the second world war (1939-45) when he kept both the Royal and the Gaiety open with entirely Irish talent. At the Gaiety there were regular seasons by the O'Dea/O'Donovan Company; the Rathmines and Rathgar Musical Society; Edwards/MacLíammóir Gate Theatre Company; and two new amateur companies – the Dublin Musical Society and the Old Belvedere Musical and Dramatic Society. When the Dublin Grand Opera Society was formed in 1941 the President, Prof. John F. Larchet paid tribute to Louis Elliman, who, when they were unable to secure a suitable rehearsal room in preparation for their first production at the Gaiety in May, 1941, put the rehearsal room at the Royal at their disposal and treated them generously from a business point of view. In addition, Louis presented his own independent productions such as the still remembered *Show Boat*.

In marked contrast to the opinions of his regular performers, whose salaries were increased when business was good, one commentator wrote – "With respect, my personal experience is that he would take the pennies from a corpse's eyes, and then come back for the coffin lid". No such invective was heaped on the head of a dodgy so-called investment consultant whose passing was noted by the fleeced author "with deep regret and affection"!

George McFall, the stage manager at the Gaiety, recalls that on one occasion the stage staff were making a collection in order to defray the expenses of one of their number for a trip to Lourdes but the shortfall was considerable so they approached Louis, who on being informed of the amount reminded them that the man would require some spending money in his pocket, and accordingly wrote a generous cheque. A fact that is not generally known is that he rescued Edwards and MacLíammóir from several sticky financial situations, and that Orson Welles left our shores for the last time, after an unsuccessful appearance as Falstaff in *Chimes At Midnight* owing Louis a considerable amount of money. He offered Margaret Burke Sheridan an open cheque to sing two songs at a concert in the Gaiety, and he and his wife Ettie were extremely kind to the Prima Donna when she was dying in a Dublin nursing home. In business, naturally, he always sought the best terms, and he was only too well aware of the fact that a contributory factor to the wholesale closure of theatres in Britain was the avarice of star performers in demanding ridiculously high fees.

He was a very private person who rarely gave interviews or agreed to be photographed. Even regular patrons at the Royal were unaware of the fact that the producer of the shows "T.R. Royle" was Louis Elliman. He was a slightly mysterious man, and the more one knew about him, the deeper the mystery became.

When he died in 1965 Micheál MacLíammóir said "He was very good to us all, to be remembered in terms of brotherhood. He had the theatre in his blood and he was a friend to us all."

Hilton Edwards said that he had known Mr. Elliman for 25 years and "this city will be the poorer without him." Maureen Potter suggested that the Gaiety should be known as the "Elliman Theatre". Brendan Smith said that the theatre must be allowed to continue as a "monument to the interest and love that Louis Elliman had for us".

Louis was, of course, human, and used his power occasionally in the dispensation of justice. Jimmy Campbell, who had made a few gramophone recordings, was anxious to do some broadcasting with the Theatre Royal Orchestra, not for the financial rewards, which would be derisory, but for the country-wide publicity that would benefit the theatre. An audition was arranged by Radio Éireann which was at that time controlled by civil servants who monitored even the records being played of Bing Crosby. After the audition, which was in itself an insult to professional musicians, Jimmy was told by these jigs and reels purists that the music he played, jazz and popular, was considered by them to be "pagan". Years later when Radio Éireann approached Norman Metcalfe to broadcast a series of programmes on the Royal Compton organ, they were very surprised when Louis Elliman proposed to charge them a fee for the use of the theatre organ, leaving a balance so small from the total budget that Norman declined the engagement. Louis felt justified not only in coming back for the coffin lid but the coffin itself!

Dance bands were very much in favour in the late thirties; they could be heard frequently on the BBC and audiences were curious to see them in the flesh. In 1937 Harry Roy and his band, Mantovani and his band, and the Roy Fox band each topped the bill at the Royal. Solo musical performers included the violinist, Albert Sandler, Charlie Kunz on his piano, and Larry Adler on what he prefers to be known as the 'mouth organ'. Helen Morgan, the star of Broadway's *Show Boat* appeared for a week, and comedy was provided by Tommy Trinder ("You lucky people"), Florence Desmond the brilliant impressionist performed her "Hollywood Party" routine. The eccentric dancer and comedian Max Wall – Professor Wallofski himself, would break off his act to welcome latecomers "Trouble with the bike? – the show hasn't started yet...I'm the compere" or deliver one liners after giving a particularly nasty cough – "I must get a room tonight....I've been using that joke for twenty years." Then becoming aggressive and almost daring the audience to like him, he would suddenly return to his normal relaxed style with the comment "That's enough of that". He finished his act with his eccentric dance act which was reminiscent of a gorilla sloping about its cage.

One of the first great Irish comedians to appear at the Royal was Cecil Sheridan, who in 1937, had won first prize in a talent contest at the Whitehall Carnival. He won cash and a weeks engagement at the Queens Theatre where he was so successful that he was booked into the Royal. Described as "The Parody King" his work was hilarious because he kept the parodies as close to the original song as possible. When his theme music was

Jimmy O'Dea

being played Cecil would walk slowly to the mike centre stage dressed in an old fashioned hearseman's overcoat with his hands stuck up the sleeves and a flat cap to complete the ensemble. Cecil had a very bad stammer in normal life, but this disappeared completely when he walked on a stage, but he found it difficult to control his nervous disposition. He once said "Everyone has nerves going on stage, but mine wear hob-nailed boots"! His was a genuine comedy creation, based on the hen-pecked husband.

"It Had To Be You"
(Parody by Cecil Sheridan)

Introduction:

Now to look at me you'd think I was an independent man
I was until I fell into the arms of Mary Anne,
She trapped me in a garage and I just could not back out
So I promised I would marry her, she hooked me, like a trout.

Chorus:

It had to be you, it had to be you,
I must have been sunk or elephants drunk,
When I married you.
You've beaten me too, I'm black and I'm blue,
Me suit's up the spout, I can't get it out,
All over you
One day out in Bray with Mrs. McKay,
Yez went out in a boat, but it wouldn't float,
You sank in the blue,
They'll both of them drown, my heart gave a thrill,
Then somebody said 'there's one breathing still',
And it had to be you, it had to be you, it had to be you.

Dance bands were still popular in 1938 and included, Nat Gonella, Jack Lewis and his Rolling Stones (the name might have been the same, but the music was certainly different!); Ray Noble and his all-American orchestra; Billy Cotton and his band (Wakey, Wakey!); Henry Hall and the BBC dance orchestra; Ambrose and his band, featuring the then little known Vera Lynn. Recordings of all these big bands are prized today in the collections of faithful old aficionados. Big Bill Campbell and his Rocky Mountain Rhythm, BBC superstars, performed their cowboy campfire routine. "Caroll Levis and his Discoveries" was a show that also had its origins in radio and was the forerunner to Hughie Greene's long running TV show 'Opportunity Knocks'. Bert Wheeler of Wheeler and Wolsey film fame appeared solo as his partner had died in 1938. There was more comedy from Naughton & Gold who must have been released from the Crazy Gang at the Palladium for a week. In addition to the hilarious 'Monsewer' Eddie Gray the Crazy Gang was made up of three independent double acts – Naughton & Gold, Nervo & Knox, and Flanagan & Allen. The latter duo was the most entertaining as a single act outside of the Crazy Gang concept. Nervo & Knox had a knockabout wrestling routine, but Naughton & Gold had a rather old fashioned cross-talk routine which did not, however, reflect upon their popularity. Charlie Naughton and Jimmy Gold had been in the business from 1900 and knew a thing or two about putting over very basic material:

Jimmy: Do you like milk?
Chas: Yes, I like that drunken milk.

Jimmy: Drunken milk?
Chas: The canned stuff, but I prefer beer.
Jimmy: Why do you drink beer?
Chas: Because I'm thirsty.
Jimmy: Because you're thirsty – then you should drink milk. Milk makes blood.
Chas: Oh, I'm not bloodthirsty.

The beautiful Evelyn Laye ("Boo" to her friends) appeared in that year. She was a Charles Cochran star, notably in his production of Offenbach's *La Belle Helene* with George Robey. She was one of an extraordinary type of English musical comedy star all of whom seemed to have the same or similar qualities, and talent. They included Jessie Matthews, Gertrude Lawrence, Cicely Courtneidge, Binnie Hale, Pat Kirkwood and Anna Neagle. They all seemed to share the same leading men, but one of Miss Laye's co-stars was Jimmy O'Dea in pantomime at the Liverpool Empire in 1946. Another young performer that year who would later have close professional associations with Jimmy O'Dea was "charming little Maureen Potter".

The highest paid star in Britain at that time, who had made several appearances in revue at the second Theatre Royal, was the now famous film star, George Formby, who appeared in conjunction with the première of his latest film *Keep Fit* at the Regal Rooms Cinema next door. The personality with the wide toothy grin which gave the impression of spontaneous friendliness sang dutifully the three numbers inevitably demanded by his audiences – "Chinese Laundry Blues", "The Window Cleaner" and "Leaning On A Lamp Post". His wife, Beryl, who was known to all by reputation but contributed absolutely nothing to the act, walked on at the end and shared in George's applause. Jimmy Campbell handed up a rather sad looking bouquet of fake flowers, Beryl mimed a mock surprised "For me?" and accepted them graciously until they were required for the next performance. George was no stranger to Dublin or indeed many parts of Ireland; as a young lad his father had sent him to train as a jockey at the Curragh, and feeling home-sick for his native Wigan for which his music hall star father, George Formby Senior, known as "The Wigan Nightingale", had invented a nonexistent Wigan pier (which even George Orwell recognised) decided to run away from the stables, but he was apprehended at Amiens Street Station, and was lodged in a cell in Mountjoy overnight, which was lucky for the young Formby because the steamer he would have boarded at Dun Laoghaire was sunk by enemy action with complete loss of life.

Another comedy duo, Clapham & Dwyer topped the bill in that year. Bill Dwyer was the straight man, and the tall Charlie Clapham, immaculate in top hat and monocle performed one of the routines which developed from situations and characters familiar to most audiences from their many radio broadcasts.

Bill: Now, do you play golf?
Charlie: No. But...er...I can't give it up.
Bill: The first important factor in the game is.....
Charlie: I suppose you've never seen my cow Cissie play golf have you?
Bill: No. I don't wish to hear this.
Charlie: Oh, it's a scream, it is, really. She played a very famous tenor the other day, you know, and – yes – it was very good...and she beat him too. He gave her – ahem – eight moos.
Bill: Eight *what*?

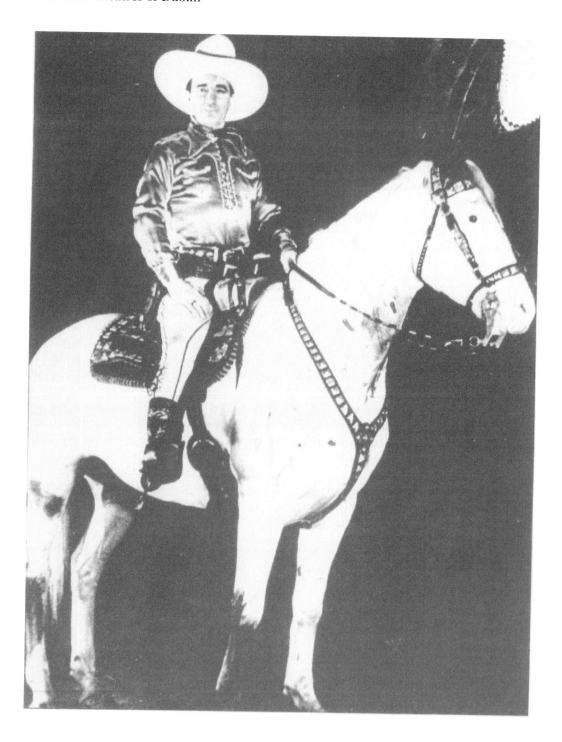

Tom Mix and his Wonder Horse, Tony

Charlie: Eight moos. You see every time he took his drive she moo'd, and he being a tenor singer, you see, of course, it upset him. You understand? These tenors do this, me-me-me....

Bill: Yes, well if you don't mind I'll continue.

Charlie: That's all right. I'm just trying to help you, you know, that's all.......

Cowboys rather than orchestras were in favour in 1939. Tom Mix and his wonder horse Tony came in January, and did some sharp shooting with a rifle, and we read later in the papers that the cowboy astride his horse entered the hallowed precincts of the foyer of the Savoy Hotel, London through the front entrance. Gene Autry, the singing cowboy, came in August during Horse Show week, which was appropriate in a way because he, too, brought his horse, Champion, "the world's most famous horse". Autry rode what was alleged to be Champion down O'Connell Street, and a mob of frenzied youngsters began pulling hairs out of the horse's tail which casts doubt on the authenticity of the 'Famous Horse'.

It is doubtful if Champion's unfortunate 'stand-in' had much of a tail left by the time it reached its stable at the back of the Royal in Townsend Street. The Autry show comprised a film supposedly depicting him leaving his ranch by stagecoach for his trip to Ireland, and to the delight of his young fans the stage coach was driven by Gene's movie pal, Smiley Burnett. The film screen disappeared into the flies, the stage lights came on, Jimmy Campbell started up the band, and Gene rode on to the stage on Champion who swished a beautiful, long, curry-combed tail, and stood on his hind legs while Gene waved his stetson to his frenzied young audience. He sang a popular song of the time which he had also taken as the title for his latest film "South of the Border". The supporting bill included Elsie Carlisle, described as a "songstress of radio". The policy of the management seems to have been a reversal to some of the features of the second theatre because three musical comedies were presented in this year. First was *The Desert Song* starring Harry Welchman, followed later on by Tom Arnold's London production of *Balalaika* by Eric Maschwitz and George Posford (who were to write George Formby's only West End show, *Zip Goes A Million* at the Palace Theatre). The third musical, which reputedly had a cast of 100 was *White Horse Inn*. Max Wall paid a return visit, and was assisted in his mayhem by a familiar local artist, Noel Purcell, who had recently left the O'D Company after playing straight man to Jimmy O'Dea for ten years. Other bill toppers were Jack Jackson & his band and Turner Layton without his partner Johnstone; Layton and Johnstone were two of the few black artists in Britain at the time but with their relaxed manner they were popular duettists, before they split up in 1935. Jasper Maskelyne was then the leading magician on the stage, and Peg-leg-Bates, who had been the star of *Blackbirds of 1934* at the London Coliseum, was something of a novelty. This handsome young black man was described as a monoped dancer. Mr. Bates, like Long John Silver, had a genuine wooden leg attached to his left knee joint, but this did not deter him from dancing, especially tap dancing, with a style, speed and grace rarely achieved by those with two perfectly good legs. Tom Walls of the Aldwych farces fame made an appearance (more than likely it coincided with some important race meeting). Alice Delysia, who was French, quite overwhelmed the Royal audiences with her flamboyant personality and seductive voice. The original Three Stooges (Larry, Curly and Moe) made their madcap appearance, and comedy of a quieter but equally crazy variety was provided by "the comedians' comedian" Jimmy James (born James Casey he started his career as 'Terry, the Blue-Eyed Irish Boy'). Although he didn't drink he had an act in which he was the perfect drunk, but he also worked with two loonies, one of whom was supposed to have a lion, a giraffe and an elephant in a small cardboard box. James Casey Junior said of his father, Jimmy James: "He was involved with these two idiots who called themselves Eli Woods and Hutton Conyers, and he believed in them – it was clear to everybody else that he was madder than they were. He'd say he'd given up his job to put the first one on the stage" Conyers would come on, interrupting a discussion of Eli's stage career – with one of the best entry lines ever written:

Conyers:	Hey.
James:	How do you do?
Conyers:	Are you putting it around that I'm barmy?
James:	No.
Conyers:	Well is it him, then? (Indicating Eli)
Eli:	I don't want any.
James (to Conyers):	He doesn't want any.
Eli:	How much are they?
James:	How much...no...it's not him.
Conyers:	Well, somebody's putting it around that I'm barmy.
James:	Did you want to keep it a secret? Your mother would have been better off with a set of spoons.

Donald Wolfit played the Mad Hatter in one of his favourite productions which he resurrected at intervals, *Alice In Wonderland* with Sara Westerman as 'Alice', and the production designed by Barbara Heseltine, in January 1940. This was followed by the Danish musical comedy star, Carl Brisson, who had, at one, time been middleweight champion of Europe. The Carl Rosa Opera Company appears to have been the last cross-channel company to play the theatre for the duration of the war. The Christmas pantomime in 1940/41 starred Noel Purcell as dame in *Mother Hubbard Goes To Town* which was directed by the stage manager, Charlie Wade, who had years of experience at the Capitol Theatre.**

The early stages of the Second World War which began in September 1939, were known as 'the phoney war', but now the fighting was in earnest, with the Nazis over-running Western Europe. This resulted in severe travel restrictions, and English acts could no longer visit Ireland. There appears to have been just one exception during the period of the war; this was Robert Donat who appeared at a special matinee at the Theatre Royal in aid of the Newspapers Press Fund on 27th April, 1941. He delivered extracts from James Hilton's *Goodbye Mr. Chips* which he had successfully filmed. The supporting bill included the Abbey Players in Lennox Robinson's one act play *Never the time and the place* with Eileen Crowe and her husband F.J. McCormick. The compere was Lord Longford. The last cross channel revue company to play in Dublin finished their season at the Olympia Theatre with a show called, very appropriately, *Farewell Dublin*.

The opportunities for Irish artists were immediately apparent, but they needed discipline, purpose and direction, and even Louis Elliman himself took some time to realise that he was the only man with the facilities at his disposal to provide them. Indeed he had to take control if his theatres were not to close. Many of his future stars were rank amateurs possessed of raw talent requiring time and experience to achieve full professionalism, and Louis had the patience to coax them and give them time.

The Walk Down: "The Jimmy O'Dea Show" with (left to right) Vernon Hayden, Ursula Doyle, Harry O'Donovan, Maureen Potter, Jimmy O'Dea, Barrie Ingham, Danny Cummins, Alice Dalgarno, Frankie Blowers and Babs De Monte

Jim Jonson's fit-up show "Titbits of 1936" at the Arcadia Gardens, Bangor, with a cast of 20 performers. Cecil Nash is third from right in the back row

VARIETY IN THE STICKS

A study of the Irish contribution to British music hall/variety, and American vaudeville would require a separate volume. So many of the so-called Irish artists were not, in fact, Irish at all, and in many cases could not even claim Irish descent – they adopted the Irish persona simply because audiences liked it, and, of course, when it was exaggerated it heightened the stage effect. In addition, pseudo Irish songs, usually of American origin, were extremely popular. "Irish" acts were popular in London years before English regional or Scottish acts were acceptable there. Nevertheless, a few genuinely Irish artists did succeed in making a name for themselves in the music halls – Shaun Glenville, Willie John Ashcroft, Joe O'Gorman (whose sons, the O'Gorman Brothers, succeeded him at the top of the bill), and Pat Rafferty. Later in the 30s the most successful Irish performer in Britain was Jimmy O'Dea, who with his own company, which included Noel Purcell, Connie Ryan, Fay Sargent, Eileen Marmion, Tom Dunne and Harry O'Donovan, made his London debut at Sir Oswald Stoll's premier music hall, the Coliseum, and went on to make films and several comedy series for the BBC. The O'D partnership should be credited with the then modern concept of ethnic Irish humour. Noel Purcell said: "He was certainly a breath of fresh air to the people in England; they never saw the likes of this little fellow".

In the dying days of variety in the 50s a few performers like Val Doonican, The Bachelors, Dave Allen and Harry Bailey made an impression. Considering the size of our population and the number of relatively few who made it to the top in either music hall or later in variety, our record is a respectable one, especially in a medium that was completely alien to our culture.

At home in Ireland, Irish performers, generally, could never rely on more than an occasional week in the plush theatres of Dublin, Cork or Belfast. Their working lives were restricted mainly to the sticks – a succession of tents, town halls, parochial halls and even barns, which gave rise to the description of these travelling companies as "the fit-ups" or "barnstormers". Each company carried all their props, scenery, costumes, curtains, and lighting system (flare lamps in the beginning), and if necessary the materials for erecting a temporary improvised stage which they would fit-up in whatever sort of venue was available. So, country rather than city folk were most likely to be familiar with the work of Irish performers as there had been a network of fit-up companies since early in the 19th century. One of the oldest and most famous companies was the J.B. Carrickford company (who did play the Queen's Royal Theatre under the management of P.J. Bourke). The founder of the company in 1830 was born in Wexford and his true name was Browne. There were at that time as few as three companies on the road – Duffy's Circus, an English opera company, and the Carrickfords. Later on, early performers in the fit-ups, like their contemporaries in the English music halls, were responsible for the composition of many well-known songs, through which they created their own distinctive tradition. The much loved Johnny Patterson, who was a clown and bagpiper from Clare who had toured America with the circus, wrote many well-known songs: 'The Stone Outside Dan Murphy's Door'; 'The Garden Where The Praties Grow'; 'Goodbye Johnny Dear'; and a song that he composed for his wife, 'Bridget Donoghue'. He did not have the protection of copyright, and like others his songs were stolen and published by plagiarists.

Another prolific performer was Thomas Patrick Keenan who was born in Dorset St, Dublin in 1866 and formed his own company called The Bohemian Minstrels. Keenan is

BEENIE DANIELLS and BEN BONO
(with " Jerry O'Sullivan ")

*Ben Bono and Beenie Daniells
in their fit-up show*

DERRY O'DONOVAN

*Most of the touring shows were family affairs. Frank O'Donovan and his wife Kitty MacMahon
(left) had a successful fit-up company. Their daughter Derry O'Donovan (right) toured in the
show as a singer and dancer, and took part in the sketches, before later joining the O'D Company
at the Gaiety Theatre*

credited with countless songs, many of which were stolen or are credited today as being 'traditional' – 'The Old Rustic Bridge By The Mill'; 'Hello, Patsy Fagan'; 'Off To Philadelphia In The Morning'; 'The Boys From The County Armagh'; 'If You're Irish Come Into The Parlour'; 'Mother Machree'; and 'Peggy O'Neill'. He wrote 'The Gambler's End' for Horace Wheatley in The Big Tree pub in Dorset St, and it was made very famous in the 1940s when it was recorded by Delia Murphy as 'The Moonshiner'.

Percy French's first composition 'Abdul the Bulbul Ameer' was plagiarised, but the former Trinity College man took care to protect his later output. All of these songs stand comparison with music hall numbers and were as enduring in their time, but they were never regarded as music hall material, their popular generic collective title being "come-all-yehs".

Over the years the numbers of fit-up companies grew until in the 1930s it is estimated that there were as many as sixty on the road, and 80% of these would have been presenting a mixture of drama and variety, so that a distinctly strong tradition of Irish type variety was established. There was an established formula for these shows from which a company manager deviated at his peril. Harry O'Donovan toured the new style revue type of show in the 1920s and lost his shirt where he was lucky and the irate patrons didn't break up the hall.

First there had to be a variety show lasting at least an hour. Then there was an interval during which raffle tickets were sold. Next, there was a melodrama, again lasting over an hour, and might be one of the stock old favourites or a completely unauthorised potted version of a popular film or book for which there would be no script; aware of the general direction of the plot, the cast made up the dialogue as they went along with all the natural Irish ability to ad-lib. After this the raffle was drawn. There followed what was billed as either a "laughable" or a "screaming" farce, depending on the faith a manager might have in either adjective. Some took no chances and used both to describe their comedy epics. The screamingly funny dialogue in "Who Died First" went something like:

"What did he die of?"

"He died of a Tuesday"

"No, I mean what was his complaint?"

"Oh, there was no complaints, everyone was satisfied"

Normally the farce concluded the entertainment, but some companies would clear all the forms and chairs to the sides of the hall, and the pianist or accordionist would thump out the music for a dance. All for sixpence.

The companies (in no particular chronology) included:

The George Daniel's Road Show; The Hayden Family of Entertainers (which included Jimmy O'Dea's future manager Vernon Hayden); The O'Brien & Ireland Company in which Dr. Cyril Cusack made his stage debut as Little Willie in *East Lynne*; The McFadden Company included Denis Franks who became famous as the thorn in the side of Ulick O'Connor on 'The Late Late Show'. Purcells' Booth (not Noel Purcell, although Noel toured his own company for a short period in the Early 40s); Harry O'Donovan's Revue Company (before he met Jimmy, but with him afterwards for short spells); The Frank O'Donovan Company with his daughter Derry; The Harry Bailey Show (which is the only way to describe Harry's activities as he toured with a circus, in variety and with a dance band); William Costello and his Bohemian Players; Ben Bono's *Irish Review*; Vic Loving and her son from England with their glamorous *Flash Parade*; Dick Forbes & Mike Nono with Dan Gibbons in *Muldoon's Picnic*; Percy Holmshaw and his wife May Royle and daughter June; Edgar Benyon and his spectacular magic show *Bamboozalem*; The Traynors; The Bow-Bell Company; Harry Lynton, Courtney and Sons, and Jim Jonson who toured pantomimes in all seasons all year round.

Many of the performers lacked technique and a lack of polish was very obvious which is not surprising in view of their rough and ready working conditions. But when the time came many helped to keep the Dublin theatres open which was, in the end, a hopeless exercise since the same theatres have since been demolished. Even the fit-ups are no more; change and eventual extinction came gradually. First, there was radio, then the silent movies, followed by the talkies, then in the 1950s the final blow fell with the widespread instillation of television. Nowadays, country folk unaware of a continuing tradition, albeit through a different medium, watch a grandson of the first J.B. Carrickford play a prominent role in RTE's *Glenroe* while out on the dark country roads the ghosts of the swaggering caravans pass silently by.

Another source of talent was the amateur company in the Father Matthew Hall, Church St, Dublin. It was a valuable training ground in its time and a highly effective theatre workshop before that term was first coined. Young amateur performers could appear in every conceivable sort of production – variety shows, Gilbert & Sullivan operettas, first rate drama, musical comedy and, of course, the annual pantomime, until he or she decided on a preference and then specialised in whatever medium suited their talents and temperament.

Several of these amateurs later pursued professional careers at the Capitol, and the Olympia Theatre (under the direction of Lorcan Bourke), and Louis Elliman engaged them when he introduced his policy of serial shows. Prominent among them were Jack Cruise, Mike Nolan, Mick Eustace, Rita Conroy, Joe Duffy, Paddy Tyrrell etc.

❦

Richard Hayward and May Devitt shared top billing at the Royal in 1940. Hayward was an actor and entertainer connected with the Belfast Repertory Company, who had made a couple of films in the mid 30s. May Devitt was to become one of the pillars of the Dublin Grand Opera Society (1941). Miss Devitt had already scored a success on her initial debut with a professional company, The Universal Grand Opera Company, at the Gaiety, in 1936. The *Irish Independent* said of her performance in *Madame Butterfly* – "May Devitt, a young Dublin guest artiste, was the 'Butterfly'. Both in features and figure she was eminently suited to play Puccini's pathetic heroine, and looked more like 'fifteen exactly' than most of the prima donnas I have seen. Her voice is light, warm in tone, and with a certain satisfying brilliance in its upper register. She played the part, I might almost say, lived the part, and carried conviction by her earnestness". May Devitt was not in the very front rank of divas, but she had great sex appeal and magnetism, two qualities that ensured a rapport with the audience in a theatre the size of the Royal.

They were followed in August by a miniature tattoo called *The Roll Of The Drum*. This was basically a recruiting show featuring 200 Irish soldiers, the No. 1 Army Band conducted by Lt. Dermot O'Hara, and the Drums and pipes of the 2nd and 5th Infantry Battalions, and scenes demonstrating Arms Drill and Physical Training. It was produced with the co-operation of the Army General Staff, and was staged entirely by Charlie Wade, the Royal stage manager. Dances and Ensembles were arranged by

Harry Bailey, Noel Purcell and "the singing duck" backstage at the Royal during "Hullabaloo"

"Sojering is Sojering"
Joe Duffy, Mike Nolan, Paddy Tyrrell and Jimmy Davenport in the Military Pageant
"THE ROLL OF THE DRUM"
at the Theatre Royal, August, 1940

Violet Hindle of the Royal Violettes whose Hussarette Costumes were designed by Micheál MacLíammóir. A camp-fire song scena, and an historical song scena featured singers, John Lynsky and Tom Peacock. Two comedy scenes – 'Sojering is Sojering' and 'Parkside Perambulations' had Mike Nolan, Joe Duffy, and Paddy Tyrrell (later of the Queen's 'Happy Gang'), straight from the Father Matthew Hall in what must have been their first professional engagements; they were joined in the comedy by Jimmy Davenport who was in fact a member of the orchestra which provided the incidental music conducted by Jimmy Campbell with A. Gordon Spicer at the organ. This special production dedicated to National Defence broke existing Dublin records for attendance during its three-week run. As the war progressed two further tattoo type shows were presented at the Royal – *Tramp, Tramp, Tramp* and *Signal Fires*.

In the following year, 1941, the first of a long series of weekly shows was presented called *Hullabaloo* with Harry Bailey (who also wrote the scripts) Sam Mooney, Josephine O'Hagan and Noel Purcell in the earlier of 14 Editions. A new show *Applesauce*, ran for four editions in October with Peggy Dell, Mike Nolan, John Lynsky, Josephine O'Hagan, and, in the final edition, Jack Cruise. Christopher Casson, who had been in *The Roll Of The Drum*, and Eire O'Reilly, who was to become identified with the Queen's, made infrequent appearances. That Louis Elliman had not yet devised a definite production policy is illustrated by the fact that in a show called *Hi-diddle-diddle* in November, he featured two legitimate actors and company managers, Stanley Illsley and Leo McCabe "in entirely different parts from any they have previously appeared in". No record of the content of this bizarre double act can be traced. In December, Jimmy O'Dea's brother, Ken O'Dea appeared in *Ducks And Drakes* with his partner, Norman Redmond, in new songs, and parodies. The bill also included Molly O'Connor and Frank Silvio, the harpist who could speak English perfectly, but posed as an Italian with fractured English by announcing that he would now play "Nella da Dean"! The pantomime in the 1941/42 season was *Cinderella* with Noel Purcell and Mike Nolan as the Ugly Sisters. John Lynsky was in the cast, and making his first appearance at the Royal, Eddie Byrne as Baron Weasle. The script was by "Namille", but since it is clearly 'Elliman' spelt backwards it is evidence that Louis was beginning to take a practical interest in the shows, although for the moment he left the actual staging to Charlie Wade.

There were three major series shows in 1942 with frequent changes of cast and some innovations. It was during this period that Eddie Byrne first introduced his popular quiz show "Double or Nothing". The casts included Noel Purcell, Eddie Byrne, Peggy Dell, Harry Bailey, Mike Nolan, Johnny Caross, Cecil Sheridan, Jack Cruise and Joe Duffy, the Thunder Brothers, the O'Keeffe Brothers, Josephine O'Hagan, the Flanagan Sisters, Chrissie Manning, Chris Reilly (dame comedian), the Violettes, and as a contemporary critic wrote... "Maureen Potter of the twinkling feet, showed that she is developing her vocal ability".

On 9th November, 1940 a young man called Sean Mooney, a baritone, was a competitor in the Radio Éireann weekly singing competition "Newcomers' Hour". He sang 'Trees', and the judge was so taken with his voice that he asked Sean to repeat his test piece. When Louis Elliman was searching for a singer for the show *Round and About* Noel Purcell remembered Sean who was now singing with the church choir at the Star Of The Sea, Sandymount. Sean auditioned at the Royal on a Tuesday morning and was on the stage singing professionally on the following Sunday afternoon. He was a firm favourite at the Royal and later the Capitol for years. In 1943 he appeared as Valentine in *Faust*

Cecil Sheridan

Eddie Byrne

Danny Cummins

Jack Cruise

with May Devitt, James Johnston, J.C. Browner, and Patricia Black for the Dublin Grand Opera Society at the Gaiety Theatre, where he also appeared in their centenary production of *The Bohemian Girl* by the Society in 1943. The pantomime in the 1942/43 season was *Red Riding Hood* (in ten scenes and a finale); Noel Purcell played Mrs. Nuala Hubbard with Eddie Byrne, described as a truly terrifying Wolf... "and proves his ability as an actor"...The cast of a hundred included Peggy Dell as Principal Boy (Robin Hood); Olive Briggs as Maid Marion; Renee Flynn as the Fairy Queen; Mike Nolan as Jimmy Green, with Jack Harrington, Jerry Dawson, Ursula Doyle (as Red Riding Hood), Johnny Caross as Felix the cat, the Violettes, Royal Raptures, Royal Rosettes. Orchestrations were by Jimmy Campbell and Arthur Bell, with Charlie Wade responsible for staging. There also appears to have been a screen attraction *About Face* with William Tracy.

Early in 1943 Louis Elliman implemented a new policy at the Theatre Royal embracing all the best features of the contributions by local artists since the outbreak of war, and he would supervise the production of these shows personally under the pseudonym, "T.R. Royle" which was intended purely for public consumption, and the added injection of mystery which he seemed to delight in.

And the mystery prevailed because few Dubliners were aware of the true identity of the obscure 'T.R. Royle'. This posed no problem for his regular colleagues and employees and artists who called him "Mr. Louis" as they had always done.

The first new series of shows was called *Royal Flush* with a cast headed by Noel Purcell and Peggy Dell; occasional guest artists were Harry Bailey and Cecil Sheridan and Sean Mooney and Mollie O'Connor provided the weekly musical spot. Eddie Byrne reintroduced his 'Double or Nothing' quiz game. During the run of this show in April, Violet Hindle made her last appearance with the Violettes. The troupe was taken over by Alice Delgarno who devised the choreography, and costumes were designed by Babs de Monte and Christine Kealy. "Mr. Louis" renamed the troupe The Royalettes.

THE ROYALETTES

In 1939 Alice Dalgarno and Babs de Monte arrived in Ireland with a troupe of dancers called the Violettes to play a booking of one week at the Royal. Most of the troupe were ex-Tiller girls and were very professional with perfect precision and timing. At that time "Mr. Louis" had been looking for a good permanent troupe for the theatre as the war was obviously going to stop the booking of Cross-Channel performers. He had tried several troupes without success so he asked the Violettes to play an extra week, and then another. Eventually, as many as could be persuaded to stay remained to form the nucleus of a troupe, and by the time he renamed them the Royalettes in 1943 they were an all-Irish line-up. There were always eighteen on hand, twelve on stage, and the balance as substitutes for holidays, weeks off etc. With Alice Dalgarno as principal dancer and choreographer, and Babs de Monte and Christine Kealy (who also made them up) designing the costumes, the Royalettes built up an enviable reputation for exactitude and innovation which won the hearts of thousands of Dubliners, and there can be no doubt that they contributed to the regular patronage of many at the box office.

An indiscreet reporter, on the night the Royal closed for the last time in 1962, quoted the legend amongst Royal audiences that at least a couple of the girls had stayed in the line until they became grandmothers. He got a strictly anonymous spokesman to concede that some were not perhaps as young as they looked! Aberdeen born Alice Dalgarno, and

71

Londoner Babs de Monte presented their first routine as the Royalettes in April, 1943 to the music of the 'Poet and Peasant' Overture, but they quickly realised that there was a limit to the evolutions possible with an unbroken line of dancers, and devised elaborate, ballet-style ensembles in which mime was an important ingredient.

So began a series of specialities which included: 'At Dingley Dell' (from The Pickwick Papers); 'The Pied Piper'; 'The Burglar'; 'The Masterpiece'; 'Bantry Bay'; 'The White Huzzars', and a total of well over a hundred more. Babs usually invented the plots; then there were discussions about the possible treatment and costumes. Movements were evolved after which Alice wrote down all the actions and steps, which would read like Greek to the uninitiated, but it enabled Alice to go along to the first rehearsal with what was in effect a choreographer's script.

The girls, average age 19 (except for the glaring exceptions), reported for practice at 10 a.m. wearing slacks and turbans (snoods were also in vogue for a time). In rehearsal rooms and on empty stages to the sound of a piano (often played by Gordon Spicer at the Royal) they went through their movements for the following week's show, their faults duly noted and corrected. Then it was home for lunch and a return to the theatre in the afternoon to do two shows.

"Actually the work was terrible" recalled Babs. "We were thinking up new ideas and new routines the whole time. Presenting something fresh each week. It was fantastic what we did. I remember once the wardrobe mistress, Christine Kealy, having to make fifty five costumes in four days. You couldn't believe it now. We rehearsed every single morning from ten to twelve. Then there was a break for lunch. The first show was after lunch, and then we had a rehearsal again before the next show. You must attain perfection. It's like an army really. To get two people together to do the same thing at exactly the same moment is difficult enough, but when you think of twelve girls.........."

But as with everything else in show business, television was to exert its influence. In 1952 Kevin O'Kelly was complaining in a write up of the Royal show for *The Evening Herald*:

> "This week's show is *Spring In The Air (Number 2)*, and as always the delightful part is the graceful dancing of the Royalettes, especially in the 'Valentine' finale, with its nice contrast in modern and old-time routines. But now, more than ever, when we're all getting used to show dancing on television, it is obvious that the girls are working under a very obvious handicap: they have no dancing partners. Is it impossible to get male dancers in Ireland? Chorus girls in top-hats and tails went out with the Big Broadway Show of 1936..........."

It was probably Father Cormac O'Daly, Chaplain to the Catholic Stage Guild, who encouraged the Royalettes to recite the Rosary in their dressing rooms between shows. No doubt this was to ensure that they would not be an occasion of sin or murky thoughts to some enchanted pimpley youth seated in the orchestra stalls while they performed their highkicking routines. It is not now known if all the girls participated in this cosy little religious observance, but some of the older ones donned mackintoshes and imbibed more tangible liquid spirits in the upstairs lounge of the White Horse on the corner of Burgh Quay in the intervals between shows. Apart from Alice and Babs the members of the troupe changed from time to time, but as near as can be ascertained, the following ladies were once in the famous troupe of Royalettes: May Boyle; Eila Browne; Grace Bourke (later Mrs Eamonn Andrews); Patsy Bolton; Eila Barlow; Josephine Barnes; Pat

Conway; Veronica Conlon; Connie Connell; Flo Clegg; Nellie Cuffe; Bridie Donoghue; Kay Fogarty; Doris Fishbourne; Rita Fagan; Jessie Fagan; Maureen Faulkner; Kay FitzPatrick; Breda Hogarty; Rita Holohan; Eileen Kelly (who also sang in some of the routines); Pauline Keogh; Ruby Kelsh; Jean Kelsh; Noeleen Kearns; Una Larkin; A. Leahy; A. Lawless; Una MacLoughlin; Jenny Monks; Terry Holloy; Alice Malone; Joan Mayne; Bridie Malone; Rita Malone; Kay Murphy; Connie Medlar; A. Martin; Valerie O'Brien; Esther O'Connor; Eileen O'Connor; Vera O'Connor; Angela O'Brien; Eileen O'Neill; Una Power; A. Phelan; Rita Smith; Helen Smith; Betty Sheridan; Rita Saul; Carmel Tuohy; E. Talbot.......

Easter 1943 saw the production of *Signal Fires* – "a cavalcade of Irish history". This was one of the successors to *Tramp, Tramp, Tramp* and the famous *Roll Of The Drum*. It featured men of the 26th Battalion and the Old I.R.A. The pageant was adapted from a script by the Abbey actor Liam Redmond, and it was staged by Charlie Wade. The cast included Eddie Byrne; John McDarby; Michael Clarke; W. (Billy) O'Gorman, and Sean O'Siotchain. Disappointed by the relatively cool reaction to *Royal Flush*, his first series of revues, "Mr. Louis" became aware of the necessity for originality and thus creativity by someone whose material could knit a more or less permanent company of performers together in regular sketches and ensemble routines, immediately identifiable as having originated at the Theatre Royal. The man he had in mind was Dick Forbes. Eventually, T.R. Royle (Louis Elliman) and Dick Forbes, assisted by Alice and Babs and later, Ivy Bourke looking after the choreography, Charlie Wade who was then stage and lighting director, Bob Slane, Stage Carpenter; Fergus O'Ryan, Scenic Designer; orchestrations by Jimmy Campbell and Arthur Bell (who had been orchestrator for Jack Payne and Jack Hylton), combined to produce some of the finest revues ever seen in Dublin, and which, in their time, compared very favourably to similar London productions at the Palladium and the Holborn Empire before it was destroyed in the nightly bombing blitz.

DICK FORBES

Dick Forbes, backed by the Louis Elliman showmanship, filled the Theatre Royal nightly to capacity during the war. A weekly visit to the Royal became a habit among Dubliners in the 1940s. It was a huge theatre, but these two men fully understood that the lovely decor and the tiers of seats were only secondary considerations. What was of primary importance was what was happening on the stage; this alone determined how many of the nearly 4,000 seats would be sold at each performance. Forbes hit upon a winning concept for revue-type shows especially written for Irish artists that succeeded spectacularly with regular audiences. The shows by themselves were not, of course, the sole attraction. A patron could go to the Royal at 2.30 in time for the feature film; after that there would be an interlude and sing-along with the Compton organ; at 4.30 Jimmy Campbell would raise his baton in the orchestra pit and the 25 piece orchestra would play the overture to the stage show which would last until around 6 o'clock. All this at a cost of 1/- (5p) before 5 o'clock. If the Orchestra Stalls and the Back Stalls filled quickly, the barriers were shifted and for their 1/- some patrons might find themselves sitting in the luxury of the Royal Circle. Noel Purcell claimed that it was cheaper to spend your afternoons in the Royal than it was to stay at home and light a fire.

Dick Forbes was born in Prince's Street, Cork, one of three sons of a master tailor. He took a serious interest in all of the plays of Shakespeare, and made his own debut on the stage with the Cork writer Daniel Corkery in one of Corkery's own plays *The Hermit And The King* with the Cork Little Theatre Company. His father opened a tailoring business in Capetown, but Dick didn't like South Africa so he was sent home to study law as a career. The War of Independence found Dick in a flying column, but he was captured in one encounter and spent 18 months in Shrewsbury Jail. On his release he toured Ireland with fit-up companies in partnership with Mike Nono. Later he formed an act with the twinkle-toed Jimmy Harvey, and they made gramophone records together relating the adventures of a character called 'Mulcahy'. He married a dancer from Hull called Muriel who opened a dancing academy in Waterford while Dick took a job as a drummer in a band, and it was in Waterford that their daughters Pauline (later a regular performer in Royal shows and at Butlin's Mosney) and Twinkle were born. Dick had started writing revue scripts for the Olympia, Dublin, and the Opera House, Cork, but his greatest success at that time came in 1936 when his play *Silver Jubilee* was produced at the Abbey. It had been placed first out of 117 entries, in a competition for new playwrights. He had submitted it under the nom de plume "Cormac O'Daly", the name of a school friend who became a Franciscan and first chaplain to the Catholic Stage Guild, Father Cormac Daly. Other Forbes plays were: *Rose of Battle*, *Saggart Son*, *No Greater Love*, and *Judas Iscariot*. Dick himself was slightly disappointed with his career as 'Cormac O'Daly'. "Listen, my friend", he remarked, "I have little use for Cormac O'Daly. I know him, of course; a rather high-brow fellow with artistic leanings and a tendency to mix with literary snobs. But the fact is, he owes me a great deal of money and so the least said of him the better. For all I know – or care – he may be lost forever in the mists that do be on the bog. Have a cigar".

In the early 40s he collaborated with Harry O'Donovan on some of the scripts for Jimmy O'Dea's BBC radio series "Irish Half Hour" in which Dick also performed – he sang an old music hall song by Robert Martin called "Killaloe" which is about a teacher of French who comes to an Irish village school:

> "We're all Irish tenants here and we're all prepared to swear
> That to the Irish language we'll be true,
> But we all wid one consent, when they ax us for the rent,
> Sure we answer them in Frinch in Killaloe".

But the pace – having to write a new show each week and the hardships endured in Shrewsbury jail – took its toll, and his health deteriorated. He died in August 1949 at the early age of 48. He had a varied career and many interests including, gold-mining, trap-drumming, tap-dancing, railway-sleuthing, seamanship, salesmanship, playwriting, scriptwriting, voice-production and the romantic details of theatrical management.

Noel Purcell, who recommended Dick Forbes to Louis Elliman, and as a result of the scripts he provided, owed him a lot in his own achievement of stardom, was asked once why so little of him was seen on Irish television:

> "No scriptwriters, me ould brown son" was Noel's reply, "That's it short and simple. There's been no one to write my scripts since Dick Forbes died. He was a tiny little fellow, as neat as a pin: soaking wet, he weighed only about eight stone, but what a brain he had and we killed him with work. He could write about anything and in beautiful English. You might say that when Dickie died, the old Theatre Royal died too....."

"Something In The Air" (1943). Theatre Royal vocalists (left to right)
Sean Mooney, Maisie Cranfield, Pauline Forbes and Frankie Blowers

The Three Stooges (from left), Curly, Moe and Larry.
After their life-threatening act of mayhem at the Royal they spent their evenings in a box at Louis
Elliman's other theatre, The Gaiety, listening to Grand Opera

T.R. ROYLE PRESENTS

Dick Forbe's first show for the Royal appears to have been called *Thro' Erin's Isle*, but it did not attract much comment. His first major series of shows were called *Something In The Air* which ran for 14 Editions, the first of which was, unbelievably for a theatre of its size, retained for a second week, such was its spectacle and professionalism – nothing like it had been seen in Dublin before. From the original introductory song written by Campbell and Bell and sung by Eddie Byrne by way of introducing members of the cast, Forbes provided original comedy ideas. Noel Purcell had a weekly 'spot' called "School Boy Howler". There was "A Dublin Cameo" featuring Noel and Eddie and occasionally Al Sharpe and Dick Forbes himself. "The Language Lesson" misinterpreted by either Noel or Eddie included most of the comedy team and divulged information such as:

"Vodka is the Russian for Red Biddy"!

Sean Mooney and May Devitt appeared in Song Scenas, and a popular addition to the cast was Frankie Blowers who really did sound like Bing Crosby and delighted audiences with numbers like: 'Sweet Sue', 'My Blue Heaven', and 'The Folk who live On The Hill'.

Noel Purcell did various impersonations and his 'Carmen Miranda' is particularly remembered. The Royalettes contributed a couple of routines each week of the very highest calibre. Their routine, to the music of Ravel's 'Bolero' was so effective that they repeated it afterwards many times in other shows.

The boxer Jack Doyle and his film star wife, the tiny Movita, appeared as guest stars in the 7th and 8th editions. They gave solo performances but back stage as a husband and wife act, they were an amazing pair. Jack would appear suddenly sporting a black eye after an argument with the tempestuous Movita, who in turn would explain that she gave it to him in order to prevent him from hanging her on a coat hanger on the wall which was his usual method of ending-an argument. In October, the show featured a tribute to Brother Michael O'Clery, Chief of the 4 masters by 'Cormac O'Daly' and it is not clear if this was by Dick Forbes or his friend the Franciscan, Father Cormac Daly, but it was stated to have been produced with the approval of the Franciscan Fathers, Adam & Eve's, Dublin. The Narrator was Eddie Byrne, but the main roles were played by two otherwise junior members of the regular company – Michael Clarke (who later starred in films with Anna Neagle under the name Michael Laurence) played Brother Michael, supported by Edward Mulhare (famous later as the Captain in the TV series *The Ghost And Mrs Muir*. He also succeeded Rex Harrison as Professor Higgins in *My Fair Lady*). A notable lady in the early editions was Kay Maher, a vivacious soubrette. One outstandingly successful edition of *Something In The Air* featured the "Royal Minstrels". A few years before Noel Purcell was playing the Empire, Belfast and he got chatting with Albert (Al) Sharpe, who was on the same bill about Sharpe's connection with the old "Dixie Minstrels', about whom Charlie Jones, the former manager of the Tivoli Music Hall on Burgh Quay wrote:

"I also built up the Dixie Minstrels, they were working men in Belfast, where I used to book an odd act, and one of the managers kept on about them; so I went to see them and booked them for a week. They were such a success that they built up two weeks next time in Dublin, and then to a month, until finally they were playing eight weeks in opposition to pantomime. Eventually they got on the Stoll circuit. They included in their company Albert Sharpe and Joe McGinnity".

Noel was enthusiastic and told Al that he might be able to sell the idea of a minstrel show to "Mr. Louis". The eventual result was the "Royal Minstrels" with everyone in the company including Jimmy Campbell and the band blacked-up. One newspaper critic wrote:

> "One would need a well-stocked garden to hand out bouquets to all who deserve them in this week's stage show. It is the brightest and jolliest edition of *Something In The Air* which has yet been presented. "The Royal Minstrels" occupying the major part of the programme offer grand entertainment. T.R. Royle, who is responsible for the production has made a grand job of his end. Dick Forbes has written a clever script, in addition to playing his part on the stage".

The show was also notable for the appearance of one of the front of house staff, the bass Morgan Hayes, making his first professional appearance singing a lullaby. It probably inspired T.R. Royle to mount his magnificent production of *Show Boat* at the Gaiety a year later, with Hayes as Joe singing "Ol' Man River".

Something In The Air inspired "Mr. Louis" to create a second troupe of dancers in addition to the Royalettes. The junior troupe was called The Rockettes, after the line-up at New York's Radio City Music Hall. They were aged around sixteen, and known to Mr Louis as "his kids" and directed by Ivy Bourke who was born in Birmingham, and had been a Tiller Girl herself, probably in the Capitol.

Ivy had only one worry – as soon as a Rockette became fully proficient she was kidnapped by the Royalettes! Some years later the Rockettes transferred to the Queen's Theatre where they replaced the Queen's Moonbeams, the resident troupe that had been directed since 1939 by the quiet and dark-haired Eileen Phelan. It is a co-incidence that Ivy was married to the Queen's stage manager, Rick Bourke, and Eileen married Rick's brother, Kevin Bourke, the boss of Strand Electric.

The Rockettes included: The Misses Doris MacDonald, Phyllis Conroy, Lily Johnston, Marjorie Mullen, Ena Whelan, Vera Boileau, Harriet Harvey, Nora Garbutt, Phyllis Farrelly, Maureen Campbell, Madeline O'Neill, Susan Johnston, Helen Connell, Carmel O'Brien Nuala O'Neill, Sadie Bailey, Doris King, Phyllis Snell, Phyllis Twomey, Rollie Flanagan, Irene Gebler, Connie Sylvester, Carmel O'Reilly, Rita Eustace, C. Connell, C. Kendellon, M. Kelly, G. Mason, T. Molloy, E. O'Neill, P. Snow, R. Smith, Irene Bradley, E. Talbot, and Maureen Cramer.

A "new spectacle extravaganza" *Passing Parade of 1943* with Jack Cruise, Joe Duffy, Martin Hendricks, Al Sharpe, Phil Donohue (who would later become manager of the theatre) Sean Mooney and Patricia Black, with the usual support, kept things going until December 19th when Dick Forbe's first Royal pantomime *Puss In Boots* was staged. It starred Noel Purcell as Dame with Eddie Byrne and Rita Conroy who played 'Puss'. Rita, like Jack Cruise, was a product of the Father Matthew Hall.

In the New Year, 1944, the rather obvious title of the first show was *Royal Salute to 1944*. Eddie Byrne was back with his "Double Or Nothing" quiz, and various guest artists were introduced like The Cooke Brothers who specialised in a cowboy routine, but one of the brothers was a bus driver in private life which inspired him to record a number called "The Yodelling Bus Man" on the Regal Zonophone label. But the most important guests were Jack Doyle and Movita in February and they took the precaution of first getting married in Westland Row. They were featured in a pretentious opening scene called 'Home From Hollywood' when the entire audience was probably aware that they had arrived only that morning from Ballyjamesduff after a tour of the sticks. They closed the show in an ensemble called 'In The Rockies' which was only slightly misleading since Doyle's more or less permanent state was 'On The Rocks'.

In April a new show *Variety Fair* introduced several new features. "Double or Nothing" continued to be popular and Jimmy O'Dea came over from the Gaiety to appear in several editions in sketches by Harry O'Donovan. Dick Forbes wrote a series of Miniature Melodramas for Bob Hennessy, Michael Clarke, Michael Ripper, Deirdre O'Meara and Seamus Locke. Noel Purcell was the principal star in "The Golden Budda" – a serial type sketch in addition to his solo 'spots' like 'The Girl Guide'. Sean Mooney and Frankie Blowers continued to provide the musical interludes, but the most long-lived innovation was the introduction of the famous 'Nedser and Nuala' comedy sketches. These featured Eddie Byrne as Nedser and Noel Purcell as his wife Nuala, with Pauline Forbes playing their daughter Finula. They were occasionally joined by others in secondary roles like Mickser Reid as their nephew, Dick Forbes in a hilarious cameo as 'Cha-shut up' and Michael Ripper as the devil. Basically, the sketches were about a Dublin couple, the hard-pressed Nuala constantly at odds with her deceitful and work shy husband Nedser, with their daughter, Finula, trying to mediate between them. The story lines were as topical as possible, and dealt with them struggling with the Census form, or when James Bridie's play *Mr. Bolfry* was playing at the Gate Theatre, the devil in the shape of Mr. Bolfry appeared to them in their kitchen. Sometimes things got too much for Nedser and he would go off to drown himself in the river only to find that the tide was out in the Liffey. Theatre critics described them as being... "As heart warming as the characters in one of the early O'Casey dramas" and... "For pure Dublin mannerism and comedy they were the equal of O'Casey at his best". In truth, although Dick Forbes provided first rate material he didn't have the time at his disposal in the weekly 8-10 minutes to give it much depth and the forceful interpretations by Noel and Eddie gave it character. Forbes wrote the material especially for them, and it would have been less successful without them.

The next series of shows *Royal Bouquet* began in July and was described by the critics as being... "Brilllant in its colour, movement and variety".

'Nedser and Nuala' were retained, and there was a return of the 'schoolboy Howlers'. May Devitt and Joseph McLaughlin sang duets from *The Lilac Domino*, *Il Trovatore* etc; McLaughlin had made his Dublin debut at the Gaiety in O'Dea's show *So What!* in August 1941. Now, in the Royal show he sang all the songs that he would later record when he achieved greater fame as Josef Locke.

A very popular weekly feature were Dick Forbes' potted extracts from Shakespeare:

Ginnette Waddell as Catherine and T. St. John Barry as Wolsey in *Henry VIII*

Michael Ripper, Ginnette Waddell and Eddie Byrne in the tomb scene from *Romeo and Juliet*.

Michael Ripper gave an excerpt from *Hamlet* – a role he had played in its entirety with Lord Longford's company at the Gate. He also appeared as Shylock in *The Merchant Of Venice* with Doris Finn and Sara Payne in the trial scene.

Eddie Byrne made an impressive *Othello* in the scene in which the Moor smothers Desdemona.

Ginnette Waddell and T. St. John Barry enacted the murder scene from *Macbeth*.

NOEL PURCELL (Shaved and bearded) with......

......Peggy Dell and Max Wall

......Eddie Byrne and Stewart Granger

......Bob Hope

*......Josef Locke and Rick Burke (Chief Barker,
Variety Club of Ireland – Tent 41)*

Jimmy O'Dea, who had played the role with Edwards/MacLíammóir Productions, repeated his brilliant performance as Bottom in *A Midsummer Night's Dream*, and Jimmy proved once again that this was Shakespeare at his funniest. The extract was treated in two scenes – the exuberant tradesmen of Athens and the 'tragedy' of Pyramus and Thisbe. Jimmy was supported by Noel Purcell, Michael Ripper, Lionel Day, Chris Markey, Doris Finn, Bob Hennessy and Grainne O'Shannon. In addition the Royalettes did an orthodox ballet to the music written for the play by Mendelssohn. Jimmy O'Dea was always amused by the Irish critics and the London film people who insisted upon comparing him to Chaplin. He said of his experiences in some British films... "To me and my friends the new Jimmy O'Dea had little appeal. The film people got it into their heads that I was a 'natural' for the role of the 'Irish Charlie Chaplin', and it would have been easier to shift the Mountains of Mourne than that notion. Similarity of stature is one of the things Charlie and I have in common, and no one has yet told me what else we have..."

Jimmy appeared in a later edition as a very lively Royal Rockette, and revived some of his Mrs. Mulligan sketches – all very far removed from Charlie Chaplin.

The Royalettes presented a particularly memorable routine in this show which one critic claimed would do credit to a C.B. Cochrane revue. This was "The Opium Dream" in which the solo dancer Alice Dalgarno, as an idol, comes to brief life.

The final show of the year was *Royal Parade* which had a stirring opening ensemble. While the principals and the rest of the company sang the opening chorus – 'Royal Parade', the Royalettes and the Rockettes in military type costumes emerged through the double doors on each side of the auditorium which led to the submarine bar, and marched up the steps at each side of the stage, drumming as they marched. It was very much a shock for some previously hopeful regulars who never thought they would be in such close proximity to 'the girls'. "Mr. Louis" tried to look after everyone! 'Nedser and Nuala' had lost none of their popularity, so they were retained once more. Dick Forbes also devised potted versions of 'Great Dramas Of Yesteryear' among which were *The Drunkard* with Michael Ripper; Bob Hennessy appeared as Matthias, Sir Henry Irving's famous role, in *The Bells*. Dick included an excerpt from *The Colleen Bawn*, and one suspects that he did so in order that he could include a mistake he had made himself in the dialogue years before – instead of saying "Get on to the rock, the boat is leaking" he said "Get on to the boat, the rock is leaking!"

One week there was a Russian 'opera' called "Cloughjordan" which was similar to O'Dea's Russian choir the 'Sneezicoughskis' except that in the 'opera' the bass singer is supposed to have lost his voice and his part is taken by a sousaphone.

Apart from "The Park-Keeper" which was the finest monologue that Forbes had written for Noel Purcell, he now provided him with a series of portraits called "The March of the Seasons" in which he recited first the dreams and ambitions and finally the memories of ladies in the Spring, Summer, Autumn and Winter of their lives. The 'Winter' monologue received particular acclaim.

The pantomime in the 1944/45 season was *Mother Goose* which has been acclaimed by the distinguished theatre critic, John J. Finegan as being...... "Beyond all doubt and argument, the greatest most spectacular pantomime Dublin has ever seen and the like of which will hardly be seen again in anyone's lifetime..." Noel Purcell was Mother Goose, and Eddie Byrne was her husband Nedser Gander. Johnny Caross, who made his own costume, was an almost human-like Jemima, the goose. The Principal Boy was Iris Lawler

Programme covers for the Royal's "Mother Goose" in the 1944/45 Season and
"Jack and the Beanstalk" the following year. Both pantos were written by Dick Forbes and starred
Noel Purcell as Dame

(she had been second boy the previous year in *Puss In Boots*) who had come from the Gate Theatre. Augustus Harris introduced music hall performers into his pantomimes at Drury Lane, London; Louis Elliman introduced legitimate actors into variety in Dublin. The rest of the cast were all Royal regulars who have been already mentioned in this account. Jimmy Campbell had left the Royal, so the orchestra was conducted by George Rothwell, who had until very recently been the Compton organist.

The pantomime, which was so elaborate that part of the back wall behind the stage had to be broken down and an extension built to accommodate the scenery, was estimated to have been seen by 258,000 people, one out of every three of the population of the city at that time, during its six week run – no doubt, some saw it more than once, and there must have been country visitors. Asked to comment on the show before it opened, Noel Purcell said:

"It's the best thing Dick has ever written, now it's up to the performers".

The performers didn't fail him.

TRADITIONAL PANTOMIME?

Pantomimes in Dublin in those days were invariably referred to as 'traditional' pantomimes. By this was meant that a number of familiar comedy routines (such as a schoolroom scene in which some simple character seated at the end of a long bench would land on the floor when the other occupants of the bench all stood up together; this was achieved by placing one leg of the bench close to the centre so that it was unbalanced with just one person seated at the end), might be expected to be seen. There was also the use of the 'song sheet' which descended from the flies and the children were encouraged to sing the simple verse written on the song sheet. But principally, traditional pantomime came to mean that the Principal Boy was played by a girl, and the 'Dame' was played by a man, and above all there had to be a breathtaking transformation scene. But fashions and fads change in the theatre and the formula for pantomime was no exception, with the result that no matter how nostalgic the pantos of several decades ago may seem, there is, in fact, no such thing as a traditional pantomime.

What we regard as traditional may in fact be the best form, but it is not the only one. This Christmas entertainment evolved from the Harlequinade which adapted characters from the *commedia dell 'arte* and in which the magical Harlequin was the principal character until the arrival of the great Joseph Grimaldi in Covent Garden (from whom all clowns derive the name "Joey") and the Clown assumed the principal role. Arthur Collins and Augustus Harris, the producers at the Theatre Royal, Drury Lane, are credited with evolving pantomime into the form as we knew it until fairly recently. Madame Celeste has been claimed as the first Principal Boy, although many actresses before her had played what were known as "breeches parts" in the theatre of the Restoration when women played men's roles. Our own Peg Woffington, who had been born in the slums of Dublin, was famous in London, apart from her association with David Garrick, for her "breeches" role of Silvia in Farquhar's *The Recruiting Officer* (a girl who disguises herself as a man) and as Sir Harry Wildair in the same author's *The Constant Couple*, and there were many other such actresses, so the "breeches" part was a well-established theatrical convention, and by 1865 Principal Boys were accepted roles in pantomime. The 'Boys' always reflected the current fashion in the female form. In Victorian times they were described by James Agate as "big-bosomed, broad-buttocked, and butcher-thighed" until in the years before the First World War they assumed a more masculine appearance which mirrored the style and aspirations of the 'New Woman'. In the post war years a decidedly more feminine image returned and its greatest exponent was one of pantomime's most famous Principal Boys, Dorothy Ward. Miss Ward, who was wife of the equally famous Irish 'Dame' comedian, Shaun Glenville, claimed:

> "When a Principal Boy swings one shapely leg forward and thumps a well-kept fist into the opposite palm, she is imitating some lost vision of man; when she adopts a resolute – and deliberately unladylike – stance, feet firmly planked apart, or hooks her thumbs nonchalantly in her belt, she is assuming postures which are meant to be recognised as manly, but she is not trying to create an illusion of manhood. In essence, she is presenting us with an attractive woman's version of how a man behaves in romantic circumstances".

A recent, but less psychologically aware, Prince Charming claimed that she was playing him "fun-loving and democratic, and I never think about my legs"!

'Dame' comedians have also changed out of all recognition, The bonnet and shawl of Dan Leno have been dispensed with in favour of the most outrageous creations to add to the fun. It is very possible that some of these unbelievable outfits are now finding their way on to the fashion catwalks of the world.

Douglas Byng (who never condescended to appear as a nanny or a cook, it had to be a governess or a housekeeper) claimed:

> "You can be more saucy as a woman than as a man. 'What he did to me' is very different to 'What I did to her'".

Anyone who has seen Danny La Rue would concur with this analysis; for a women to play 'Dame' is to try to make sense out of nonsense – it is a paradox, but there can be no such thing as a female 'Dame'. In a production of *Cinderella* at the Royal Strand Theatre in 1860 the character of "Buttons" first appeared, so called because of the close-sewn row of small brass buttons down the front of his page-boy jacket. The original reason for introducing the character was so that there would be someone to comfort Cinderella in her kitchen because he is in love with her despite competition from Prince Charming. The role of Buttons can provide a comedian of genius with a real tour de force. It was, however, a long time before Buttons was established as the important character he can be made to be today. In a Fred Karno production of *Cinderella* at the Gaiety, Dublin in 1905 the character is called 'Pepper' – the Baron's page, and at the Theatre Royal, Dublin in 1906 he is referred to as 'Peter' – the Baron's page. Since then he has been played as Buttons by the star comedian or sometimes as a secondary character if the star comedian chooses to play one of the Ugly Sisters.

The most blatant break with tradition (or a reversal to another older tradition) was the introduction of the male Principal Boy. This vogue started in modern times in the 1956/57 season at the London Palladium when Norman Wisdom played the title role in *Aladdin*; he was quickly followed by Frankie Vaughan as Francesco in *Puss In Boots*; Cliff Richard as *Aladdin*; Frank Ifield as *Robin Hood*; Englebert Humperdinck as *Robinson Crusoe*; Jimmy Tarbuck as Jack in *Jack And The Beanstalk* and Edward Woodward as *Robin Hood*. Just as music hall artists had come to dominate the pantos at the turn-of-the-century, now it was being influenced by stars of television and as *The Stage* newspaper reported it, "a host of rock 'n' rollers and recording artists were making their pantomime debuts throughout the country". Recently, at Nottingham in a production of *Robin Hood And The Babes In The Wood* the role of Robin Hood was played by Leslie Grantham (Dirty Den of "Eastenders") about whom a local critic wrote that "Robin Hood, played by Leslie Grantham, was even more sinister than the Sheriff of Nottingham".

Evelyn Laye, a famous Principal Boy, expressed her distaste for male Principal Boys 'because of their knees'; questioned as to who would worry about Robin Hood's knees, a rather shocked Miss Laye replied in all seriousness, "I hope Maid Marion". And the perceptive Miss Laye was, no doubt, thinking about the legions of disappointed dads who only took the kids to the panto in happier times for the sole purpose of seeing Robin Hood's knees. This new vogue had at least the redeeming feature of being based on an earlier, though short lived tradition. In 1912 at the home of pantomime, Drury Lane, the role of Principal Boy was given to a man, Wilfred Douthitt, and this drastic change of policy continued until 1916 when the role was returned to the ladies in the person of Madge Titheradge, but elsewhere the impeccable music hall star Randolph Sutton, famous for his song "On Mother Kelly's Doorstep" played Jack Goose in *Mother Goose* and played 'Boy' for nearly twenty years.

The practice was, unfortunately, introduced into the Gaiety, Dublin in the 1966/67 season by Fred O'Donovan who cast Austin Gaffney as the first Irish male Principal Boy (which is really a misnomer) in the role of *Robin Hood*. Louis Elliman, a real man of the theatre who was well aware of the short life of gimmicks, wouldn't countenance breaking faith with his public and continued to feature Noel Purcell as 'Dame' and a succession of shapely ladies as Principal Boy. There are accounts of many famous Principal Boys and some are remembered affectionately in living memory, but none of them are males.

The pretentious, penny-pinching, dull and lifeless pantomimes of the past several years are alleviated only by a visit to a theatre like the Palace, Manchester, where the comedy genius of the last of the greatest, Ken Dodd, can still present a panto in the old style with breathtaking production values. Proof perhaps that we are still young at heart and that real entertainment still soaks in a lot more deeply than we suspect.

Otherwise the trend is to feature fading or dimly remembered soap stars in what are described as 'politically correct' versions of the old stories. Cinderella is portrayed as a victim of child abuse who ends up rejecting the hand of the Prince in favour of Buttons, preferring a "new man" to an arrogant one. Worse still, Captain Hook has been portrayed as a misogynist and Peter Pan as a bisexual.

The influence of feminism has permeated the story lines. In another version of *Cinderella*, she is portrayed as a tomboy and in *Robin Hood* the Maid Marion wears Adidas trainers and is physically stronger than the hero. Muscle-bound men and women known as The Gladiators on TV are distributed all over the country, one or two per show.

But all is not lost; the TV interlopers invariably get bad notices because they can't act and they can't sing and it is reported that patrons write in to the theatre managers complaining about how terrible they are. They suit their respective roles in the soaps but it takes years to learn the art of pantomime. Today's Dick Whittington, who frankly enjoys having her legs admired by a legion of dads, probably started out in a troup of cute kiddies chaperoned by their mums many years ago and worked her way up to the role of Principal Boy.

Jimmy Campbell, Max Elliman and Eddie Byrne on the roof of the Theatre Royal

Panto at the Theatre Royal

The new show at the end of January 1945 was *Royal Review*, which featured Noel Purcell in a new series of solo appearances called 'Round The Royal' which began with Noel as a Charlady. There was a 'Historical Vignette' which featured incidents from Irish history like the case of James Fitzstephen Lynch, Mayor of Galway, who in 1493 condemned his own son to death, and gave the word 'lynch' to the English language. Niall Lawlor and Michael Ripper played in this episode. Other regular appearances were made by Sean Mooney, Renee Flynn and Frankie Blowers. Dick Forbes abandoned 'Nedser and Nuala' and replaced them with a new series called 'At The Widda Duffy's' with Noel as the Widda, Eddie Byrne as her son, Blinker (who was, perhaps, supposed to be a tram conductor) and Pauline Forbes as her niece, Josephine. This new format wasn't really successful. Forbes, at that time, seemed intent on changing the format of the entire show and departed from the serial type revue. He submitted three 90 minute long original 'book' shows, like musical comedies, to "Mr. Louis", who, perhaps also sensing a need for change, agreed to stage them. These were: *Trouble In Troy*, *Castles In Spain* and *Frolics In Spring*. They were not hugely successful, and the following advance publicity account of one of them, may give a clue as to why not.

> *Trouble In Troy*, the 'revusical' which inaugurates the new Royal policy of a musical show with a story, makes a big change from the ordinary type of revue. It is much more necessary to see the show from the beginning, as the plot which is set in a modern Troy and not that of Greek mythology is more than a trifle involved. It all begins with the arrival of Longodds Ellis (Eddie Byrne) and wife (Noel Purcell) to the court of Archduke Schropolus (Dick Forbes). Longodds is a Dublin bookie to whom "it's a pleasure to pay" and also a pleasure to collect little debts as the impecunious Archduke discovers at the expense of the Crown Jewels. The jewels are pawned for £100 and the whole sum used for a bet on the State's annual greyhound race. After this the gentle art of the double-cross has quite delightful play.

One critic noted that..."Comedy is forced to take rather a back seat as the plot requires a good deal of 'straight' dialogue to explain – the best wise-crack was "Nothing is rushed in Ireland except bills through the Dail" (this had to be a topical joke). The Royalettes received the best applause of the evening for their 'Horse Of Troy' scena which was really artistic....

At this time in 1945 Mr. Max Elliman, house manager of the Theatre Royal died after a brief illness. One of the best known and popular figures in the Dublin theatre world he was in the entertainment business since he was 14 in the days of the first "flicks". He was manager of the Corinthian Cinema, and the Queen's and Royal Theatres in turn. The growth of the entertainment business in Ireland with the emphasis on accommodation and comfort for patrons were due mainly to him. Liam MacGabhan of the *Irish Press* wrote:

> "Maxie was especially liked by pressmen. He had a casual off-hand manner that hid a rare generosity, and a reporter was always welcome in any of the theatres he managed. When pressed for a story of the theatre world he gave the details quite frankly with nothing 'off the record', trusting his man implicitly as to how the copy be treated. He took criticism of his shows and films pro or con, with fine good humour. He himself had a keen sense of appreciation. He never kept a pressman waiting. We shall miss him".

Jack McGrath, who had been invalided out of the British army after a spell as a prisoner of war, with the rank of Colonel, returned to the Royal in his old capacity of house manager as replacement for Max Elliman. He was assisted by another of the Elliman brothers, Jack, who was publicity director and deputy manager.

Later, in July of that year "Mr. Louis" returned to the old serial type revue with *Royal Brocade*. Newcomers to the cast were Maurice Keary, the tenor who had starred in a revival of *Show Boat* at the Gaiety, and Norman Barrs, a legitimate actor poached from the Gate Theatre, although Norman did on occasion appear as an illusionist calling himself 'The Gay Deceiver'. Dick Forbes abandoned 'The Widda Duffy' and left her to live on her pension while he revived the perennially popular 'Nedser and Nuala'. The regular company were working as hard as ever. Dick Forbes continued to write a new show for each week, always comprised of different elements. Everyone in the company had three shows to deal with at the same time. First they had to know and perform the current show, which was not to be confused with last week's show, and then every Sunday afternoon Dickie distributed the scripts which had to be committed to memory for the following week's show. When Danny Kaye appeared at the Royal later in 1952 he commented on this work load: "I used to do that when I was very young. I used to work in a stock company in America, and I think a great many people were trained for their respective professions in the stock companies, having to do a new show every week. I think it prepared a great many of us for being able to walk out on a variety stage and being entertainers." (Which explains why there are so few entertainers or comedians today).

The Royal was a very special place that needed expert management and stage skills. It contained everything that a theatre needed – it was a self-contained world with its own special community of workers of every description and artists who lived, ate and slept the Royal. One of its few surviving artists, Sean Mooney commented; "We were all one big happy family – from the front of house staff, ushers and usherettes, the orchestra, the backstage staff of scene shifters, electricians, carpenters, scene painters to the performers – everyone was friendly. There were no rows, no animosities. Most were known by their Christian names, but respect was given where it was due".

The last revue of that year was *Confetti* with Nedser and Nuala disturbing the neighbours with one of their few parties or Nedser trying to explain how he happened to come by a large sum of money. Cecil Sheridan appeared as his Dublin character Martha Mary-Anne Magee while Frank O'Donovan sang about the pleasures of 'Sitting On The Bridge Below The Town'. The last edition was notable for the appearance of the old barnstormer, entertainer and character actor, Val Vousden, in a character study from Dickens' 'Bleak House'. After a long absence Eddie Byrne's 'Double or Nothing' was reintroduced.

The pantomime that year (1945/46) was *Jack And The Beanstalk*, which opened on 20th December. Noel played 'Dame' as usual, Eddie was 'Baron Graball', Eire O'Reilly was 'Jack', and the Baron's henchmen, Twister and Hookey were Seamus Forde and Norman Barrs. Cecil Sheridan had a role as the 'Sorcerer' specially written in for him, and he enjoyed himself popping in and out casting spells: "Abra-from-Cabra, Killamechanic – that'll get them into a panic". For those who regarded themselves as still young and enjoyed the spectacle, the costumes and the laughter, it was great fun. Many a grown-up denied the fact subsequently and claimed that his visit was for the sake of the children, but the real child whom he escorted to Fairyland was within his own heart.

DOUBLE OR NOTHING

This quiz show had a simple format. The orchestra played the theme music and the combined Royalettes and Rockettes did a dance routine as they sang the theme song:

> "If it's 'Double or Nothing' you've been waiting for
> Then here is Eddie, who's ready to give you some more,
> If you can answer questions right you know –
> He'll give you two, four, eight, sixteen or so......."

Those figures were used merely to suit the rhythm of the song, the actual cash prizes for four correct answers progressing from 2/6 (12½p) to £1, but the contestant could collect his winnings at any stage. If someone after three questions had won 10/- (50p) it was his for the taking. There were four contestants (usually the first four in a mad rush to the short row of steps on to the stage; a £1 was a lot of money in those days) who were seated in front of the quiz master who was himself standing at a podium with a cup-like attachment at the side into which he dropped the money noisily as it was won.

The show was devised from an original series of film shorts called "Take It Or Leave It" which was more elaborate than the Theatre Royal version. For instance, there was a visual element like models coming on dressed in fur coats, and the question was to name the furs; or different sorts of dogs were paraded, and the contestant was required to name the breeds. In the Royal all that was required were the answers to four straight-forward questions, but on Friday night the big prize was a Vauxhall car. The first quiz master was Eddie Byrne, impeccable in evening dress and the epitome, then, of the perfect compere. Although Eddie could give the impression of being somewhat aloof or tetchy, he was never condescending or unfair to a contestant. In Dublin, however, rumour spreads on its own lubricant of malice, and is usually started by someone who is jealous of or dislikes the victim. Soon the city was in no doubt that on one afternoon in the Royal a young lady in reply to Eddie's usual question, informed him that she was a parlour maid, to which Eddie is supposed to have remarked: "you mean you are a skivvey!" The fact that many people had the mistaken impression that Eddie had the sort of manner capable of making such a remark did not help matters, and he went to the trouble and expense of placing advertisements in the newspapers asking for information about the origin of this rumour. Gay Byrne, who was probably working with Joe Linnane in radio at the time, was in the Royal Circle bar one evening after the show when Eddie came in for a drink. There were two dear and charming old ladies seated behind Eddie, and one of them approached him with hand outstretched

> "Mr. Byrne this lady here is my friend, Alice, and we want to shake your hand. We are so thrilled to meet you" she gushed. "You know we come here every week to see you in 'Double or Nothing' – we wouldn't miss it for the world"
> "That's very nice of you" said Eddie "I hope you enjoy the show"
> "Oh, yes. We're along every week, isn't that right Alice? We never miss a week"
> "That's very nice to hear" said a slightly bored Eddie, "But tell me why do you come absolutely every week?
> "Well" said the old lady confidentially, "We know that one of these nights someone is going to beat you up, and we want to be here to see it"!

When Eddie was booked for a lot of film work in England, Eamonn Andrews took over the quiz show, and in his experience of it —

> "There was always a great family atmosphere in the Royal. Always the same faces especially in the bars after the show. Eddie was away in films and Jimmy Sheil (who was by then house manager of the theatre) invited me to take his place. It was an extraordinary experience. I had done all the concerts in the Father Matthew Hall and the C.Y.M.S., but to walk on to the stage of the Theatre Royal, a 4,000 seater....even to get your feedback, it was like trying to send a shot up to Mars, and you had to wait to know whether you were received or not. Weird. You gradually got used to it even though you had an orchestra between yourself and your audience. But the quiz itself was great fun and had been made a tremendous success by Eddie. The motor car was on the stage all week in readiness for Friday night. I was never privvy to all Eddie's secrets, but I'm sure the management wanted desperately to make sure that nobody won the car in one week. There are nearly always ways of making it difficult for people who are competing, not unfairly, but you'd always have to try to spin it out to get value for your money. [Author's note: Royal Manager, Jimmy Sheil, who was a personal friend of Tommy McCairns, the agent for Vauxhall Motors, has stated that he could have obtained these cars for nothing because of the publicity value to McCairns Motors, but "Mr Louis" insisted upon paying the going rate]. I have since met people who have told me that when they were students at Trinity or U.C.D. if they were short of a pound they would go to an afternoon show at the Royal which cost them only 1/- (5p), and they would enter the quiz and win the top prize of £1; sometimes there might even be an extra bonus if you did something spectacular like leaping over a chair backwards. Peter O'Toole, he must have been a schoolboy then, told me that on one occasion he was short of cash and went up, answered all the questions and got his pound. I thought he was pulling my leg, but apparently it was true".

Eamonn was the most unsatisfactory quiz master ever to compere a show. He had no personality, which he disguised by assuming a Mid-Atlantic accent. He lacked repose and confidence and his attempts at humour were abysmal.

When Eamonn moved on to greater things at the BBC in terms of financial rewards, 'Double or Nothing' was taken over by Roy Croft (Harry Roycroft) who had been resident at the Capitol Theatre for four years. His outstanding memory is of Friday night and the Vauxhall car.

> "On Friday night the house lights came on, and you stood on the stage looking out at 4,000 people. Every one of their half-admission tickets were in a drum, and as you drew them out you had to get a check-back from the usherettes in the various stalls and circles. They had to let you know where the holder of the second half of a ticket was sitting by giving a green flash from their torches indicating that, someone in their section had it. I don't know how I did it – I couldn't do it today".

Although Roy Croft had his own distinctive personality and technique, he was the only one who could put the show over with Eddie Byrne's style. It all ran to an almost set routine, and even the type of patron could be predicted. In those days the different trades like butchers, barbers, drapers etc took their weekly half-holiday on different days when their practitioners would be found in the Royal on their afternoon off, battling for one of the four places in the quiz show.

J. Arthur Rank, later Lord Rank, was a British flour magnate who took an interest in films in the 1930s with the objective of promoting wide-spread interest in religion. He took over so many production, distribution and exhibition companies that by the 1940s he was accused of monopolising the industry. Always anxious to break the Hollywood influence and secure guaranteed releases for his Ealing films, he and his accountant John Davis turned their attention to Ireland. The result was control of the Savoy Cinemas in Dublin, Limerick and Cork (Irish Cinemas Ltd) and the Metropole, Dublin which was renovated beyond recognition, the famous print of a four in hand stage-coach whose horses the customers in the Long Bar had named Tea, Toast, Tacit and Tambourine, disappearing forever. Flea pits like the Picture House, Dun Laoghaire and the Broadway, Manor Street were demolished, but the greatest prize of all – the Theatre Royal, Dublin, property of the Dublin Theatre Co, became Rank's (or Odeon Ireland Ltd) in 1946 and was amalgamated with Irish Cinemas Ltd.

Mr. Rank started off exceedingly well with his new Irish employees, and exuded an air of paternalism. Their immediate bosses were the same and "Mr. Louis" was managing director of the Irish operation; central control of finance, film booking, publicity, and catering, was situated on the top floor of the Royal, the last stop on the elevator leading from the foyer. On the first Christmas after the Rank take-over, every employee received a double week's wages, but this was never repeated, and in time, pension schemes were introduced, but few ever benefited from them.

The shows presented by 'T.R. Royle' continued as usual, and in that year *Royal Spotlight* and *Cap & Bells* were presented in the usual formula. Norman Newman was the new musical director, and the only regular member missing from the cast was Eddie Byrne who was away filming. Cecil Sheridan continued to have his running battles with "Mr. Louis" over his scripts. Cecil in particular had to submit his scripts for scrutiny each time he played the Royal, and invariably these would be returned heavily blue-pencilled, causing Cecil to complain – "Submitting a script here is like throwing a bone to a pack of savage dogs!" On one occasion he was rehearsing a sketch set in a police station when 'Sergeant Sheridan' instructs 'Constable Mickser Reid' – "Change the single bed in the prisoner Murphy's cell to a double bed, he's expecting a visit from his wife this evening". "Cut, that's out" roars "Mr. Louis" sharply from the stalls. "Change that to a holy picture," says Cecil, "I forgot it's only his girl friend"!

Foreign artists were soon streaming back, now that the war was over, Elizabeth Schumann, the classical soprano, was the first to give a celebrity concert in August, 1946. She was followed by Jeannette McDonald (without Nelson Eddy) and Grace Moore, the opera star. The pianist Louis Kentner gave a recital and Sir John Barbirolli conducted the Halle Orchestra. The Oscar Rabin Band took over the stage for a week to be followed soon by a flood of cross-channel performers. But "Mr. Louis" did not forget his old reliables, and they continued to appear regularly. One evening in nostalgic mood and facing competitive times ahead, Cecil Sheridan dashed off an appreciation of the old days that were now at an end – He used the tune of 'Thanks for the Memory'

"Thanks for the memory of stars who played the Royal,
Frankie Blowers, Freddie Doyle,

Jimmy Campbell's band with his carnation and his style,
Thanks Jim, so much.
And thanks for the memory of 1942, the film and revue,
Three hours of entertainment, that was just a bob to you,
And thank you so much.
Pauline, Sean, Noel and Eddie,
Dickie Forbes brilliant pen at the ready,
Royalettes with precision so steady,
Alice and Babs – my parodies perhaps?
And thanks for the memory,
I'll be judged when day is done, when St. Peter says 'ouldson'
Purcell washes whiter, but I can't swop two for one,
Thank you so much.

Colonel Jack McGrath did not retain his post as manager for very long as he succumbed to a nervous disorder, and the new joint managers were Jimmy Shiel and Charlie Wade whose specialist services as stage director would be required less frequently. Incidentally, the bars manager at this time was Bill Margey, who would be replaced by John Bible and finally Tim Dawson.

The pantomime in the 1946/47 season was *Cinderella* by Dick Forbes. If *Mother Goose* was his masterpiece this must have been the worst piece of writing for which he was responsible. No expense seems to have been spared, but expertise may have been misdirected. Hamlyn Benson and Ria Mooney are credited with Dialogue Direction, but it remains a mystery as to what these classical actors would know about pantomime slapstick, material, or timing.

Eddie Byrne had a weird role as The Demon Of Disobedience in which he cavorted around the stage dressed as a policeman wearing black tights and waving a truncheon for no obvious reason. Nigel FitzGerald tried to up-stage everyone, and Billy Percy, a British comic, as Buttons, was lightweight for a theatre the size of the Royal. Undoubtedly his personality, performance and old fashioned stage business would have been successful in a smaller, more intimate variety theatre.

Jimmy O'Dea recalled an occasion when he, Harry and Noel Purcell went on a cruise to Tangier. No one knew them on the ship and they were careful not to reveal their theatrical connections, but one fellow holiday-maker puzzled them; not by what he did or said but by his theatrical 'stamp'. They guessed that he was a member of their profession, but they had no means of confirming their deep suspicions. After days of clear blue skies they were coming out of the Bay of Biscay when they saw their first great black and threatening rain cloud. Normally, theatre people liked to see the clouds rising as they drove the patrons in and often ensured an extra £20 or so to save the night. Jimmy was leaning on the ship rails when this little stranger came up to him and said:

"There it is, Boss – there's your £20 shower"

He, too, had recognised their theatrical 'stamp'. He became a well-known variety player called – Billy Percy.

Dick Forbes and T.R. Royle were not praying for £20 showers, only thunderstorms would have filled the Royal that Christmas. Cyril Raymond was the musical director.

On the celebrity concert circuit in 1947 there were visits from Sir Malcolm Sargent, and the Liverpool Philharmonic. Sir Thomas Beecham called Malcolm Sargent "Flash

Harry", and Harold happened to be Sargent's true name, but Sir Thomas thought that "Flash Harry" suited Sargent's personality and life style. Other celebrities that year were the pianists Moura Lympany and Pouishnoff. On the variety side Sandy Powell was one of the top liners with his disastrous ventriloquial act. The much lamented Eric Morecambe and his partner Ernie Wise admitted to having pinched the idea for their own vent act from Sandy Powell. What Eric and Ernie did was to develop Sandy's act and make it their own. In the end, it was a Morecambe and Wise routine inspired by Sandy Powell. Powell had another act in which he blacked up like Al Jolson and sang, "Mammy" complete with exaggerated gestures of the arms until very gradually audiences began to realise that Sandy's arms were being extended to ridiculous lengths until they touched the floor.

Sandy was, of course, famous for his amusing human touch every time he made one of his frequent radio broadcasts. Practically his first line was "Can you hear me mother?", as if the broadcast was entirely for her benefit.

Noel Purcell and Eddie Byrne reached a high point in their careers in this year. A film in which they both had important roles, and for which they received worldwide critical acclaim, was *Captain Boycott*, which received its world première at the Theatre Royal in September, 1947. The stars of the film – Stewart Granger, Cecil Parker, Mervyn Johns, Kathleen Ryan, and a contingent from what was known as the Rank Charm School, which encouraged potential new British stars, were introduced on stage and the ladies were presented with bouquets from the Royalettes. Apart from the various civic, Government and judiciary V.I.P's, it was a proud moment for the regular Royal audiences to be able to see two of their most loved performers featured in both the film *and* the stage show in the cine-variety programme in the same week; actually it attracted capacity audiences to the huge theatre for four weeks. T.R. Royle had devised a special revuette, *Many Happy Returns* in which Noel and Eddie appeared in top hats and tails to sing an old Harry O'Donovan number "Thank Heaven We Are Living In Rathgar".

Sir Thomas Beecham paid two visits in 1948 with the Royal Philharmonic Orchestra to play afternoon concerts. Joe Loss, whose band played popular music, were topping the variety bill that week, and he asked the dry-witted Sir Thomas for permission to hear the Philharmonic rehearse on the Saturday morning. Sir Thomas very graciously assented with the warning – "It's a bit different to your sort of stuff". When Sir Thomas stood on the podium he raised his baton, paused, glanced down at the figure of Joe Loss in the front row, and deliberately stamped the floor four times with his foot in the manner of a dance band leader starting up a set. Anton Karas playing the theme music from *The Third Man* on his zither was unusually popular at that time, possibly because everyone was fascinated by the strange and unusual sound of the stringed instrument. The manager of the Royal, Jimmy Sheil, who delighted in off-beat humour, and knowing that he would get a memorably caustic reply, asked Sir Thomas what he thought of Karas and his zither. Sheil was delighted to learn that the great man compared it to a canary "seducing its own cage" (except that he did not use the word 'seducing').

The pianist Corot and the tenor Lauritz Melchior gave recitals, and the other inevitable dance bands were those of Carroll Gibbons and Eric Winstone. There is a very strong theory that Nude Shows helped to hasten the end of variety in England, but dance bands, which had become predictable and boring should be made to take their share of the blame for the wholesale closures.

"The Russian Quartette"
Johnny Caross, Noel Purcell, Albert Sharpe and Mike Nolan

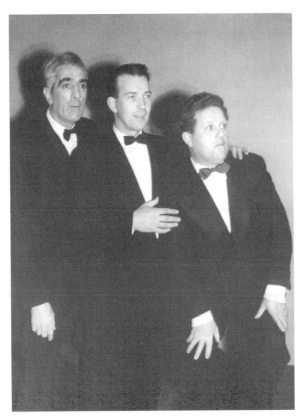

Noel Purcell, Jack Cruise and Harry Bailey at the Royal

Noel Purcell had a major starring role in the film *The Blue Lagoon* and in the week that it received its Irish première at the Savoy Cinema in April, 1949, T.R. Royle had him in a revue at the Royal. Called *Easter Cavalcade* it also featured Eddie in a return visit with 'Double or Nothing'. Noel's major contribution was a Dick Forbes' monologue "The Man In The Street" from the Hysterical History series featured in *Royal Bouquet* in 1944. The year was also notable for the engagement of Alan Beale, who had appeared first as a solo act at the Queen's playing clarinet, as musical director. He was succeeded at the end of the year by the famous Roy Fox, late of the Kit Kat Club, London, who also became producer of the stage shows for a short period.

In the Christmas season 1949/50 the theatre was reduced to presenting a circus on the stage.

Jimmy James and Dorothy Squires appeared in 1950 as well as the 100 strong American Airforce Band. In November, Emile Littler's stage production of *Annie Get Your Gun* made its Dublin debut and played the Royal for eleven nights. The male lead was played by Shamus Locke, who had been one of the Royal resident company in the 40s, and the cast also included newcomers Lionel Blair and his sister Joyce, in minor roles. In December the celebrated Beatrice Lille appeared in concert in aid of the Sunshine fund.

There was another Grand Christmas Circus in 1950/51 including:

Chipperfield's Royal Bengal Tigers, Herd of Elephants, Percheron Stallions, Royal Cream Ponies. As might be expected the performers and clowns came from all over the world – France, New Zealand, Denmark, Sweden, Spain, and Australia. Indian and Chinese acts often presented problems for the stage-management. Although the famous Ostinellis Italian Restaurant was situated beside the Royal and Regal buildings there were, at that time, no other ethnic restaurants in the city with the result that the strange aromas of curries and other exotic dishes frequently wafted from the dressing rooms into the back-stage corridors while some Oriental act prepared their meals on a fire lit on the concrete dressing room floors. Apart from any other consideration these make-shift arrangement were unlikely to meet with the approval of Austin McDonald, the Corporation fire officer.

Jack Cruise wrote the script for a new T.R. Royle revue, *High Times* in 1951. Noel Purcell shaved off his famous beard to appear as Mrs Mahockey, mother of John Joe Mahockey, played by Jack Cruise. Unfortunately, during the run of the show Noel received an urgent call from the director, Betty Box, to appear in a film *Appointment With Venus*. Noel had to grow the beard again – fast, and as it sprouted he tried to conceal it with heavy greasepaint, but the problem became acute, and in the end Noel and Jack reversed roles with Jack now playing Mrs Mahockey.

In January, Eileen Joyce appeared at an afternoon concert, but to the less classically minded, the return in April of Jimmy Campbell, complete with the inevitable red carnation, after such a long absence, was a matter for rejoicing among the regular punters. In May of that year a celebrity of a different calibre was to delight Royal audiences with his more universal appeal. This was Bob Hope, accompanied by the lovely Marilyn Maxwell, and supported by Sid Field's straight-man, Jerry Desmond. Hope swaggered on to the stage and looked around the vast theatre – "This is some garage" he marvelled (at a later show he said – "This sure is some hangar!"). At one point he looked belligerently into the wings and informed the audience "There's a guy standing there at the side called Harry Bailey, and he's writing down all my gags". Hope was a cold, glib

No Business Like Show Business: The Royal accommodated Boxing in 1945 and Irving Berlin in 1950

performer, and Grouch Marx claimed that he was not a comedian, but merely an interpreter of others' jokes. Admission prices were doubled for a week in July when the 29-year old Judy Garland played twice nightly. It had been said of her:

> "She seemed unable to stand the pace of her own success; but her resultant personal difficulties only accentuated the loyalty of her admirers"

The Theatre Royal soubrette, Pauline Forbes, gave an understanding verdict on the show:

> "It was a great show, but it didn't go down quite as she wanted it to go down. She was having a bad time in her personal life with her husband, Sid Luft. People who came loved her and she did encore after encore, but she wasn't as good as they'd hoped she'd be. The house was fairly packed but not enough, you have to be turning them away before they believe they're doing well. She was a wonderful performer. She had what we took to be a drink of water in the wings, and they dared me to drink some; we thought she might be on drugs or something, and they kept saying – "I dare you", so I had a sip, and it was Scotch and ginger ale. There were some very moving moments. At one point she took her shoes off and sat at the edge of the stage in just one spotlight and sang "Over The Rainbow" – vocally, not so good, but because she was who she was it was very moving".

Noel Purcell was back as Mrs Crusoe in *Robinson Crusoe* for the 1951/52 panto season with Eddie as Captain Hook. They were supported by some of the Queen's Happy Gang, who had been turned out of their theatre in 1951 in favour of the Abbey Players, whose theatre had been destroyed by fire. The old Queen's stalwarts included Cecil Nash, Frank Howard, Freddie Doyle and Mick Eustace.

The successful 'Royal Minstrels' show which had been featured in *Something In The Air* in 1943 was revived in 1952, and the critics gave the show a warm welcome:

> "The Royal Minstrels show bears the stamp of lavish setting and expensive production. It is made the occasion to signalise the return to Dublin of that great old comedian, Al Sharpe, who resumes a long-standing partnership with Noel Purcell. Jimmy Campbell, complete with black face and white suit, and his black-faced band keep the show moving at a smart pace".

Noel was, of course, busily employed making films between these sporadic return visits to the Royal, and Al Sharpe shortly afterwards went to New York where he was to triumph in the starring role of Finian in the original Broadway production of *Finian's Rainbow*, with Jimmy Logan's sister, Ella Logan as Sharon. After Al's New York triumph he went to Hollywood where he appeared in many films, notably Walt Disney's *Darby O'Gill And The Little People* with an old friend from Dublin as his co-star – Jimmy O'Dea. Another Royal performer who was doing extremely well in films was Eddie Byrne, who, at that time, had the leading role in a very amusing film called *Time Gentlemen Please*. Described as "Quite a nice little picture" by Karel Reisz, it was, of course, given its Irish première in the Royal.

Katherine Dunham and her exhilarating Caribbean dancers came in May of 1952 (was the struggling newcomer, Eartha Kitt, a member of the company?). Danny Kaye's visit for a week in June was as a result of a promise he had made to Louis Elliman in

Programme cover – Danny Kaye (1952)

Hollywood in 1950, but heavy stage and film commitments had prevented him coming to the Royal until now. He arranged to leave America a week ahead of his intended schedule in order to fit in his Dublin visit before going on to the London Palladium. Jimmy Shiel had to employ extra staff to deal with the flood of postal bookings which reached the theatre when the week of two shows daily was announced. Danny Kaye was a most charismatic performer, and as is usual with such people of genius, his various films did him less than justice. This is the strongest, irrefutable argument in favour of live theatre: the bond and rapport between audience and performer, in which the audience responds either cooly or to degrees of enthusiasm according to the personality, charisma and degree of sympathy (or rapport) displayed by the performer. The artist, of course, surpasses himself consistent with the degree of acceptance. The important element with intelligent artists is 'mind', one mind eliciting the approval of each and every mind in the audience, until 'he has the audience eating out of his hand'. This is by no means an easy thing to accomplish, and it might even succeed one night only to fail dismally on the following one. At each performance there is a one to one situation, the collective mind of the audience responding to the quirky, surreal, nonsensical, gormless or even apparently disinterested mind of the artist. Danny Kaye did nothing spectacular, indeed that was the charm of his act. Audiences were not invited to sit back and marvel at the talent of this famous film star. He talked amusingly, and would suddenly sing "Ballin' The Jack" complemented by extraordinarily graceful movements, giving the song a dignity that it never really possessed. A spotlight would focus on his hands held high above his head, and he sang "The Ugly Duckling", and gradually, unbelievably the weaving hands magically became the duckling. It was all bewilderingly enchanting, and the patrons at the second show of the evening got the better part of the bargain. They encouraged Danny to give them more and more, and he would sit on the edge of the stage and warn them – "The last buses will be leaving shortly", and the huge roar from the audience was "We don't care". Danny would tell the band to go home (he must have been appraised of "Mr Louis's" aversion to paying unnecessary overtime) and he would continue with his pianist, Sam Praeger, until nearly midnight. He had a deceptively easy style, but he regarded the Royal as a daunting prospect, and was really frightened at the prospect of playing it for a week when he stood on the empty stage on his first morning and saw the enormous size of it. Towards the end of his week he began to receive letters of thanks from grateful Dublin taxi drivers who told him the week he played the Royal was the best they had ever had, taking patrons to their homes after his final midnight curtain.

On the classical side Jussi Bjorling sang in a concert in November, and in the same month a somewhat nervous Betty Hutton, whose life was to take a very tragic turn of rejection of her talents in later years, arrived to play a week. The last Royal stage manager, Billy Kelly, remembered Betty on her first night – "She was just a bundle of nerves, in fact she collapsed on the stage. After that, she'd come to me before each performance and say 'How's the crowd, Billy?' and I'd say 'Wonderful'. She was scared of making a bad impression, I think. And sure enough, after each show she'd rush in, give me a hug and a kiss, and say 'You're a darling'. So was she!"

In the pantomime season 1952/53 the subject was *Babes In The Wood* with Noel Purcell as Dame Wimple of Waffle. *The Sunday Press* critic wrote:

> "The Theatre Royal's version of *Babes In The Wood* is the best show from Hawkins Street since the late Dick Forbes's *Mother Goose*. Additional dialogue by Tim O'Mahony, says the programme. Take a bow, Mr. O'Mahony. We hope to hear more of you. Noel Purcell, as the Nurse, is

back to the top of his form (all seven or eight feet of it); he even has little fragments of dances which recall his riotous ballet, "Spring Song". In Eddie Byrne, Jack Cruise and Phil Donohue he has a trio of double-dyed gold-plated villains to contend with."

That was the year Noel got a vicious bite from one of the senior members of the W.H. Wilkie's Chimpanzee Family, and after a bout of whiskey drinking, it was assumed that the rigid little form of Mickser Reid was dead, until someone whispered in his ear that 'the show must go on'!

After the pantomime, Noel stayed on in January 1953, to star in another T.R. Royle revue *Royal Travelcade*. Maurice Chevalier gave two performances of 80 minutes each in the same month, and the printed programme listed scores of Chevalier's songs from which it was noted Mr. Chevalier would choose as the spirit moved him. According to the Royal manager, Jimmy Sheil, Chevalier was a very complex man, although he admitted that the apparent complexity might not be unconnected with the Parisian's presence in a cold, wet, overcast and generally depressing day in Dublin.

Jimmy took Chevalier shopping for a white *báinín* type jacket, after which they had lunch at the Gresham, which was eaten in virtual silence. Afterwards, he took him to see the trees along the Liffey and the *pissoires* on Eden and Burgh Quays in the hope that this would stir memories of Paris and the Seine, but the reaction was morose and unresponsive. Chevalier stood in the wings that evening as his theme music was played, and what a transformation: suddenly there was a wide dazzling grin, his straw hat was almost balanced on his nose, and he stepped on to the stage, the epitome of the debonair song and dance man, he was charming, he was gallant to the ladies in the front rows, and how he enjoyed singing. This man was happy!

Other visitors that year were Frankie Laine, Allan Jones (the singing film star and father of Jack Jones), Jean Sablon, the French vocalist, Edgar Bergen, the film ventriloquist, and his dummies, Charlie McCarthy and Mortimer Snerd. The inevitable big bands took over the stage: Geraldo and his Band; Harry Roy and his Band; Joe Loss and his Band; and Stan Kenton and his band, who were booked to play for one Sunday afternoon by the Dublin Crystal Ballroom owner, Bill Fuller. Kenton's was an American outfit which couldn't play in Britain because of some internal wrangling between the American and British Musicians' Unions. Fuller took advantage of this and booked the band into the Royal for the afternoon and had them playing at a dance that evening in Bray. Advertising in the music press ensured that a specially chartered boatload of fans arrived in their hundreds at Dun Laoghaire on the Sunday morning of the concert.

Bob Hope returned for a two day engagement in September, 1953, succoured on this occasion by the lovely Gloria de Haven and his usual straight man, Jerry Desmond. Hope informed a reporter at the airport – "I played the Royal before, but I found it safe to come back. They've probably forgotten by now"!

There was no pantomime in 1953/54, nor would there be one until 1955/56.

The Taoiseach of the time, Sean Lemass, launched the idea of a national festival in 1953 which was known as An Tostal, and was designed specifically to attract tourists in the early Spring, with inducements like fully licensed bars open until midnight. T.R. Royle responded with a specially mounted show called *Trumpet Call*, with Officers, Non-Commissioned Officers, and men of the defence forces, Army Trumpeters with Massed Pipe and Drum Bands.

Programme cover – Roy Rogers

The civilian cast included Jack Cruise, Eddie Byrne, Phil Donohue, Bob Hennessy, and the Royalettes. Noel Purcell sang his recently recorded song by Leo Maguire, "The Man Me Mother Married", and of course he had to sing Leo's other song "The Dublin Saunter" ("In Dublin On A Sunny Summer Morning") as an encore. With memories of *The Roll Of The Drum*, *Tramp, Tramp, Tramp* and *Signal Fires* it was almost like old times at the Royal.

In the following year 1954, the former manager of the Queen's Theatre, P.R. Gogan, became manager of the Royal. Paddy Gogan had once raised the hackles of "Mr Louis" (T.R. Royle) by announcing in a newspaper ad. that the Queen's show was being presented by T.R. Queen!

The visiting artists that year were Nat "King" Cole; Vivian Blaine, the American musical comedy and film star; Lena Horne, Ronnie Ronalde, and Yma Sumac, the Peruvian singer. Gracie Fields appeared for one night of what she claimed was her farewell tour. On the stage since 1911, she would then have been 56, and still protesting that it was ridiculous for a woman to sing a song like her all-time favourite "Sally". At the end of her performance to a packed theatre her fellow Lancastrian, George Formby, who was then living in Foxrock, flat-footed his way on to the stage and gave her a bouquet of flowers. Another visitor was Guy Mitchell supported by the George Mitchell Choir, and Bill Fuller exploited the row between the British and American Musicians' Unions by booking Woody Hermann and his Orchestra (The Fourth Herd?) into the Royal for one performance on Sunday afternoon 2nd May, to the delight of British fans who again arrived by the boatload at Dun Laoghaire. Relaxing after a gig in Bray on the Sunday evening Hermann's involved theory that music is somehow merely a matter of advanced mathematics went completely over the heads of his listeners. Roy Rogers, "The King Of The Cowboys" on his golden Palomino horse, 'Trigger' billed as "the smartest horse in the movies" gave two shows on 18th and 19th March 1954. Of secondary importance to Trigger was Roy's wife, Dale Evans, who appeared with him in his movies, and could be relied upon for a song backed by the Whipporwills. Many a young fan left the theatre in tears as Roy and Dale sang their theme song "Happy Trails".

On Easter Sunday of that year, while Lemass's tourist festival struggled for life, the best man at his wedding, Jimmy O'Dea, presented *Fun On Tostal*, by Harry O'Donovan. Jimmy himself appeared in the opening as 'The Tostal Spirit' (probably a Dimple Haig), Danny Cummins was 'A Little Dash Of Dublin', Jimmy Kennedy sang and took part in the sketches with Vernon Hayden, Derry O'Donovan and Maureen Potter, and the Royalettes appeared with the Royal Oultons in 'A Celtic Tableau'.

In the Christmas 1954/55 season T.R. Royle presented a dazzling spectacular show, *The Bells Are Ringing*, with Harry Bailey, Hal Roach, Mick Eustace and the Four Ramblers. Mick Eustace, who was an accomplished and popular pianist who probably made more money playing at weddings than he did on the stage, complained about the frequency and length of rehearsals for the show. "They were" he said "interfering with his weddin's!" The Four Ramblers had started life as the Donnelly Singers on a commercial radio show for sausages. They later became the Four Dots and a Dash at the Capitol Theatre, and dispensing with the Dash became the Four Ramblers, one of whom was Val Doonican, and also at one stage, Brendan O'Dowda. Also on that Christmas bill was a determined lady called Koringa who presented 'a jungle rhapsody' which included an array of crocodiles and snakes which she treated deplorably, and wore the snakes about

*Poster cards for Cine-Variety and
Panto at the Royal*

her person like furs. But only Koringa could inflict these indignities on such treacherous reptiles, and one afternoon a snake escaped. An extremely cautious search was conducted by the stage staff without result and Paddy Gogan visited each dressing room to warn the fearful occupants about the very dangerous member of 'the jungle rhapsody' company who had decided to go solo. Val Doonican was on the stage that evening singing the sad story of "Jimmy Brown" with the other three Ramblers:

"When the chapel bells were ringing in the little valley town"
(Boom, Boom, Boom)

Suddenly he saw a movement out of the corner of his eye, and looking round between harmonies of 'Boom, Boom' he saw the snake sliding towards them from behind. Only too well aware that one of them might be joining Jimmy Brown in the chapel on the hill very shortly, he continued bravely and tried to signal into the wings when to his relief Koringa herself, dressed in a leopardskin cloak, appeared on the stage and hauled the huge snake around her shoulders and proceeded to admonish it with sharp smacks on its nose, demanding to know "Where have you been you naughty boy; how dare you disappear like that in the middle of a matinee..." She waved reassuringly to the audience, ignored the Four Ramblers, and went off to prepare for her next 'Jungle rhapsody'.

The amusing incidents that were continually happening back-stage kept the staff entertained since they were due mainly to misunderstandings or the nature of the business. For instance, the Radio Éireann Symphony Orchestra, with soloist Louis Kentner, were booked to do a Saturday afternoon concert in 1953. It so happened that a Scottish comedian had been booked in to appear in the following week and he had been warned by his agent to bring a full set of band parts as the Royal orchestra had a complement of twenty five musicians. The comic arrived back-stage on the Saturday morning to prepare for his opening on Sunday afternoon. The Radio Éireann Symphony Orchestra were on stage rehearsing for their afternoon concert. The stupefied comic gazed at the huge orchestra and was heard to say aloud – "Bugger this Jimmy, I've worked with big orchestras, but this is fuckin' ridiculous..."

Johnnie Ray, with the Vic Lewis Orchestra, cried his way effectively through his act for two days in April, 1955. Pianist Claudio Arrau, and Segovia, the Spanish guitarist, gave recitals. There were also appearances from Rawicz and Landauer, the Continental pianists; Vic Oliver, a violin-playing comedian, and star of the London Hippodrome's *Starlight Roof*. His true name was V. von Samek, and he was supposed to be an obscure European Baron. Dickie Valentine played a week as did the Four Bachelors, who before achieving huge success in Britain started their careers in the Royal as The Harmonicords. Billy Cotton kept everyone wide-awake with his cry of "Wakey! Wakey!" before launching into his band show featuring Alan Breeze. Josef Locke, who was now a big star in Britain, and known particularly in Blackpool as "Mister Blackpool" which he often played during the summer seasons, played the Royal for a week in March. Royal audiences remembered him better as Joseph McLaughlin from T.R. Royle's wartime shows, but when he first went to London, Jack Hylton booked him into the Victoria Palace, in a Crazy Gang show, and on the opening night Joe searched for his name in the billing in vain. Hylton explained to him that the name Joseph McLaughlin was too long to fit on a poster card, and in any case it was a name that English audiences would have difficulty in pronouncing, so he changed his name to Josef Locke. The pantomime in 1955/56 starred a clean shaven Noel Purcell as *Mother Goose*. "Mr Louis" still hadn't lost

From the mid-1960s to the mid-80s, Royal veteran Maureen Potter continued to very successfully fly the flag for Variety and Panto at Dublin's Gaiety Theatre. Pictured here with Patricia Cahill in "A Couple of Swells".

his magic touch and commissioned Michael O'Herlihy to design the scenery, which was described as having an Edmund Dulac quality and in itself made the panto worth a visit. It was almost like old times with a cast including Pauline Forbes, Jack Cruise, Hal Roach, Frank Howard and Cecil Nash. Johnny Caross was there again as the goose that laid the golden eggs. Sean Mooney, Frankie Blowers and Renee Flynn led the Royal Singers, and the personable May Devitt sported an urchin-cut style hairdo as Principal Boy. *The Irish Times* critic reported:

> "Film, stage and radio success has not changed Noel from what he essentially is, the typical, warm, unaffected Dublin man in the street. One of the best of all Irish pantomime dames, his power over children is one that many parents will envy".

"Mr. Louis" made certain that there was a song-sheet and Noel, Jack, Hal and Cecil had no difficulty in getting the children to raise the roof with:

> "We must be ever so, ever so QUIET,
> Don't make a noise it may lead to a RIOT,
> Can't you hear the tick of the clock –
> Dickory, dickory, dickory dock,
> We must be ever so, ever so QUIET,
> Hush, Hush, Hush."

THE DEATH OF VARIETY

Readers will have noted that many of the acts booked into the Royal in the 50s were American. Some English acts still topped the bill like:

ALBERT WHELAN, the veteran Australian artist who is reputed to have invented the 'signature tune' for he always came on stage in full evening dress, and as he slowly removed his top-hat, white silk scarf, overcoat and gloves he continued to whistle from his entrance a tune called "Der Lustige Bruder". He then continued with his normal act about the three trees (One there, one there and one there). He finished his routine with the opening business in reverse as he put his evening clothes back on again. There was only one word to describe it – "style"!

PAYNE & HILLIARD was a crazy act. He came on dressed as Napoleon and threw frequent handfuls of confetti into the air and complaining to her "God what a night!" (presumably Napoleon was supposed to be in Russia). He would then announce that he would give an impression of Napoleon crossing the Alps, at which point the back drop, on which some hills were painted, would be lowered to the floor, and he would merely step over it throwing more confetti in the air ("God what a night"). Next he complained "An old gypsy woman told me I'd find a letter in the snow. She's a liar, there is no letter...." At this point he would surreptitiously fling an envelope on to the stage behind his back where he would 'discover' it – "I'm wrong there is a letter...More confetti, "God what a night!" And so the madness continued.

SCOTT SANDERS came on wheeling a genuine knife sharpener complete with sharpening stone, singing "Walking round the world looking for the sunshine, that never seems to come my way" He had a great personality.

THE TWO LESLIES Leslie Holmes on the Piano and Leslie Sarony, author and composer of countless well-known songs, sang and danced.

JIMMY EDWARDS with the walrus moustache; he played a trombone which he called 'A slush pump'. He sometimes worked with TONY HANCOCK in a lighthouse sketch, and if they were not getting the laughs he would whisper to Hancock – "Do the Look!" which was a cue for the young Hancock to pull a most grotesque face which was supposed to look like Robert Newton as Long John Silver and mutter "Ahr there Jim me lad"!

But people were becoming increasingly reluctant to leave their homes and go and see these old reliables. Better shows were on the way on television, and it was difficult for any management to compete with say "Sunday Night At The London Palladium". Humour was changing too, and many of the old routines were considered old hat compared with "The Goon Show" on radio, the creation of a comedy genius, Spike Milligan, who changed the face of comedy forever and influenced the creation of shows like "Monty Python's Flying Circus".

Rowan Atkinson has said that "Fashion and fad are just as great a part of comedy as they are in clothes. That's why comics like Benny Hill and Frankie Howerd went through such cycles in their appeal". Variety theatres everywhere began shutting their doors, or theatres began to decay. The former glamour of showbusiness which desperate managers still pretended to exist. Backstage the performers were only too well aware of bleak dressing rooms and general squalor.

In 1957 when Bill Haley and the Comets visited Britain (and the Theatre Royal) most adults felt threatened by the loud and raucous sound of Rock-and-Roll, with the result that Haley's audiences were mostly teenagers who sat in boredom through the usual supporting acts – no future for them with the new generation!

"Mr Louis" did his best to give new talent a chance, and frequently booked local semi-professionals like Chris Casey, Eddie Bannon – who described himself variously as Eddie Bannon, "No Ban On" or "The thief of bad gags". The diminutive Tony Kenny got himself into trouble with "Mr Louis" by cutting his act short by three or four minutes one afternoon when there wasn't a very full house. When it was discovered that the programme was running four minutes out of sequence, Louis despatched a messenger to the film renters in Abbey Street in order to secure a four minute Bugs Bunny cartoon to make up the time. Frank Carson got one of his first professional engagements at the Royal in 1958 and doubled in cabaret at the Georgian Rooms in the Metropole.

There had been a time when gramophone recording was reserved for the highest quality performers. There was even a hierarchy in existence in the recording companies. Certain artists would be dignified by having their records pressed on a coveted colour label, while others were given a colour exclusively to themselves. With few exceptions an artist had to be pretty good to merit the distinction of having himself recorded. These records were very highly prized in most homes and compared with present day values they were not cheap.

Suddenly, it seemed that anybody and everybody was making records. They were all aimed at the teenage market which is still notoriously fickle. A singer who might find herself at the top of the charts this week, would next week disappear into oblivion. Some of these 'chart toppers' appeared at the Royal at the top of the bill. It was an act of desperation and by that time Louis Elliman was beginning to lose interest in what he foresaw as a losing battle. He left the stage shows to the new manager, Phil Donohue. Paddy Gogan had left to become an A&R man for a record company as Jimmy Sheil had gone to join the Bill Fuller Group. Louis offered Phil Donohue little assistance, and even when Phil suggested a revival of 'Nedser and Nuala' Louis replied that there would be trouble about the copyright with Dick Forbes's wife, Muriel, who claimed that the copyright was her property, and Louis was damned if he was going to pay for the same material twice. A couple of Phil's chart toppers come to mind: Shirley Ryan and Annette Kluger "where are the songs we sung when we were very young?"!

It was a sad experience to visit the Royal in those days. Most people sat through the stage show in the forlorn hope that someone resembling a variety act would appear. The films were usually so bad that many took refuge in the bars, which were at least livelier than the stage shows.

WILSON, KEPPEL AND BETTY

To the bored teenagers awaiting the appearance of Bill Haley and his rock 'n' roll, the appearance of Wilson, Keppel and Betty can only have increased their irritation. Yet this was the most loved and famous speciality act ever seen on the British stage. They would later be brilliantly parodied by Morecambe and Wise with Glenda Jackson in one of their early TV shows, although the parody had first developed during their days in variety. The bare essentials of their act was simply an eccentric sand dance performed in pseudo-Egyptian style. They didn't consciously play for laughs, but they radiated enormous genuine happy amusement which was evident from the broad grins on the faces of their audiences.

JACK WILSON, Liverpool born, was taken to America by his parents when he was a lad.

JOE KEPPEL, who was born in County Cork, Ireland, also went to the USA when he was young.

BETTY was the name given to eight young ladies who joined the act as it developed into the best speciality act in the business. Jack and Joe met and teamed up together before the outbreak of the First World War. After the war and a tour of Australia with the Colleano Circus they returned to America and a period of odd dates in burlesque until in Pasadena an agent suggested they should add a girl to the act, and conveniently he had the very girl. She had been working with a fellow called Jack Benny, who played the fiddle, but couldn't get any work. So, Betty Knox joined the new act which eventually became known internationally (they had no dialogue) as "Cleopatra's Nightmare". The music they selected for the act was Luigini's 'Ballet Egyptian' (popularly known as 'The Old Bazaar In Cairo'), and they enquired as to whether anybody locally could arrange it to fit their routine. They were told about "a bloke down at a local bar who plays piano, and would do it for them pretty cheap". The piano player turned out to be an unknown composer called Hoagy Carmichael (he doesn't mention them in his autobiography "Sometimes I Wonder") and that arrangement continued to support "Cleopatra's Nightmare" all round the world for the next four decades including three Royal Variety Shows.

When the variety theatre was dying in the 50s this great act came to represent the epitome, the personification of all that was tawdry and at the same time glamorous and courageous in show business. These two lean, starved looking men with thin hairy legs and long drooping moustaches on their staring serious faces, wearing short, tatty toga-like costumes with a fez, shuffled automatically in a hilariously funny sand dance around the beautiful Betty as Cleopatra in the warm stage lighting highlighting the

Gaels of Laughter – Comedians at a Royal Charity Concert.
(Left to right) Jimmy Harvey, Harry O'Donovan, Jack Harrington, Cecil Sheridan, Jim Jonson,
Jimmy O'Dea and Mike Nolan

Wilson, Keppel and Betty

backdrop which represented a large Sphinx. Betty's main function was to be carried on in all her glamour to occasionally sprinkle a little sand on the stage for the two zombies who made a shuffling noise on the sand as they moved with a determined intensity in perfect unison, with a single-mindedness that made the comic dance look even more hilarious, but compared to the lovely Betty they were derelicts. Somehow, when the end was near they reminded one of some of the grottiness that existed behind the spotlights. Dressing rooms with naked bulbs some of which might work, peeling paintwork in bare utilitarian places with cracked mirrors and cold taps dripping into ancient hand basins. Cold places with a single bar electric fire, broken chairs, and nails hammered into walls on which to hang costumes and clothing. The inevitable notice from the management:

> "Ladies are requested not to use the basin for purposes other than washing and the hand laundry of underwear.
> Sitting in the basin is expressly forbidden. Do not wash your feet as it might break the basin. By Order"

But saddest of all might be a pencilled scrawl on the wall – "I died the death here last night" followed by a date over a decade ago and the signature of some anonymous hopeful whose name never appeared on another bill. Robb Wilton recalled towards the end of variety that an old friend asked him if he believed that variety was dead he replied "I wouldn't be at all surprised, it was very ill when I was in Barnsley a few weeks ago". His friend was critical of Robb, "Why do you do it?" he asked, "you have been decades in the business and you must have put by a few bob, yet here you are playing to practically empty houses, and dressing in this dirty grotty dressing room where the facilities are absolutely minimal". The lugubrious Wilton stroked his chin, stuck his tongue into his cheek and replied "I don't rightly know – perhaps it's the glamour".

None of this applies to the Theatre Royal which was as well appointed backstage as it was in the front, but it is a picture that did obtain in countless poverty stricken halls throughout Britain that had once gloried in the names of the Palace, the Empire, the Hippodrome or the Grand.

Soon, they and Wilson, Keppel and Betty, with all they represented for thousands of people, would have to go and make way for changing taste as dictated by a different medium.

After "Mr. Louis" decided to transfer a long running and popular Radio Éireann show called "Living With Lynch" to the stage in 1955, renaming it *Laughing With Lynch* and starring as on radio, Joe Lynch, Charlie Byrne, Pamela Duncan and Ronni Walsh, nothing notable happened in 1956, apart from the appearance of some local artists. During the Dublin Theatre Festival in May, 1957 the Royal Ballet paid their first visit with Margot Fonteyn in a full length *Swan Lake*.

In the pantomime season of 1956/57 T.R. Royle presented Cecil Sheridan in *Red Riding Hood*. The script was by Cecil Sheridan; Stage Direction by Phil Donohoe; Scenery by Michael O'Herlihy and James Mahon; and Dolly Sparkes directed The Gaiety Girls (the Royalettes, were in *Cinderella* with Jimmy O'Dea at the Gaiety). Cecil played Grannie Grapefruit supported by Cecil Nash, Mick Eustace, Mickser Reid, Billy Livingstone and, making her debut, was Cecil Nash's daughter, Veronica. Maurice Good and Twinkle Forbes who were later to marry were also in the cast.

The new combined services of Radio and Television to be known as Radio Telefis Éireann (RTÉ) was set up by the state in the next year 1958, and following the BBC

THE VARIETY CLUB OF IRELAND

Tent 41

In Co-operation with Dublin's Theatres

Presents

OVERTURE - - - - JIMMY CAMPBELL AND THE
THEATRE ROYAL ORCHESTRA

1. EMERALD GIRLS PIPE BAND - - BID YOU WELCOME
2. JACK CRUISE - - - TO TELL YOU OF VARIETY
3. URSULA DOYLE, PADDY BEDFORD - - "IT"
4. ALEX MATISON - - - - The Professor
5. DENIS CLAXTON - - THE VOICE OF THE AGE
6. THE WALLABIES - - THRILLS AND SPILLS
7. JACK CRUISE AND COMPANY - - MODERN MUSIC!
8. JEAN AND PAT - - - TEENAGE HARMONY
9. TRIO SPARKES - - - SPEED AND GRACE
10. STAN STENNETT - - Certified Insanely Funny
11. LOU CAMPARA - - WIZARD OF THE ACCORDEON
12. DANNY CUMMINS - - - DUBLIN'S OWN
13. ALICE DALGARNO, BABS DE MONTE,
    THE ROYALETTES - - - - AMERICANA!

14. INTERVAL
    with
    FRED BRIDGEMAN AT THE ORGAN

DON'T FORGET YOUR TICKETS FOR THE RAFFLE—3d. EACH OR 5 FOR 1/-

8

SHAKE HANDS WITH THE IRISH

The Show of the Century

15. THE CADWELL TROUPE - - IRISH DANCING AT ITS BEST
16. TOMMY KELLY - - FROM OVER THE BORDER
17. JIMMY O'DEA AND MAUREEN POTTER - - YOU GUESS
18. JOSEF LOCKE - - - HEAR MY SONG
19. PRESENTING THE STARS from 'SHAKE HANDS WITH THE DEVIL'
    MICHAEL ANDERSON   GLYNIS JOHNS
    Producer-Director

    DON MURRAY   assisted by   DONAL DONNELLY

20. THE ROYALETTES   introducing
21. THE ONE AND ONLY

JAMES CAGNEY   -   -   THE YANKEE-DOODLE-DANDY

22. FINALE - - - - ENTIRE COMPANY

NATIONAL ANTHEM

THE ORGANISERS RESERVE THE RIGHT TO ALTER PROGRAMME AS CIRCUMSTANCES DEMAND

9

In "Shake Hands With The Irish" (1958), James Cagney returned fellow Irish-American George M. Cohan to his spiritual home

pattern of taking over a theatre like the Shepherd's Bush Empire to use as studio space, it was suggested that the Theatre Royal should be taken over for the same purpose. It was a pity that the deal fell through – the Royal would still be standing.

Pop star Terry Dene came in that year, and on his first visit to Dublin, the comedian Stan Stennett, on whose show Eric Morecambe would collapse and die while making a solo guest appearance in 1984. Others who topped the bill in that year were Russ Hamilton, Tommy Steele, Diana Dors, and Jimmy Shand and his band with his Scottish Presentation of Country Dancers and Singers. The Royalettes were once again in evidence in all of these shows and Tommy Dando at the organ invited everyone each week to "Keep Your Sunny Side Up". In 1958 Louis Elliman was elected Chief Barker of The Variety Club of Ireland (Tent 41), and when the Annual All Star Variety Concert came round great things were expected of Ireland's leading showman. At that time the film *Shake Hands With The Devil* starring James Cagney was being filmed at Ardmore Studios, Bray, so on Sunday evening 9th November, 1958, Louis presented his show *Shake Hands With The Irish* at the Royal. The bill included Patrick Bedford, Jack Cruise & Co, Stan Stennett, Jimmy O'Dea, Josef Locke, Glynis Johns, Donal Donnelly and closing the bill in a breathtaking Grand Finale, James Cagney performed his famous song and dance routine exactly as he did it in the film *Yankee Doodle Dandy* with enthusiastic support from Jimmy Campbell and his boys. It was one of the really memorable nights at the Royal.***

Asked at that time who was the greatest showman he ever saw in the Royal, Phil Donohoe (who was co-manager with Phil Clarke) did not hesitate:

> "Liberace. He came to the Royal just after his court case in England; you remember he got £10,000 damages for libel. That press conference I held was the biggest ever in this city. A lot of top English newsmen came over just to have a look at this freak. Yet, throughout, he remained perfectly calm and unruffled. The first afternoon he went on at the Royal, he faced a most hostile audience. Any man who sings to his mother, as you can imagine, would not be exactly popular with our gallery. Yet by 5.30 he had that audience eating out of his hand. We could not get him off the stage. He could sing, tell jokes, play anything from boogie to Beethoven, and was always there when you wanted him. There's another thing I found – the bigger the star the better the person...."

The last Royal pantomime was *Old King Cole* with Vic Oliver and Ruby Murray in the season 1958/59. Frankie Vaughan headed the bill in 1959 although his song "Give Me The Moonlight" had been known to Dubliners for years as the twinkle-toed Jimmy Harvey had been using it in his song and dance routine at the Queen's and the Royal. The Golden City Dixies, were coloured performers from South Africa. The Festival Ballet came with Alica Markova and John Gilpin. The Ballets were "The Enchanted Stream" by Micheál MacLíammóir and "London Morning" by Noel Coward. The Sistine Chapel Choir was warmly welcomed, as were Antonio and his Spanish dancers. Donald Peers paid a return visit, but the gyrations of a young pop performer, hungry for notoriety and headlines, brought protests from some members of the audience. This was Billy Fury, who substituted indecency for talent – a one day wonder of gross behaviour. Phil Donohoe recalled his visit:

> "Before he came we had heard about this objectionable part of his act. He arrived at the Royal at 2 o'clock on a Sunday afternoon. The show was

opening at 3 o'clock, so we had no time to run through. However, we told him firmly to make sure that IT was not in. That afternoon he was perfect, and again that night. Monday was the same. Tuesday he started moving around the stage in what we considered an indecent manner. We warned him that if it happened again he'd be blacked out. Wednesday he was O.K. but on Thursday he did it again, and again we warned him, and quite honestly we thought that would be the end of it. But on Friday he repeated it, so we blacked him out and I fired him. It is a very strange thing, but during all the time I talked to him and warned him he never said one thing to me. Nothing. For a while, I thought he couldn't speak, only sing".

A young man called Barry Cryer, 'the new personality' appeared in 1959, but his real claim to fame was as a scriptwriter on TV and radio; he wrote some of the Morecambe & Wise shows when they left the BBC and went to Independent television.

Johnny Dankworth and his band were visitors in 1960, and music of a different calibre was provided by the National Orchestra of Monte Carlo and the Sicilian Symphony Orchestra. In the week commencing 25th September, 1960 T.R. Royle presented *Royal Jubilee* – A 25th Birthday Celebration. "Mr Louis" supervised the cutting of a large cake on the stage and presented gifts to members of the staff with 25 years service to the theatre. Although she had broken service, Babs de Monte had appeared with Francis A. Mangan's troupe of 24 London dancers in the first ever show at the third Theatre Royal in September, 1935. The Jubilee show featured, as was proper, a very representative cast of Irish artists who had helped to keep the theatre open during its darkest days: Cecil Sheridan, Jack Cruise, Danny Cummins, Cecil Nash, Frank Howard, Mickser Reid, Peggy Dell, May Devitt, Pauline Forbes, Willie Brady, The Harmonichords (later The Bachelors), The Comerford Troupe (who were familiar to audiences every St. Patrick's Day) Frankie Blowers, and Alice Dalgarno with the Royalettes. Tommy Dando was at the organ and Jimmy Campbell, who had conducted the orchestra in 1935, presented his orchestra on stage in a Grand Finale. Jimmy, who was dressed in a black tuxedo complete with red carnation, left the stage briefly to be quickly replaced by a young man dressed in a suit of white tails. This was Jimmy Campbell Junior, looking and dressed exactly like his father twenty five years previously. It was a clever piece of showmanship and the audience rose to the nostalgia of the occasion. In retrospect it is inevitable that a programme note is now read with great sadness:

"We Look Forward to Your Continued Patronage In the Years to Come"

The promising Irish comedian with the quirky style, Dave Allen, who had been on an Australian tour with Sophie Tucker, made his first appearance in 1961. Russ Conway was another visitor, as were the Scandinavian duo, Nina and Frederick ("There's a hole in the bucket"). The last Christmas Show at the Royal in 1961/62 was *Christmas Revels* with Jack Cruise, Patricia Cahill etc. And so to 1962 and the last six months of the Theatre Royal. Irish artists like Hal Roach and Marie Conmee were there until the end fighting to keep the doors open.

"Mr Louis" paid huge salaries to star artists whose drawing power in Dublin was in many cases to say the least very disappointing. Some of these acts were paid thousands of pounds which was in marked contrast to the salaries paid in the early days of the Royal. – Tom Mix and his company were paid £300, while the *Desert Song* London company got more than twice that sum, with, of course, a bigger cast. The Three Stooges received

£350, while Jack Hylton and his band, which must have been a guaranteed attraction, were paid £1,000 and one third of the gross takings. The huge, jolly xylophonist, Teddy Brown got £350, and Max Wall was paid £80. Dorothy Squires got £25 (and there are those who would claim that she was over-paid). Jasper Maskelyne, the magician, was paid £75, and Billy "almost a gentleman" Bennett was worth £150. Later on Joe Loss and his band were worth £500 for the week.

Louis Elliman secured most of the big names that visited Europe from America, and many played the Royal before they ever appeared at the London Palladium. But there are stories about some whose services were declined. At a time when Frank Sinatra's career was at a low ebb in Hollywood, he was escorting Ava Gardner through Europe in the early fifties, and appearing in unprestigious halls like the Finsbury Park Empire; and the Bristol Hippodrome, where the prices had been doubled, lost £8,000 on the Sinatra week, and took less money than they had the week before with Billy Cotton at the top of the bill. Word came to Dublin that Frank and Ava would like to play the Theatre Royal together. Their agents, the Lew and Leslie Grade Agency, were informed that because of the notoriety then attached to the couple, Ava would be welcome at the Royal, but not Frank. Dublin, in those less open, pre-permissive days would not take kindly to the errant Frank, although it must be stated unequivocally that many so-called "public protests" were organised by *ad hoc* committees of right wing Catholic groups. Even Orson Welles, who was alleged to have Communist leanings, despite Hilton Edward's assurance to the mob that as long as he had known Orson he had been making every effort to become a capitalist, was jeered and subject to abuse and was lucky to escape physical violence by a militant religious group. Neither Frank nor Ava came to the Royal, but years later Dubliners relented and welcomed 'old blue eyes' on many occasions in their thousands. There was a story about a projected visit by Elvis Presley for a week at the Royal to coincide with a similar engagement at the London Palladium. The question of salary was mentioned and the figure of £10,000 crept into the conversation. "Impossible" said Mr Louis "The Royal couldn't possibly hope to attract a box office that would justify a fee of £10,000 a week". He was further enlightened, "No, not £10,000 a week, but £10,000 a performance!" The Royal and the Palladium immediately lost interest in Elvis Presley, who never did perform outside of the American continent.

The accumulation of many factors resulted in the eventual closure of the Theatre Royal:

The abnormally high fees demanded by visiting artists, who were not always even sure fire attractions.

Constantly rising overheads.

The coming of television.

There had been a five-week strike (which also affected the Gaiety and the Olympia) in May-June 1961, which was followed by another pay demand.

Variety was well and truly dead and when the few who survived began working the clubs like 'Jollees' in Longton, Stoke-on-Trent, it was estimated that there were only about eight or ten acts left who were guaranteed to put bums on seats – the greatest attraction being Ken Dodd; he unfortunately has never played Dublin, except for a Sunday evening concert in the Shelbourne Hotel for the Irish Bloodstock Breeders Society, which brought him down from Belfast where he had been playing the Empire.

Louis Elliman apprised the Rank London headquarters, where the accountants were well versed in Dublin property values at the time, of the situation, and the reply came back

THEATRE ROYAL, DUBLIN
SATURDAY, 30th JUNE, 1962, at 8 p.m.
"ROYALE FINALE"

1. "PROLOGUE" ... ... Jimmy Campbell and the Theatre Royal Orchestra.
2. "SHOW BUSINESS" ... ... Frankie Blowers, Peggy Dell, Royalettes, Jimmy Campbell Singers.
3. "TREBLE TROUBLE" ... Cecil Sheridan, Mickser Reid, John Molloy, Derry O'Donovan.
4. "MUSICAL COCKTAIL" ... Jimmy Campbell Singers.
5. "A ROYAL OCCASION" ... Cecil Sheridan and John Molloy.
6. ENSEMBLE ... ... Alice Dalgarno, Babs de Monte, Royalettes, Cora Cadwell Dancers and the Jimmy Campbell Singers.

INTERVAL:

"ROYAL CABARET"
OUR GUESTS :

Frankie Blowers	Edmund Browne	Jack Cruise
Paddy Crosbie	Danny Cummins	Ursula Doyle
Val Fitzpatrick	Pauline Forbes	Vernon Hayden
Frank Howard	Josef Locke	Sean Mooney
Jimmy O'Dea	Harry O'Donovan	Noel Purcell
Milo O'Shea		

Mickser Reid   Cecil Sheridan

Choreography and Design : Alice Dalgarno and Babs De Monte

The Jimmy Campbell Singers :

Kay Condron   Denis Claxton   Claire Kelleher   Bill Golding   Dolores Murphy

The Royalettes

JIMMY CAMPBELL and the THEATRE ROYAL ORCHESTRA

TOMMY DANDO

"Royale Finale". Programme for the final night of the Royal, June 1962

114

– "Close the place!" The last revue at the theatre, called, inevitably, *Royale Finale* which commenced as part of a cine-variety programme on 24 June, 1962, would end an era of only 26 years and nine months, but whereas all the previous Theatres Royal had been rebuilt and loved by Dubliners for their own new distinctive qualities, and none more so than the last Royal which had helped to keep their spirits up during the dark, deprived days of the 'Emergency', now the entire block was to be the site of high-rise concrete and glass offices. The Royal, the Regal, Ostinelli's and the Kosmo Bar on the corner were to disappear and be replaced by a monstrosity called Hawkins House. In the words of Micheál MacLíammóir: "Dublin's talent for destroying valuable and irrecoverable things amounts to genius". Cecil Sheridan's company had the sad honour of presenting the last revue and included Peggy Dell, Frankie Blowers, Mickser Reid, John Molloy, Derry O'Donovan, Alice Dalgarno, Babs de Monte and the Royalettes; Jimmy Campbell and the Theatre Royal Orchestra and the Jimmy Campbell Singers (Kay Condron, Denis Claxton, Claire Kelleher, Bill Golding and Dolores Murphy). It was a strange coincidence that Cecil Sheridan's show *Gossoons from Gloccamorra* was scheduled to close the famous old London music hall, the Metropolitan in the Edgware Road, but it was reprieved for a short time longer. These largely needless demolitions bring MacLíammóir's description of "this strange frenzy of some demoniac reign" to mind when it is considered that when the Metropolitan was finally demolished to facilitate some road widening scheme, it was discovered that through some surveyor's error, the ground it stood upon was not required, and stood useless until they built a police station on it.

There was to be no brief reprieve for the Theatre Royal and on Louis Elliman's instructions invitations went out to past performers (mostly his discoveries and creations) to appear one last time in a gigantic special show on the last night:

> Dear......
>
> For the closing of the Theatre Royal, we are presenting a special Show for the final night, on Saturday, 30th June '62 at 8 p.m. and as you have been associated with the theatre for a great number of years, we would like to invite you to fill a 'Star Spot' in this final performance.
>
> We would appreciate it if you would let us know as soon as possible if you will be able to accept this invitation.
>
> The rehearsals for this show will be on Saturday morning, the 30th instant.
>
> Kindest regards,
>
> Yours sincerely,
>
> Phil Donohoe
>
> Manager
>
> THEATRE ROYAL.

Naturally, scores of performers passed through the stage door in Poolbeg Street for the last time on that Saturday morning for the final rehearsal of all time with a visibly agitated Jimmy Campbell taking the band call.

At the booking office tickets were sold for the last night with priority going to regular patrons – the people who had booked the same seats permanently every Sunday night for years, and who, it was claimed, passed the right on, when they died, to their close relatives to claim the seats for themselves.

There was no film on the final night, but as patrons passed through the foyer to claim their seats they were surrounded everywhere from the plate glass entrance doors and into the foyer itself by neat little artistic plaques each bearing the name of a famous film star, musical or operatic star, classical musician, or variety star. They were all of the very highest rank and they had all appeared at the Royal, evidence of the very highest standards and quality that still lives on in folk memory conscious of a fine tradition. Cecil's company presented their usual revue and then there was an interval during which the bars were crammed to capacity with patrons very much aware of the historic occasion reminiscing nostalgically to complete strangers each vying with the other to recall some marvellous show or performance that the other hadn't seen. Louis Elliman who was sitting in Row D of the stalls with his wife Ettie, rose from his seat and took a last walk through his packed theatre. It is significant that the special give-away programmes printed for that night do not mention the name of "T.R. Royle". That name was synonymous with bright lights, colour, gaiety, laughter and life in the theatre – not its demise. "Mr Louis", the saddest man in the theatre that night, dazed and heartbroken wandered aimlessly around the theatre, wanting to see and remember everything but seeing nothing but the faces of strangers to whom he nodded and smiled as if in recognition, his natural reserve shattered by extreme emotion. Patrons with pent-up emotions struggling for service at the bars, did not recognise the dapper, balding, cigar-smoking figure as the mysterious T.R. Royle.

When the second part of the show, called *Royal Cabaret* started, Cecil Sheridan was standing in the wings listening to a tenor overcome by the occasion give an over-emotional rendering of a popular song. When the singer came off stage he remarked, to Cecil, "You know that song haunts me". "So it should" stammered Cecil "You're after fuckin' murderin' it!"

Peggy Dell sang "A Little Sprig Of Shamrock" which she had first sung 26 years earlier; Danny Cummins – 'A Dash of Dublin' gave his nimble tap-dance in topper and tails; Jack Cruise as John Joe Mahockey, and Pauline Forbes as his new bride, were suitably shy in their roles; Sean Mooney caused memories to come flooding back with the 1940s wartime song "Lili Marlene"; Alice Dalgarno and Babs de Monte danced with the Royalettes as if it were the opening of a new show; Frankie Blowers was cheered to the roof when he sang his special favourite "Buddy Can You Spare A Dime"; Milo O'Shea performed one of his amusing comedy mime routines; and Val Fitzpatrick sang and played his guitar; John Molloy and Mickser Reid supported Cecil Sheridan in a comedy routine which included a special song Cecil had written for the occasion; Josef Locke sang "Goodbye" from *The White Horse Inn*. When Noel Purcell came on to deliver his Dick Forbes monologue about the old park-keeper he was accorded a welcome which was conclusive proof of the affection in which he was held by his old reliable audience at the Royal. And so it went on – a throat-catching and heart tugging experience as a host of artists whom audiences had come to regard as old friends, followed one after the other to give a brief performance and then bid farewell. Tommy Dando played, "Keep Right on to the End of the Road" on the organ then the dapper leader of the variety theatre in Ireland (and Dr. Cyril Cusack would have included the legitimate theatre too) Jimmy O'Dea, came over from the Gaiety to deliver the valediction:

> "I was asked to close the Empire in Belfast; now I'm asked to close the Royal. I hope this won't become a habit, although I'm told that 160 variety theatres have closed in Britain. It was said that this was a won-

derful theatre but too big; Bob Hope called it "a magnificent garage". This has been a great place where a great many people came to see a few give them enjoyment. Louis Elliman has kept it going for the past two years under great difficulties. I suppose all theatre springs from Greek drama, but when I talked to one of the ushers tonight about the closing, the word he used wasn't Greek. It might have come from *Lady Chatterley's Lover*......"

Up in number one dressing room, a bare, utilitarian place with the occasional cracked mirror and dripping taps, Cecil Sheridan was telling old colleagues who were arriving in numbers:

"When you close a place like this it's like digging a hole and carting away the top soil. There's nothing to fill the gap. Listen, they're in such a hurry to close places like this that one day they'll be crying out for office blocks to be turned into theatres. It is not television that's doing it, you know, it's a matter of how much more money you can make out of a square foot of property".

Cecil had a theory that the wheel always turns full circle and that people would tire of gimmicky films and television and return to live shows. It was something that he would never witness himself, as he died in January 1980, but he continued to produce a regular series of shows called *The Good Old Days* at the Eblana Theatre, Dublin, in addition to touring whatever dates remained in Britain.

Phil Donohoe, who had, with Phil Clarke, been theatre manager since 1954, and had been a performer there in his time, came on to the stage and thanked the audience for their enthusiasm over the years and then introduced representatives of all sections of the staff, front of house and backstage. Some members of the Royal staff had been featured as solo acts by "Mr. Louis" following the production of their own shows, *It's The Business* and *See Dublin First* which were written and produced for them by the present author in the SFX in 1948. Ushers, usherettes and boilermen like John Brierton, Cleo Savage, Joe McLaughlin, Josephine Lynch, and Chris Gibson found themselves in the spotlights for a week. Finally, Jimmy Campbell expressed in music "What I cannot say in words!" – "Now is the Hour".

The audience joined hands spontaneously and sang "Auld Lang Syne". The gold tasselled curtain rose and fell a half dozen times and finally the heavy safety curtain covered with advertisements familiar to regular patrons for years descended for the last time. The time was 10.40 p.m.

There were a few efforts to take away souvenirs – Exit signs, Directions to the bars etc were the most easily detachable items. Cecil Sheridan managed to save the key to number one dressing room and Jimmy Campbell's baton.

There had been few tears on stage during the show but a little later at a staff party, there were tears aplenty. "Mr. Louis" final order had been: "Let there be a fitting wake; let the staff and the artists drink the bars dry".

A contemporary observer wrote at the time:

"Only variety artists and members of the staff could quite appreciate what it meant when the Theatre Royal closed its doors forever. It was probably akin to having your ancestral home burnt to ashes or demolished to the ground. It resulted in an utterly different way of life for hundreds of people whose tangible memories had been cruelly swept away".

As the theatre emptied, many of the performers were asked to sign autographs at the stage door which was besieged by fans. The little dwarf Mickser Reid was there with his great friend and protector, Cecil Sheridan, and when the demolition ball went to work on Monday morning, Mickser Reid was back again as the site tea boy!

Life, subsequently, wasn't easy for the jolly, inoffensive little clown. He was the butt of cruel jokes about his size, but the site foreman got to hear about this and remonstrated with his men, and instructed that Mickser must be left in peace and respected like any other worker on the site. He took Mickser aside and informed him of developments, assuring him that the lads had just been having a bit of fun and really meant no harm. Mickser listened carefully with his Woodbine in the corner of his mouth, and assured the foreman that he was accustomed to being laughed at, although he had previously been paid for it, but they were decent lads, and he understood. Just as the foreman was about to leave Mickser added, "Tell them it's O.K. and in future I'll stop pissing in the tea"!

Now there was a real student of Dickie Forbes. A minuscule Avenger – Mickser and Goliath!

EVENING PRESS, THURSDAY, SEPTEMBER 26, 1968.

Final curtain for Mickser Reid

By Adrian Mac Loughlin

Mickser Reid left here yesterday. We won't see him, or anyone quite like him, ever again. It's hard to define a "character", but it is almost impossible to define the almost unique bond of affection that existed between this funny, bouncy little man and his native city. Almost as impossible as to define Mickser's personal stage touch, his poignant appeal as a clown.

Who among us can presume to say what makes a child laugh so heartily that adults envy him his innocence? Or where is the old cynic who doesn't feel better when the big, involuntary guffaw suddenly bullets out from his bowels and cracks the tired mask? Just what we needed, a good old-fashioned laugh.

Mickser Reid knew how to make the kids' sides ache and he knew how to make their parents feel like kids again. He belonged to the tinselled fairyland that usually only comes once a year, with the turkey and the plum pud. and the sequined cards and the goodwill. The Olympia pantomime was as much an institution as the carol singers in Dame Street and Mickser was as legendary a character as Santa Claus.

Constant

He was a constant character to people of my generation, linking past and present. He made us laugh when we were all pink and dimpled, and he was still doing it when we were all drink and pimpled.

MICKSER

Good-bye, little pal,
The curtain is down.
Dublin hearts will remember
Its well beloved clown.
With each tumble and chase
Kiddies screamed with delight.
And the dads and the mums
Knew you made their lives
bright.

Mickser was never the star, and he didn't sing. You took him for granted as you did the clowns in a circus, and you never tried to analyse him. Who wants to analyse spontaneous bedlam? Had he been a comic genius like Jimmy O'Dea, it would have been different. With Jimmy, the tear ducts were generous, and the other side of the mask was never far behind. But Mickser was purely a clown, and like a true clown, he wore the same comic mask all his life, whether he was cantering hilariously across the Olympia stage in an incongruous bobby's uniform, or knocking out Noel Purcell in a "fixed" fight at an Inkblots v Crackpots match in Dalymount.

Nights out

You thought of the squirting smell of oranges in the gallery when you saw him, and pubs with wooden floors and gold lettering, and the honest

So thank you my friend,
On behalf of us all.
And I know in my heart,
When you take your last call
In God's Book of Life,
He is sure to record
Welcome home little Mickser,
You've earned your reward.
—With fond affection, Cecil
Sheridan.

laughter of crowded Saturday nights out, when the happy breather of a week of toil was squeezed into a few hours at the end, and the war years and the jokes about rationing—that kind of an old Dublin.

And then, when the bulldozers moved in to tear down the mighty Theatre Royal and give the old city a heart transplant it didn't want, Mickser was a silent figure from the old days, working as a "nipper" on the site. One more change in a clown's adaptable life.

Mickser Reid loved children as much as they loved him, and to them he was a big man. If I knew him properly, he also loved life. And being so physically small, it must have been all king-size to him, and I like to think that he saw the whole wonderful scene on a far bigger scale than we ever will.

But the sad thing is that Mickser left here yesterday.

The death of Mickser Reid, reported by The Evening Press in 1968. The photo shows Reid working as "tea boy" on the Hawkins Street site

* There is an unsubstantiated story that a patron, a little the worse for drink, was undetected in one of the Circle toilet cubicles when the house was checked before closing one night, and at some period during the night in the darkened theatre the unfortunate man groped his way towards the front of the Royal Circle and fell over into the stalls below where he was found dead on the following morning.

** Mother Hubbard Goes To Town was devised entirely by the Royal staff. It was the first Elliman pantomime and it was a hybrid affair as it featured at least ten of the principal characters from six other pantos. It starred Noel Purcell and Peggy Dell, with John Lynsky, Eily Murnaghan, Paddy Tyrrell, Freddie Doyle, Joan Flood, Tommy Byrne and Kay Lynch. The Abbey School of Ballet, The Violettes, the Rosettes and Jimmy Campbell & the orchestra. It opened on December 22, 1940 and was seen by 87,000 people in two weeks so it was retained for a third week after which it was succeeded by Heckenberg's Famous Circus in The Circus Comes To Town. "Mother Hubbard" was supported by a 55 minute film called The Bride Wore Crutches.

*** James Cagney has written in Cagney by Cagney (Garden City N.Y.; Doubleday & Company, Inc 1976):

"I did specialty dancing jobs for the next few years, winding up in a vaudeville three-act that needed a replacement for one of their number. This act was Parker, Rand and Leach, and Mr. Leach, now known to history and admiring film fans like myself was Cary Grant. When he left, it became Parker, Rand and Cagney.... It is vital for me to say that it is vaudeville that has had the greatest single effect on my life, both as an individual and as a performer. I still think of myself essentially as a vaudevillian, as a song and dance man. The vaudevillians I knew by and large were marvellous people.... they had a vivid something or other about them that absolutely riveted an audience's attention. First of all, those vaudevillians knew something that ultimately I came to understand and believe – that audiences are the ones who determine material; they buy the tickets. It's only in their opinion that a thing is good or bad".

Looking at James Cagney on that memorable night in the Royal one could well believe that he enjoyed being a hoofer.

The Queen's Theatre

Exterior of the Queen's Theatre

THE QUEEN'S THEATRE
Previously the ADELPHI THEATRE – Built 1829; Demolished 1844

QUEEN'S ROYAL THEATRE
Built October 1844; Demolished (as QUEEN'S THEATRE) April, 1969

Unlike the art of the sculptor, the painter or the composer whose work has a permanence that keeps it alive to battle against the vagaries of taste and fashion, the art of the performer is an ephemeral one which dies even as he is performing it, and its last vestiges disappear with the memories of those who have witnessed it. And we must take at face value the opinions of contemporary critics who, at best, give a very poor idea of what a performer actually did with his material, much of which may still be read on the printed page, and pretty insipid stuff it is too...

We have no alternative but to accept the opinion of E.V. Lucas on Dan Leno:

> "Dan Leno's greatest triumph was that the grimy, sordid material of the music hall low comedian, which, with so many singers remains grimy and sordid, in his refining hands became radiant, joyous, a legitimate source of mirth. In its nakedness it was still drunkenness, quarrelsomeness, petty poverty, hunger even crime; but such was the native cleanness of this little, eager, sympathetic observer and reader of life, such a gift of showing the comic, the unexpected side, that it emerged the most suitable, the gayest joke. He might be said to have been a crucible that transmuted mud to gold".

We know what Mr. Lucas means, he elevates Leno to the status of a serious artist, but we don't know what it was like to experience his artistry. George Bernard Shaw admired Marie Lloyd, but often wondered why someone didn't write humorous songs for her. Her songs, according to GBS, were very funnily sung but were not in themselves particularly funny. Arnold Bennett said rather prissily that all Miss Lloyd's songs were variations of the same theme of sexual naughtiness – no censor would ever pass them, and especially *he wouldn't pass her winks and her silences*. But that is exactly what happened – Miss Lloyd sang her songs (without the winks) for a board of stage censors which found them faultless, but Miss Lloyd, in retaliation, scandalised them with her version of a drawing room ballad, complete with winks and silences, Tennyson's "Come Into The Garden Maud", which was very familiar to their wives and families at cosy musical evenings.

How will our own Irish performers fare in the eyes of posterity? There can be no doubt that their position and importance has been debased by the more popular media of film and TV. Still, if the reputations of the performers mentioned above managed to survive over the decades, why shouldn't Jimmy O'Dea who had been compared to Dan Leno by the English, and Noel Purcell, and particularly those who had invented a stage persona for themselves like Cecil Sheridan, be remembered in their own country? Waves of nostalgia for some thing or another come crowding back at intervals, and when the turn of Irish music hall comes round many names will, no doubt, be examined with curiosity.

It is quite an unique experience to stand on the stage of a theatre like the Royal or the Queen's at the end of the show at night, quite alone and undisturbed. The tabs and the safety curtain are down and the only light is provided by a single low wattage bulb. The strange atmosphere is similar in all theatres (including the Theatre Royal, Drury Lane and the London Coliseum), there is an intangible energy which permeates the silent, vacant stages. The dedicated lover of the theatre does not attribute this to some romantic notions of the imagination. The enchanted observer allows himself to be influenced by the unseen power and energy of past great performers that still lingers and surrounds him. When one enters a cinema one is conscious of the prepackaged automated entertainment to come at the press of a button when so many frames of film will pass through the gate of the projector per second to be flashed on to a screen – a process that can be repeated indefinitely and in thousands of different venues. Anyone who ever enters a theatre is invariably struck by a strange indefinable atmosphere as if one were entering a church where the ritual and the language will be variable, but essentially familiar, and the performers of the past contribute to this in some inexplicable way. The sense of spirituality is enhanced by the fact that many theatres genuinely lay claim to being haunted, and this certainly applied to the Queen's Theatre. Just one witness of many, Danny McShane, who was related to Kitty McShane, wife and stage partner of Arthur Lucan, of Old Mother Riley fame, lived over the Queens, and acted as theatre watchman and fireman, was checking an open window backstage in the early hours of the morning when he saw a figure cross the stage whom he recognised as a former, deceased manager of the theatre named Rube Walshe. Danny swore to the truth of this on his life.

The Queen's Theatre was opened by its proprietor, John Scott as the Adelphi Theatre in December, 1829 in Great Brunswick Street (now Pearse Street) on the site of what is now Pearse House. The opening performance was a double bill – *The Old Oak Chest*, a melodrama, and a pantomime, *The Three Enchanted Girdles*.

When in 1830 Mr Calcraft became the lessee of the Theatre Royal he did not relish competition from the new theatre in Brunswick Street, so he rented the Adelphi for £250 with the sole intention of keeping it closed in order to stifle opposition, and it stayed closed for four years. The theatre re-opened in 1835 under the direction of a Monsieur Last, but it was sold in 1844 to John Charles Joseph who demolished it and built a new one on its site. He obtained an official patent, which the Adelphi had lacked, and opened the Queen's Royal Theatre in October, 1844 with three pieces: *The Devil's In It*, *The Lottery Ticket* and an after-piece *The Miller's Maid*. Joseph's management was unsuccessful and he let the theatre to John Harris but became jealous of the latter's success and expelled him in favour of Charles Dillon in 1852. Bram Stoker, the author of *Dracula*, who was Henry Irving's manager for 28 years, records that Irving appeared unsuccessfully at the Queen's in March, 1860 as Lartes in *Hamlet*. Dublin made amends years later. Irving's close friend of later years, J.L. Toole, the famous comedian (1832-1906) played the part of the First Gravedigger in *Hamlet* under the management of Harry Webb. The Queen's management made every effort to keep their theatre in an orderly fashion. When a seat in a box cost a maximum of 3/- (15p) the last assistant manager at the Queen's, Bill Bailey, claimed that he came across an old poster which read in effect that...

> Children in arms cost one guinea. The public were advised that there were police in attendance. Bicycles were stored free, and gentlemen in bare feet were not admitted!

A playbill dated 4th July 1904 for The Queen's Royal Theatre.
The Tyrone Power mentioned is the father of the famous filmstar
(Courtesy of The British Music Hall Society)

Dion Boucicault's plays were extremely popular at the Queen's during the management of J.W. Whitbread around 1889, and the scenic and musical effects were outstanding.*

"The successful young Irish comedian" Mr. Tyrone Power took the leading role in *Rory O'Moore* in April, 1900 and again in *Theobald Wolfe Tone* in 1901 under Whitbread's management.

London managements were aware of the importance of pantomime as a means of keeping their theatres solvent with a healthy treasury in the event of 'flops' later in the season, and Dublin managers were not slow in adopting the same policy. Pantomime was always popular at the Queen's, although its format, with the inclusion of a Harlequinade, would appear strange to present day audiences. Panto survived even when the resident Happy Gang were evicted in 1951 in favour of the homeless Abbey Players who nevertheless continued to present pantomimes based on strange themes and bizarre subjects in the Irish language until 1966.

It is of interest to note that the panto in December, 1911, was *Jack and the Beanstalk* and that it was written by J. Hickory Wood, famed for the pantos he wrote for Drury Lane, London. The ever changing misnomer of "traditional pantomime" is neatly illustrated by another Queen's panto *Dick Whittington and his Immortal Thomas*, from the more familiar *Dick Whittington and His Cat*. In 1912 the Queen's panto was *Mother Goose* with the lugubrious Robb Wilton, the Liverpool comedian as Dame. Wilton became famous for his sketch in a fire station and later for his brushes with 'the wife' and his letters to Churchill during the war:

> "The day war broke out my missus said to me – 'You've got to do something'. I said "Who?", she said "You!", I said "Me!". Well I wrote a letter to Churchill about it, I don't know if he ever got it......."

Also in the cast with Wilton was a performer called Jack Judge who played 'Muggles', the village squire, and in the second half of the show stepped out of character and informed the audience:

> "To-night I am going to sing for the first time a song I wrote myself" –

SONG: "It's A Long Way To Tipperary"

Paddy wrote a letter to his Irish Molly-O,
Saying – 'If you don't receive it, write and let me know'
If I make mistakes in spelling, Molly dear, says he,
Put the blame upon the pen, don't put the blame on me.

Chorus
It's a long way to Tipperary, it's a long way to go,
It's a long way to Tipperary, to the sweetest girl I know,
Goodbye Piccadilly, farewell Leicester Square,
It's a long long way to Tipperary, And my heart lies there.

It was not until the outbreak of the First World War that this song, allegedly first sung in the Queen's, Dublin, achieved its phenomenal popularity.**

Under Whitbread's management in the early 1900s, the theatre attracted English touring companies in melodramas like *The Down Express* and everything was grist to the

Robb Wilton played Dame in "Mother Goose" at the Queen's in 1912

Some of the 'Queen's Happy Gang' in rehearsal: (left to right) Liam O'Connor, Lollie Flanagan, Ronan O'Casey, Kevin Casey, Mick Eustace, Bill Brady

mill. Previously, in 1894, for instance, the famous boxer, James J. ("Gentleman Jim") Corbett appeared in a comedy-drama, *Gentlemen Jack* billed as 'Direct From Drury Lane'. Corbett must have been very popular and successful as he returned on a number of occasions over the next ten years.

The most productive period at the Queen's coincided with the arrival of James W. Whitbread in 1882. Whitbread was a young English producer, manager and actor; he was also a prolific playwright, and for a man of his background he appears to have used Irish nationalism to its full commercial potential. Among the many plays he wrote the following were produced at the Queen's: *Shoulder to Shoulder*; *The Nationalist*; *The Irishman*; *Lord Edward Fitzgerald*; *Theobald Wolfe Tone*; *Rory O'More*; *The Ulster Hero*; *The Insurgent Chief*; *The Sham Squire*; *Sarsfield*; *The Irish Dragoon*.

Later on it might have seemed that a young Irish manager, P.J. Bourke, founder of the Bourke theatrical dynasty, had a greater claim to the subject with plays like: *When Wexford Rose*; *For Irelands Liberty*; *In Dark and Evil Days*; *Kathleen Mavourneen* (a play which he successfully adapted into a musical); *For the Land She Loved*; *Ulster In 1798*.

These works taken together with Boucicault's *The Colleen Bawn*, *The Shaughran*, *Arrah-Na-Pogue* and *The Octoroon* prompted J.M. Synge to write about the Queen's in 1904:

> "Some recent performances of *The Shaughraun* at the Queen's Theatre in Dublin have enabled local playgoers to make an interesting comparison between the methods of the early Irish Melodrama and the Irish National Theatre Society (The Abbey). It is unfortunate for Dion Boucicault's fame that the absurdity of the plots and pathos has gradually driven people of taste away from his plays".

But in the years of the First World War Arthur Lucan and Kitty McShane were appearing, not in their later act of Old Mother Riley, but as individual performers in their first Queen's panto *Little Jack Horner* in 1916/17 with Moira Breffni (mother of the late Dr. Cyril Cusack) as the second 'boy'. Lucan was Dame and Kitty the Soubrette. Others in the cast were Cathal MacGarvey, humourist, singer, and song writer with a wonderful effervescent personality, and the Lennox Troupe of Dancers from which would emerge some years later the greatly talented young star, Eileen Marmion (later Mrs Noel Purcell). In the following year Lucan and McShane were re-booked for *Babes In The Wood* with Power and Bendon. Walter Mc Nally was a popular artist at the Queen's appearing in both Opera and Variety. His first really big success was at the Queen's as Danny Mann in the first performance of *The Lily of Killarney* by the Brisan Opera Company.

In January, 1974 when Seamus de Burca was researching his invaluable book on the Queen's – *The Queen's Royal Theatre*, the theatre critic, Gabriel Fallon wrote to him:

> "Believe it or not, I first saw your father in Sherrard Street in Whitbread's *The Siege of Limerick* (Sarsfield). I was fourteen at the time. I thought he was the best actor in the show, which he possibly was. Father Conlon was the founder of the Pioneer Dramatic Society. Shortly afterwards (or was it before?) in the same place, I saw McHardy Flint (who remembers him?) as Hamlet. His daughter played Ophelia. Thanks to Eily Murnaghan I was introduced to the "sides" of the Queen's at a time when Roberto Lena and Company were on the boards. There for the first time I met that fine actor Breffni O'Rorke and his wife Moira Breffni (or Cusack). I seem to have seen much of the Queen's during the First

Children's Matinee

Interior of the Queen's Theatre

PANTO TIME
Above: An expectant matinee line for "Aladdin"
(Queen's Assistant Manager Bill Bailey at front)
Below: Peggy Dell and Jimmy Harvey in "Dick Whittington and His Cat"

World War. I remember pantomimes, and of course the Brisan Opera Company (Vincent O'Brien, Noel Sands) with McNally, Joan Burke etc. etc. in *Maritana* and of course *The Bohemian Girl*."

The date 1909 appeared on the frontage of the Queen's that was eventually demolished, but this date refers merely to the fact that the theatre was closed between 1907 and 1909 when it was completely reconstructed. The result was a cosy, horseshoe shaped auditorium, and to a newcomer performing on the stage, the close proximity of the audience in the boxes, parterre and dress circle must have been frightening. Seamus de Burca had another view:

"The Queen's had many faults as a theatre. There were seats in the Dress Circle that if you sat comfortably in one you saw nothing except the back of the person seated in front of you. I don't know the name of the architect who was responsible for the reconstruction between 1907 and 1909 [the architect was R.J. Stirling – Author] except to repeat what George Wilde [later his father's partner – Author] said, that he was a Trinity College man who had boasted that he never designed a theatre before in his life. I hope he never designed another one...."

Mr. de Burca continues:

"I'm afraid anyway that (it was) no improvement on Whitbread's theatre. There were far too many staircases....the Upper Circle had two flights of stairs going either side of the main facade. There were too many entrances...four apart from Boxes. The Queen's was literally a warren of stairs, worthy of a king's palace. But acoustically the Queen's was perfect. You could hear a pin drop."

The pervading smell of the Queen's recalls the alibi of the actor Philip Yale Drew who was arraigned at Reading on a charge of murder. Drew claimed that he was in a local theatre when the murder was committed. When Counsel asked him if it was his habit to spend the afternoons alone in an empty theatre, he replied that it was his habit as he loved the smell of the theatre. The smell of the Queen's for instance, depended on the part of the house you were in. The dressing rooms smelt of humanity and grease-paint, the toilets were no worse than the people who might use them. But across the footlights when the curtain rose wafted the smell of paint size that I never found offensive. Commenting on the Queen's smells, Cyril Cusack, being a poet said – 'the major smell was of romance of the period and the presence – very potent – of a romantic tradition, a theatrical tradition and a patriotic tradition all combined'

The Queen's will always be remembered as the home of the old Irish melodrama, long before the opening of the Abbey Theatre. J.M. Synge writing about the Queen's in 1904, the year in which the Abbey opened, commented upon the high standard of acting frequently to be found in the older theatre. It is not surprising, therefore, that the names of future Abbey players of the early years may be found listed on old Queen's playbills. P.J. Carolan and May Craig were frequent performers there and in September, 1917 Fred Harford and Barry Fitzgerald presented their Celtic Comedy-Drama Company in the famous play *Pike O'Callaghan* with Barry Fitzgerald in the name part. Fred O'Donovan appeared in two productions of *Two Little Vagabonds*.

Peter Judge, a young civil servant from Skerries made his first Queen's appearance under his own name with Ira Allen's Company of Irish Players in June, 1912 in *Father*

Murphy. When P.J. Bourke asked Peter to appear in his play *When Wexford Rose* (in which Harry O'Donovan, using the name Harry Kildare, had previously appeared), Peter agreed on condition that his true name would not appear on the playbills as his father, a farmer, did not approve of his involvement with the stage. It is more likely that he was concealing his private activities from the civil service like his fellow civil servant, Barry Fitzgerald, whose true name was William Shields. Peter Judge did not know what name the impresario had chosen for him until he saw it in a shop window – it was F.J. McCormack under which name he would later become world famous at the Abbey Theatre and give a legendary performance as Shell in the film *Odd Man Out* with his name slightly altered to F.J. McCormick. Subsequently, he made many appearances at the Queen's. When he joined Barry Fitzgerald, May Craig, and P.J. Carolan at the Abbey they were the original creators of many of the famous O'Casey roles.

In the Christmas season of 1923/24 Jimmy O'Dea made his debut in pantomime at the Queen's when he appeared as 'Buttons' in *Cinderella* and stopped the show each night when he sang a duet "Bridget Donohue" with little Florence Sullivan, daughter of the house manager, Jack Sullivan.

In January, 1928 P.J. Bourke and George Wilde took over the lease of the theatre from Bertram Productions. Bourke already had close contacts with the theatre where his No.1 company had often appeared, and in 1920 J.B. Carrickford of the famous touring company, produced and appeared in two of Bourke's plays, *Kathleen Mavourneen*, and *For the Land She Loved* with Dorothy and Kitty Carrickford in the cast.

P.J. BOURKE was born in Dublin and was an orphan by the time he was twelve years old. He was reared by relatives in Kildare and Wicklow, but by the time he was eighteen he returned to Dublin and was employed as a vanman in Arnotts of Henry St. (another employee in that establishment had been Sean O'Casey), where he met Margaret Kearney, sister of Kathleen, the mother of Brendan Behan, and they were married in 1905. At twenty he was producing an Irish-American play *Green Bushes* in the basement of the Royal College of Surgeons in St. Stephen's Green. Mrs. M. Glenville, mother of the Dame comedian Shaun Glenville, and husband of the famous Principal Boy, Dorothy Ward was, in addition to managing the Mechanics Theatre (on the site of the present Abbey Theatre) a theatrical costumier offering costumes, scenery and wigs for hire from her premises in Little Denmark St. With the help of his wife Margaret, P.J. Bourke opened in opposition as a theatrical costumier in Lower Dominick St. transferring later to North Frederick St. and finally to Dame St. which only recently closed. He died in 1932 aged 49 years leaving the management of the Queen's to his eldest son Lorcan, who began his career at the Masterpiece, an early Dublin cinema, and had been associated at different times with the Capitol and the Tivoli. During the Second World War he worked wonders as impresario at the Olympia and finally became managing director of the Gaiety.

When Joseph Howard, who had been stage manager at the Queen's from 1909 until 1931 retired, he was replaced by Lorcan's brother, Rick, who was stage manager until the Abbey took over in 1951. P.J. Bourke's other sons remained closely identified with the theatre: Jimmy (Seamus de Burca) is a well-known playwright (*The Last Of Mrs. Oblong*; *Family Album*; *Find the Island* etc.) and novelist (*Limpid River*) in addition to writing the biography of his uncle, Peadar Kearney, author of the National Anthem. Kevin Bourke was managing director of Strand Electric; Billy managed the Four Provinces Ballroom and Banqueting Suite, and Peadar, the youngest, ran the costume hire business in Dame St. with his sister Maureen, who is now the mother of Gerry Ryan, the unpredictable TV

"Robinson Crusoe": Frank O'Donovan and Jimmy Harvey (Top)
Danny Cummins and Cecil Nash (Bottom)

and radio star. In 1928/29 Noel Purcell appeared in his first professional panto at the Queen's as the pirate king in *Robinson Crusoe*.

Lorcan left the Queen's in 1935 when it was taken over by the Elliman family and the theatre was managed for a time by Maxie Elliman, but in 1937 the chairman, Maurice Elliman appointed P.R. Gogan as manager. He had been, like his colleague Jimmy Sheil, a representative for Urney chocolates, and it appears that Maurice Elliman, who would have met them when ordering supplies for his cinemas, poached them from the chocolate firm. Maurice seemed to have a talent for selecting the right men and this was true in the case of Frank Dowling who had been manager of the Savoy Cinema, but fell foul of the then newly appointed general manager, Hugh Margey, who saw Frank as a definite rival for his job and gave him the sack. Frank was reduced to supporting his family by working as a labourer on the new housing scheme in Marino until one fine afternoon as he was walking down O'Connell St. he was grabbed by the arm by Maurice Elliman who told him that he had been looking for him everywhere and wanted him to take over the management of the Metropole Cinema immediately. A mixture of films and cine-variety seems to have been the main policy at the Queen's until the outbreak of war in 1939. Periodically, a show like the Frank O'Donovan Revue Company would be featured, and audiences always welcomed Frank with his original songs like "Sitting On The Bridge Below The Town". Desmond Rushe of the *Irish Independent* wrote after Frank's death on June 28, 1974:

> "Frank O'Donovan and Anew McMaster were two of the great joys of my youth, and memories of both are strong and deeply affectionate, for each brought to country life a peculiar type of magic which the gilding process of nostalgia has fashioned into mellow permanence. McMaster exercised his magic over a far longer period of touring, [McMaster first toured Ireland with the O'Brien & Ireland Company during the First World War – Author], but in its own way, the Frank O'Donovan Revue won hearts and full houses with equal facility. Looking back on it now, it was a remarkable show and it could not happen today. It was full of sketches, music, singing, dancing and novelty acts, and it brought laughter, delight and colour to relieve austerity. Frank O'Donovan and Kitty McMahon, his wife, shared top billing and invariably appeared together in the sketches Frank had written. In addition to featured solo performers there was a troup of roughly a dozen dancers and an orchestra of equal strength. There was also young Derry O'Donovan – to me a vision of exquisite beauty as she sang and danced. I fell into starry-eyed, teenage love with her, and worshipped hopelessly from a hard seat near the back of a village hall".

When the combined forces of radio, films and finally television left the touring companies without an audience, Frank decided 'if you can't beat them, join them' so he started an entirely new career in television and became famous in every household in Ireland, which included people who had never seen him on the stage, as Batty Brennan, a sort of odd-job farm hand in the RTE weekly series *The Riordans* with several old friends from 'the fit-ups' in the cast. Frank, was of course, a brother of O'Dea's partner Harry O'Donovan.

P.R. Gogan very wisely engaged the services of a permanent script writer, a young man who was sub-editor on one of the city papers called Ernie Murray. Ernie, who was

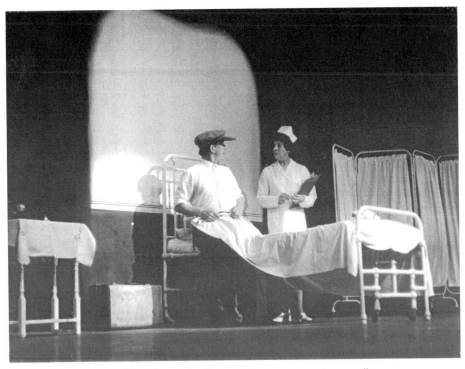

"I'll bury the peak of my cap between your two eyes"
Jack Cruise (seen here with Patty Ryan) as John Joe Mahockey from Ballyslapadashamuckery,
started his career at the Queens

Cecil Nash and Danny Cummins in a sketch by Ernie Murray

one of nature's gentlemen, had as a young lad spent some time as call-boy in the Tivoli Variety Theatre. One of his first shows for the Queen's was called *Dublin Laughs* which he wrote for Harry Bailey who had secured a week at the Queen's on the recommendation of his brother in law, Ben Bono, who was married to Harry's sister Beenie. The series ran for three months with Paddy Tyrrell as straight man. After pantomime, Ernie wrote another show for Bailey *Broadway to Connemara*. Harry Bailey, who had done everything in show business and circus became a comedian by accident. He had been a clown in a circus, but his real forte was the fiddle and when one night he went on stage to play a violin solo the E string broke so he had no option but to tell a few gags. When the audience laughed at him, he said –

> "That's O.K. you can laugh at me – I laughed at you when you were coming in. You should have seen me when I was living. Here's a little song entitled 'She sits among the cabbages and peas!'; Did I tell you about my mother, she used to play the piano on the Titanic. That went down well. Just before they hit the iceberg she ordered a whiskey on the rocks; after the collision she said 'I just asked for ice, but this is ridiculous'. I must tell you about my friend Casey. Casey has a farm down the country – well he wouldn't have it in Cabra would he? I saw him outside his cottage one day sawing a piece of timber, 'How are you, Casey?' says I. 'I'm fine' says he 'but the wife has a bad cold'. 'Is that her coughing?' I said 'No' says he 'I'm buildin' a hen house'".

Harry had a habit of telling a joke and following it with the remark 'And now I'd like to play a little solo on the fiddle' which he never played. This so exasperated one member of the audience one night that he shouted up in rage – "Will you for Christ's sake play the shaggin' fiddle". Harry went on to become a firm favourite in Britain and up to the time of his death admirers like Jimmy Tarbuck and Ken Dodd were known frequently to ask after him. Ernie Murray's next task was to write a series for a promising young comedian from the Father Matthew Hall, Jack Cruise, who had created his own original 'culchie' character called John Joe Mahockey from Ballyslapadashamuckery who dressed in a very recognisable cheap blue striped suit obtainable only from Burton's for £8, huge brown boots and a red tie with the narrow end hanging down over his waistband, but Cruise completed this sartorial elegance with a crowning glory which was a master stroke. He wore a normal size flat cap, but it had a peak which was at least nine inches long and was obvious to the eye long before Jack's face came into focus. He also affected a country accent that was his exclusively, and has never then or since been heard in any part of Ireland. Cruise was puritanically whistle clean regarding his material, but he was mortified one night in the Theatre Royal when things went slightly wrong. His act was going well one night (which was a blessing for a virtual novice in a theatre the size of the Royal) when Jack came to reciting one of his little poems and became over-excited or anxious, a lone figure in front of 4,000 people.

> "I wish I were a little frog,
> I'd have such blinkin' fun,
> I'd climb up all the rocks and trees –

The next line should have been: "And climb down on my hands and knees". But Jack in his excitement said what would have been regarded as unspeakable (especially in front of a mixed audience) in those days:

> "I'd climb down on my bum"

Jack's embarrassment and his obvious regret expressed in sincere apologies caused the entire audience to embrace him when they had recovered from the shock and stood to give him a cheering standing ovation. Nowadays a line like that would be more or less expected and shrugged off as very weak comedy.

In the thirteen week season of *Serenade to Happiness* in which Jack starred with Eire O'Reilly, Ernie Murray firmly established the character of John Joe Mahockey. He teamed Jack with a young soubrette who had recently won a singing competition, Patty Ryan, as John Joe's wife Mary Kate, and each week they had hilarious adventures – on their Honeymoon; at the Museum; at the Zoo; at the Waxworks etc. Jack's great delight was in knocking the establishment (especially the Gardai, with whom he was really on very friendly terms) so that people left the theatre saying: "I wish I had said that!". He had one story about a shopkeeper who is approached by a garda sergeant for a subscription towards a wreath for the funeral of a dead policeman. "How much are you getting?" enquires John Joe "All the shopkeepers are giving a pound" the sergeant tells him. "Here's a fiver" says John Joe, "Keep the change and bury four more of them".

Gradually, a permanent team of performers were assembled and christened The Happy Gang by Danny Cummins. They could not compare or compete with the famous Crazy Gang, but the name gave them a certain cohesion and identity. Ernie continued to write the scripts which were described as being "racy of the soil" and occasionally he came up with some real winners. In 1944 for instance, his show *Swanee* was the biggest musical success in the city and it ran for 72 performances. He wrote all the Christmas pantomimes and his *Aladdin* in 1945/46 was his finest panto script beaten only by Dick Forbes's *Mother Goose*.

The Queen's Moonbeams choreographed by Eileen Phelan usually opened the show, but they were replaced later on by the Rockettes from the Royal when cut-backs were being made there.

The original Happy Gang team were: Jimmy Harvey, Danny Cummins, Bill Brady, Cecil Nash, Mick Eustace, Gloria Greene, Paddy Tyrrell, Kay O'Toole, Liam O'Connor, Tom Glavin, Frank Howard and Kevin Casey. There were occasional guests like Ronan O'Casey (who gave a much publicised impersonation of the new film comedy sensation, Danny Kaye, which was a disastrous flop. O'Casey couldn't even have his hair tinted in the proper shade). Seamus Forde met with much greater success in his extracts from old melodramas like *Smilin' Thru* and *The Monkeys Paw*. Lollie Flanagan was an attractive soubrette, and a late comer to the Happy Gang was the stylish Freddie Doyle.

The regular members of the 'Gang' took parts in sketches as required, but in addition each had to be a solo performer in his own right.

JIMMY HARVEY was the epitome of the top-hatted song and dance man. Hilton Edwards selected him to play the role of Banjo (a caricature of the real life Harpo Marx) in his first production of *The Man Who Came To Dinner*, at the Gate. P.R. Gogan returned the compliment some years later by engaging the young Gate actress, and Micheál MacLíammóir's niece, Sally Travers, to star in Ernie Murray's show *Susie*. He was Frank to Kay Maher's Ellie in *Show Boat*.

DANNY CUMMINS did double acts with Jimmy Harvey in addition to his own solo spots, which were usually very topical. The film at the Royal one week featured a young

Joe Duffy and Mick Eustace

Grand Finale: The cast of "Aladdin" 1945-46.
(Front, left to right) Lollie Flanagan, Mick Eustace, Molly Murphy, Bill Brady (Widow Twankey),
Liam O'Connor, Danny Cummins (Washee), Phyllis Cook (Principal Girl),
Nora Anfield (Aladdin), Jimmy Harvey (Wishee), Cecil Nash (Abanazar),
Tom Glavin, Kevin Casey, Ronan O'Casey

brooding, menacing Marlon Brando as the leader of about thirty leather-clad hoodlums on motor cycles. The film was called *The Wild One*. On the following week Danny walked on to the stage of the Queen's dressed in a scruffy sports coat with bicycle clips on his greasy flannels. He was wheeling a decrepit, rusty bicycle. Pausing centre stage he stared at the audience defiantly and said "They call me the Wild One!". Danny went on to star in Gaiety Theatre revues and musical comedies, and Hilton Edwards talked him into playing a role in Donagh MacDonagh's *God's Gentry*.

BILL BRADY never played anything but a Dame role, and Ernie wrote a series of sketches for him each week in which he played a Dublin character, 'Magso'. Bill's timing was needle sharp, but it was said of him that his 'Dame' characterisation was too perfect.

CECIL NASH who was known as "the Bishop" was born in Monmouth, South Wales of a line of "stiff-collared, deep-rooted, non-whistling Protestants". In his early days he had understudied Jack Buchanan and Sir John Martin Harvey (in *The Only Way*). He came to Ireland in 1927 and stayed to play in every city, town, village and cross-roads in the country. He was a man of enormous versatility, and he also wrote some shows for the Queen's, the most memorable of which was *Back Your Fancy*.

MICK EUSTACE was an accomplished pianist and a good tenor, but his most effective role was as 'Mickser' a clown-like figure whose trousers were far too short, black jacket over a collarless shirt was far too large, and the black bowler seemed to emphasise the chalk whiteness of the face underneath with the eyes picked out in heavy black liner. All 'Mickser' had to do was to fix his great black blazing eyes on some unfortunate in the front row and threaten him with – "Hey, you, go by the wall and tickle the bricks, I'll tell me granny on you!"

GLORIA GREENE had been an usherette in the theatre until P.R. Gogan discovered that she played the cello very well and featured her thereafter in a musical interlude. This developed into a series with Paddy Tyrrell called "Thanks For The Memory" in which they sang duets each week requested by the patrons.

PADDY TYRRELL Apart from his series with Gloria Greene and his sketch work, Paddy was happiest playing straight man to Harry Bailey with whom he appeared on the TV music hall show *The Good Old Days*.

KAY O'TOOLE had been a member of the Moonbeams troupe, but graduated to roles in sketches.

LIAM O'CONNOR had a pleasant baritone voice and helped to popularise songs like "Moonlight In Mayo".

TOM GLAVIN was the tenor much given to appearing in the stage ideal of Ruritanian uniforms to sing selections from *The Chocolate Soldier* etc.

FRANK HOWARD was a product of the 'sticks' with a blustering type of humour and always signalled that he had finished a gag by sucking in air at the side of his mouth. His heart was out in the 'fit-ups' and bore out Hazlitt's insight into the heart of a performer to whom "nothing could be more intoxicating than unlooked-for success in a barn".

KEVIN CASEY known as 'the Prince of parody' to distinguish him from the King who was Cecil Sheridan. Kevin's parodies were not particularly funny, and none are remembered, but Kevin didn't particularly care so long as they rhymed.

CECIL SHERIDAN had made his first professional appearance at the Queen's in 1937 singing his clever parodies and although he was not a permanent member of the

"Smarter than any girl they know". Cecil Sheridan as Martha Mary Anne Magee

company (his home grounds were the Royal and the Olympia), he returned occasionally to regale Queen's regulars with the adventures of a Dublin 'wan' Martha Mary Anne Magee.

Grotesquely dressed and heavily made-up with rouge and lip slick Cecil would totter on in high heels to his introductory music:

MARTHA MARY ANNE MAGEE

Martha, Mary Anne Magee; smarter than any girl you'll see
Although I'm over forty I'm the best of company,
And you'll know that I'm not haughty, I'm happy, gay and free,
Smarter than any girl they know, when they take me out to supper or a show,
When they're home on leave, who have the boys got on their sleeve?
Martha Mary Anne Magee.

"Well how are yez, it's lovely to see yez. I just thought I'd get out of the house to cheer myself up. You'd be sick of the house missus, wouldn't you? There's me poor father at home sick in the bed. Wastin' away missus. Skin and bone. The woman next door says to me this mornin', 'How's your father?' 'Wastin' away' says I, 'the cat had him out on the landin' twice already'. And me brother he was in the bed next door cleanin' his bicycle, and I says to him 'Did you see that ad in the paper, Drink Canada Dry'. He was nearly away on the next boat. He was sittin' in the corner in the pub the other night drinkin' his pint when three teddy boys came in and ordered three glasses of whiskey and a pint for the cripple in the corner. I'm no cripple says me brother – they told him, 'You will be if you don't pay for the whiskey'. He got a job collectin' for a bob-a-week furniture company; you know missus, a pound down and fifty p. a week. Well, he was up in Ballymun and he knocks on this door, and this one in a revealing, oh, a revealing, undressing gown opens it. 'Excuse me ma'm' says he, 'I was wondering if you could let me have a little something on the sofa'. 'Oh, come on in' says she, 'I thought you were looking for money'. Talkin' about money missus – the bingo, do you ever go to the bingo? Up in our hall they're callin' the numbers out in Latin so that the Protestants don't stand a chance. But I was tellin' you missus (loosen your corsets and you'll feel more comfortable), I was tellin' you that I poshed myself up a bit to get out of the house. I was lookin' in the mirror and I says to myself, what's wrong? The teeth – they were every colour missus. All I wanted was another white one for a snooker set. I dropped into the dentist on the way down. I said 'I want me teeth out'. He said 'You want your gums out. Open your mouth' Oh, it was terrible, terrible missus. 'He said there's a very bad cavity down there, down there... I said 'Don't keep repeatin' yourself' He said 'No, that's the cavity, there's an echo off it' He said 'Do you want gas?' I said 'Of course'. Well you would missus, I wouldn't have him muckin' around in the dark. I was very nervous missus... Don't you know, I was shakin', I was goin' like that, I said 'I'd rather have a baby than have me tooth out'. 'Well make up your mind' he says 'before I take out me pliers' Well missus......."

Before the end came for the Happy Gang the policy seemed to be to repeat old sketches interminably, but they still got full houses. It was more a matter of style than of material; it was not so much what was said and done as how they said and did it. On a weekly visit to the Queen's Dress Circle one had the strange impression that everything about the place was of another age. First one would have met the assistant manager, Bill Bailey who, upon recognising a regular patron would stop for a chat with all the hall-marks of old world charm and courtesy. Bill stayed on at the Queen's as bar manager when the Abbey took over, and although Alex Fryer the musical director went to the Savoy Restaurant with a musical quartet, both he and Bill Bailey had each given thirty years service to the Queen's and when they both died on November 23, 1952, their coffins stood side by side in Haddington Road Church.

Ernie Murray's last pantomime at the Queen's was in the 1950/51 season with *Aladdin*. The Happy Gang continued as a resident team until September, 1951 when the Abbey Theatre Company took possession following the destruction of the Abbey by fire in July of that year.

The Happy Gang had a loyal and regular patronage from all classes of society which appreciated their brand of entertainment, simple and unsophisticated though it may have been. On the morning before their final performance *The Irish Times* reported:

> Over 1000 people who have been lucky enough to book seats will have the bitter-sweet experience tomorrow night of being in at the end of an era – the final performance of the Queen's Theatre Company. Thou-sands of others will regret missing this performance. The Queen's achieved its popularity through the provision of its special brand of light-hearted humour, and just as it had this tradition, so there was a tradition among thousands of people who paid it a weekly visit. Among these regular patrons there was a genuine feeling of regret when it was announced that the theatre was to be leased by the Abbey Company until such time as it builds a new theatre of its own. Mr. P.R. Gogan, the Dublinman who became manager and producer of the Queen's in 1937 and so successfully guided its affairs, told an Irish Times reporter last night that he could have booked every seat ten times over for the per-formance on Saturday. He said, "We had thousands of regular patrons – I knew seventy-five percent of them personally and they all seem to want to be here when we close down. The Players will be among friends when they take their last curtain call and there will be many other friends in other parts of the city regretting that they cannot be here". Mr. Gogan is proud that, although the humour at the Queen's was designed for the average Dublin family, the theatre had just as many patrons in Mount Merrion as in Crumlin or Kimmage......"

Members of the Happy Gang obtained sporadic engagements at other venues but as the grand old trouper Val Vousden had once said to Seamus de Burca: "The actor like the soldier seeks the bubble reputation even in the cannon mouth". Though that is rhetoric there is a good deal of truth in it. It is possible to be the toast of the town on the stage today and to be forgotten next year. Perhaps no art is so transient as the art of the actor. Dublin is merely a village, but so is London, and so is Broadway. All of the Happy Gang are dead, scarcely remembered. To quote Alfred Lunt lamenting the passing of American vaudeville:

"Their sincerity was greater than their artistry – their eagerness to please was beyond their capacity to please but they gave their hearts and their lives and it was not their fault that that was not enough. God bless them, every one".

The Abbey company wasn't, in fact, light years removed from what the Happy Gang had been doing for years. Farces by John McCann became the staple diet and Hugh Leonard's first play *The Big Birthday* was produced although it had already been produced by an amateur company, Lancos Productions, under the title of *Nightingale In The Branches*, which resulted in acrimonious exchanges between the author and the *Evening Mail* drama critic R.M. Fox.

The Abbey Company vacated the Queen's in 1966, and for three years various plans were mooted for the theatre. Hilton Edwards had been interested, but the most persistent rumour was that it was to be converted into a venue on the style of the now defunct "Talk Of The Town" in London with food, cabaret and dancing. A regular *Evening Herald* correspondent who signed himself "The Sham Squire" suggested that the theatre should be taken over by the new TV station, which seemed sensible enough. In April, 1969 the Rank Organisation (late of the film industry and now property speculators) which had all along been looking for a buyer for the site, allowed the demolition squad to put up its hoardings and go to work with the pickaxes.

From the moment that the work of destruction began the solitary figure of Ben Bono mounted a token protest, and carried a placard bearing the forlorn message "SAVE THE QUEEN'S THEATRE". His was the only protest. Nothing could prevent the rise of the monstrosity known as Pearse House – it hasn't even the merit of being a fitting tribute to the patriot whose name it bears.

On May 12, 1975 Siobhan McKenna laid a wreath on the site of the former Queen's Theatre in Pearse St. once the home of the Happy Gang and the Irish variety theatre. Watched by actors Bill Foley and Cecil Nash the ceremony was part of the campaign for funds to rebuild the Olympia Theatre. Actors and variety artists were determined that the Olympia would not go the way of the Royal, the Capitol and the Queen's. Thanks to their efforts the Olympia is still with us.

A large card on the wreath read:

> QUEEN'S THEATRE
> HAPPY GANG
> GONE BUT NOT FORGOTTEN
> ONCE REFUGE OF THE ABBEY THEATRE

Perhaps there wasn't enough room on the card to record that the Queen's was also the cradle of native Irish Drama and training ground for its finest actors and actresses and that during the war years, like the Royal it evolved a distinctly Irish genre of light entertainment.

---

* George M. Cohan's biographer, John McCabe, asserts that Boucicault's stagecraft had an important influence on Cohan, notably in the "transformation" device during the "Give My Regards To Broadway" number in his 1904 musical *Little Johnny Jones*.

** A more reliable account as to the first performance of "Tipperary" relates how Jack Judge upon leaving the stage door of the Grand Theatre, Bolton one evening in 1912 bet a colleague five shillings that he could compose and write a song and sing it the following evening at the theatre. Once back at his 'digs' Judge set to work, and the next morning he persuaded the musical director to write out the score and thus enabled his to sing the song that evening.

The Tivoli Theatre

Exterior of The Tivoli Theatre (1898–1928)

THE TIVOLI VARIETY THEATRE

Originally THE CONCILIATION HALL (1843)
GRAND LYRIC HALL (1897)
LYRIC THEATRE OF VARIETIES (1898)
TIVOLI VARIETY THEATRE (October, 1901)
CLOSED in 1928 and subsequently housed *The Irish Press*
newspaper.

In 1897, the year in which Dan Lowrey's (which had opened as The Star of Erin) was renamed The Empire Palace, there was no opposition from radio or cinema. The Gaiety and the Theatre Royal were not in direct competition as they presented straight plays which included Shakespeare, old classical comedies and grand opera which alternated with musical comedy. The Queen's Royal Theatre delighted its audiences with an endless diet of melodrama and nationalist historical plays. All three theatres presented a Christmas pantomime or Harlequinade (Harlequin's and the Clown's contribution became much reduced with the passage of time until eventually they disappeared entirely). The Round Room at the Rotunda specialised in concerts and musical evenings, but did not balk at the occasional exhibition or circus, and Buffalo Bill's Wild West Show was presented there, but there is a convincing argument that it was not the original Buffalo Bill Show which featured Annie Oakley.

The Mechanics' Hall which operated as a music hall from 1874 to 1902 seems to have been a pretty shoddy establishment according to the few existing accounts, but it had the distinction of an appearance by Sean O'Casey in *The Shaughraun* in 1895. Clubs and societies organised regular entertainments known as "smoking concerts" in venues all over the city: the Antient Concert Rooms (later the Palace Cinema) where James Joyce and John McCormack sang, and the favourite Dublin comedian of his day, Pat Kinsella, was billed in March, 1900; the Molesworth Hall; the Dublin Coffee Palace Hall in Townsend St. and the concert halls in the Gresham and Grosvenor Hotels. These concerts featured a mixture of amateur and professional performers, and in the words of Barnum, the public were always assured of "a colossal aggregation of talent of every description". Private residences were even pressed into service, and the elocutionist who taught Jimmy O'Dea how to form his vowels at Blackrock College frequently announced 'Mr. & Mrs. McHardy-Flint's Character Recitals at their home, 31 Haddington Road, Dublin'.

The Empire's greatest commercial rival was situated on Burgh Quay, where the *Irish Press* offices now stand empty, when the Lyric Theatre of Varieties opened in 1898 a year after the refurbishment of the Empire. The Lyric had originally been the site of the old Conciliation Hall, built in 1843 as a meeting place for Daniel O'Connell's Repeal Association, and which was rebuilt as a concert hall called the Grand Lyric Hall, opening on November 24, 1897 with an elaborate new facade topped by a statue of the Goddess of Music. A year later it became the Lyric Theatre of Varieties under the management of the popular Charles M. Jones, a 24 year old native of Rochdale of Welsh parentage. Mr.

PROGRAMME.

WEEK COMMENCING

Monday, September 10th, 1906,

And during the Week.

| General Manager ... | MR. CHARLES M. JONES. |
| Secretary ... ... | MR. H. A. MURPHY. |

1 Overture	" Pompey "	(Herold)
2 FRANK NEWBURY		Siffleur
3 JOHNSON & PELHAM		Comedy Act
4 FLO CECIL		Comedienne & Dancer
5 TOM PARKER		Comedian
6 GUSTAVE **FASOLA**	The Famous Indian Fakir, and Oriental Wonder Worker	
	Selection—	
7 Interval	"A Gaiety Girl" *(Suite de Valses)*	(*Sidney Jones*)
8 BROS. SMART		Comedy Acrobats
9 THE HAVERLEYS		American Song Illustrators
10 3 TIVOLI GIRLS		Comediennes and Dancers
11 TOM CRAVE	Flying the Revolving Wheel	
12 TIVOLI BIOSCOPE		New Pictures

| Tivoli Orchestra. | E. J. TAYLOR, Conductor. |

The Public can leave the Theatre at the end of the Performance by all Exit and Entrance Doors, which must open outwards.

The Fire Resisting Screen in the Proscenium Opening will be lowered at least once during every Performance to ensure its being in perfect working order.

All Gangways, Passages, and Staircases, must be kept free from Chairs or any other obstruction, whether permanent or temporary.

LYRIC. NIGHTLY, At 7.45 LYRIC.
General Manager : CHAS. M JONES.

CONTINUED SUCCESS.. EVERY EVENING.
MARION AND VEDDER,
American Comedy Team
M O T R A M O S,
Musical Grotesques.
Two Graces. George Formby, Edmunda, Olive Trio, Sisters Harries, Kitty Olive.
CLEOPATRA THE SNAKE CHARMER.

MONDAY, APRIL 2nd, and following Nights,
8   STELLA TROUPE   8
EDIE MADISON. | PERCY MEYE.
THE DANBYS.
W. J. CHURCHILL.   LEO TELL.
MINNIE MORAN.   BROS. DE KOCH.
MARION AND VEDDER.

Popular Prices : Stalls, 1s. 6d. ; Balcony, 1s. ; Pit, 9d ; Gallery, 3d. ; Private Boxes from 15s. to 5s.. After 9.30 admission to Stalls only 1s. Booking at Cramer's

A Tivoli bill including the Bioscope

George Formby Senior. As the bill above for the LYRIC Theatre (1910) (later the TIVOLI) shows, he had not yet earned his rightful place at the top of the bill

Jones was also General Manager of the Palace Theatre, Cork from 1900 when it passed into the hands of a Dublin syndicate. The Palace, Cork had originally been constructed by Dan Lowrey in 1897. Acts booked for the Lyric, Dublin, automatically moved down to the Palace, Cork in the following week. Of all the artists who performed in those theatres very few of their names survive in the annals of music hall: Morny Cash; J.W. Rickaby; Karno and Lester – patter comedians (Karno is not remembered as a performer but rather as the creator of the sketch "Mumming Birds" in which Stan Laurel and Charlie Chaplin appeared thus becoming part of "Fred Karno's Army"). Alice Lemure was the first to sing "Her Golden Hair was Hanging Down Her Back", but it is the song rather than Miss Lemure that is vaguely remembered today. George Formby Senior ("I'm coughing well tonight!") was always assured of a welcome, and one lady who topped the bill was a Lillie Reed – Champion Lady Ball Puncher and Negro Buck Dancer. The mind boggles!

Admission to the Lyric stalls had been 1/6 (7½p), but this was reduced to 1/- (5p) after 9.30 and late arrivals were known as 'half-timers'. There was nothing unusual in this practice and it operated in the Theatre Royal, Drury Lane, London, the first theatre in the kingdom. In April, 1896 Dan Lowrey had given the first public showing of moving pictures in Ireland in his Star of Erin Music Hall, but technically it was not a success. By 1900 the cinematograph was beginning to insinuate itself on to the bill in music halls. In April of that year there was an almost throw-away item on the bottom of a bill headed by Bransby Williams:

LATEST WAR PICTURES

> General Trenche's march to Kimberley; Troops in action; The fight with the Boers; The very latest from the seat of war; Queen Victoria's visit to Dublin (specially taken).

In less than thirty years this novelty would be housed in huge *art deco* picture palaces of its own and would lead to the closure of many variety theatres especially after the arrival of 'the talkies'. The Lyric Theatre of Varieties closed on August 31, 1901 and re-opened as the Tivoli Variety Theatre on October 28, 1901. Many were the complaints about the behaviour of the denizens of 'the gods'. They were, it appears, given to pelting the occupants of the circle with orange peel and other equally objectionable missiles from the safety of their top gallery. It was suggested that the presence of a policeman might curb their enthusiasm for displaying the opinions of the *hoi polloi* of the knuts and the nobs in the more salubrious parts of the theatre. A protecting board from the base of the railing of the gallery, such as existed in the old Star of Erin theatre was also suggested as a protection for the more civilised parts of the house from the rather unpleasant attention of 'the gods'. Of the First World War Charlie Jones has written:

> "The first war was a difficult enough time for artists, owing to travel or other difficulties and often they would not appear at the last moment. I kept a 'nest' of artists together in Dublin and would assemble them every Monday morning while awaiting the usual urgent messages from theatres in Dublin, Cork, Belfast, Limerick and other places that so-and-so had failed to turn up. I would then go along the line saying: 'Off to Cork'; 'Catch the first train to Belfast'; 'Ten pounds this week at the Tivoli', and always managed to complete the dates this way. Some very popular acts were built up by this manoeuvre, including 'Power and

*Still remembered by a few old timers in Dublin, Pat McNamara, a popular
song and dance man in his time*

Bendon', who were so popular with their door-mending act. Arthur Lucan and Kitty McShane with their first 'Dame and young daughter' act also came under my wing. I also built up the Dixie Minstrels".

Charlie Jones was by this time, of course, a booking agent for theatres throughout Ireland. After the war, in which Val Vousden had been promoted to the rank of Regimental Sergeant Major on the field of battle, Jones frequently engaged Vousden to perform his one man shows of monologues and recitations. Vousden was born William Maher MacNevin in Carlow around 1880. He intended to become a Jesuit but joined the 'fit-ups' instead and as a tribute to an old time Dublin entertainer and wit who had been popular from 1860-1880, Valentine Vousden, William MacNevin decided to call himself Val Vousden. His stage presentation was similar to that of Percy (who on his death in 1920 left most of his monologues to Val) without the music. Above all he displayed some of the appearance and the characteristics of 'Mr. Jingle' in Dickens' "Pickwick Papers". Val was also very partial to whiskey and delighted in relaxing with a bottle in some convent parlour after a Sunday night special recital for the sisters. On one occasion, however, Val was not so lucky. During the course of a Sunday night concert in a convent, "refreshments for the artists" as they are known in the profession were supervised by a naive little nun who beckoned each performer as they finished their turn, and escorted them to the parlour. Val finished his recital of "The Four Farrellys" and followed the beckoning nun expectantly. Upon entering the parlour he was quick to observe that every one of his fellow artists was eating thinly cut sandwiches and cake accompanied by cups of tea in fine bone china. One or two who were aware of his preferred refreshment, raised their eyebrows, glanced meaningfully at the tea cups and generally conveyed silently the sad news that this was all that was available. Later, after his second cup of tea which had been pressed upon him reluctantly, Val enquired of the little nun, "I observe a very fine portrait of one of the Sisterhood, over your mantlepiece, who would that be pray?" "Oh, that" said the little nun proudly "is our Foundress, Mother Mary Aikenhead".

"I see" mused Val, and confided in a stage whisper to his nearest neighbour – "Well, she certainly didn't get it here!"

Val Vousden, the epitome of the old style showman and barnstormer, died at Clonskeagh Hospital on Wednesday June 6, 1951.

The Tivoli, with a capacity of 1252 seats, was a cosy theatre, a fact that probably made it unviable with the advent of the all singing, all dancing, all talking movies. It closed its doors for the last time in 1928.

Charlie Jones was himself absorbed into the film business as manager of the old Grafton Cinema in Grafton Street, but he hadn't quite finished with the stage for he was one of the first to present, on the Grafton stage, The Dubliners with Ronnie Drew, and the cabaret artist Agnes Bernelle, in their earlier Dublin appearances.

Albert Sharpe. He started his career in a minstrel show at the Tivoli and went on to star in "Finian's Rainbow" on Broadway and co-starred with Jimmy O'Dea in Walt Disney's film "Darby O'Gill and the Little People"

The Abbey Theatre

The original Abbey Theatre (1904–1951) in Marlborough Street, Dublin

THE ABBEY THEATRE

Opened: 27 December, 1904; Destroyed by fire: 18 July, 1951
Foundation stone for new theatre laid 3 September, 1963.

Without the Fay brothers, William and Frank, and the generous financial support of Annie Horniman, the Abbey Theatre would probably never have materialised.

William Fay had some practical professional experience as he had left school at the age of eighteen and bitten by the theatre bug joined a touring company as advance manager, a not very important position in the small towns around Ireland, but by the time the company moved to Scotland and Wales he was playing small parts and really learning the business. Meanwhile, his elder brother, Frank took a safe secretarial job and made acting his hobby with the Ormond Dramatic Society. When Willie came home Frank persuaded him to take a more secure job as an electrical engineer, and they both spent their spare time in amateur theatricals, although Frank retained some of the aura of the actor-manager. For instance, appearance in local concerts included *The Irish Tutor* by Mr. W.G. Fay's Comedy Company; in a J. Dudley Digge's concert Mr. W.G. Fay and his talented combination "kept the house in one continuous roar of laughter in a clever production of Wilke's famous farce, *My Wife's Dentist*". Mr. W.G. Fay's Comedy Combination presented the laughable farce, *The Boots At The Swan*, at St. Theresa's Temperance Hall, Clarendon St., and in the Town Hall, Clontarf in May 1900, Mr. W.G. Fay's Comedy Combination were "vastly amusing in the farce *The Secret* with Mr. Fay displaying a wealth of quiet comedy in his clever and unforced character study of Thomas, a talkative butler, his expressive face being remarkably droll. Mr. Frank J. Fay, as a stuttering porter, also caused much hearty laughter".

Ambitious for greater things, the brothers formed W.G. Fay's Irish National Dramatic Company, composed entirely of Irish players of great talent, many of whom would later become world famous. The Fay's were absolutely clear in their objectives. Frank was one of the first pupils of a professional actress, Maud Randford, who taught the art of speech, and he passed on his knowledge to Willie, who was, in the meantime, studying the methods of a small group of amateurs in the Norwegian National Theatre and in particular the work of Andre Antoine, in Paris, where in a barely-equipped back-street hall he had created a Theatre Libre. These were William Fay's inspiration. He knew from the failure of the Irish Literary Theatre that if there was no one in Ireland who could genuinely act, there would never be an Irish National Theatre. Maire Nic Shiubhlaigh (Marie Walker) wrote in "The Splendid Years": "A popular error still identifies W.B. Yeats with the training of the Irish players and the establishment of the acting tradition which had kept the Abbey Theatre alive through the last fifty years. If the poet was alive now he would be the first to disagree with such a theory. To Frank Fay must go the credit of training the actors. Without Willie Fay there might never have been a competent one".

Yeats concept of a rehearsal was idiosyncratic; the theatre diarist Joseph Holloway said that he was "a strange odd fish with little or no idea of acting, and the way he stares at the players from within a yard or two of them, as they act, would distract most people. You would think he had a subject under a microscope he stares so intently at them".

Yeats liked to think of himself as 'distinctly dangerous'. "Somebody must be a devil" he declared, and apparently considered himself ideally suited to the role. In 1899 the Irish Literary Theatre (Yeats, Lady Gregory, George Moore, and Edward Martyn) had presented some 'literary' Irish plays at the Antient Concert Rooms and the Gaiety Theatre, the most successful and incidentally, the most realistic of which was Edward Martyn's *The Heather Field*, but they had to send to England for performers. Now, the Fays with their own Irish company were working on George Russell's(AE) play, *Deirdre* in a cold, draughty, smelly, leaky hall squeezed between a fish and vegetable shop and a butcher's, in Camden Street. It had room for an audience of no more than fifty and the seats consisted of long school-room benches. Yeats (who was a friend of Russell) gave his *Cathleen Ní Houlihan* to fill out the bill, and to Willie Fay's admiration and delight the title role was to be played by the beautiful Maud Gonne, who was presumed at that time to be Yeats' lady friend. The three performances in April, 1902 at St. Theresa's Hall, Clarendon Street could easily have extended to a week particularly due to the performance of Maud Gonne who charmed the ordinary working class people, rather than the usual sort of theatre audience. On the strength of these performances the Irish National Theatre Society was formed with W.B.Yeats as president.

Miss Annie Elizabeth Fredericka Horniman, an eccentric, chain-smoking Englishwoman arrived in Dublin in 1903. She had been a willing unpaid secretary to Yeats, particularly during the period relating to their Masonic and spiritualist activities relating to the Order of the Golden Dawn whose membership included Aleister Crowley. Yeats also enjoyed the company, gaiety and humour of the Russian born Madame Blavatsky, who was trying to rescue her reputation after being denounced by the Society of Psychial Research as "one of the most accomplished, ingenious and interesting impostors of history". Under the influence of Yeats Miss Horniman looked through the mystic Irish mists to a world of perfect light and beauty; a world of the imagination that had nothing to do with the real world. In time she grew to despise the Irish.

She was invited to Ireland on the understanding that she would supply the material, and design and execute, free, the costumes for the forthcoming production of *The King's Threshold* at the Molesworth Hall, which had seating for three hundred. Meanwhile, rehearsals continued in the hovel in Camden Street, and Marie Nic Shiubhlaigh remembered Miss Horniman as a likeable person with great experience of the theatre. How great it was was known to few. For instance, she was a source of great support to Bernard Shaw when nobody recognised his talent and she secretly financed a production of *Arms And The Man* with Yeats' *The Land Of Hearts Desire* as a curtain raiser at the Avenue Theatre, London, on 29th March, 1894. Now, although it was not exactly 'the land of hearts desire' that she had anticipated, Annie would sit by the stove in Camden Hall, busily sewing and displaying great interest in the Irish style of acting which they claimed was entirely their own, although years later when a curious Barry Fitzgerald had the Method school of acting explained to him he replied that "for Jasus sake they had been acting in that style at the Abbey since 1904!" Annie was more experienced than the players as she had seen many more productions all over the world, and in addition she could read plays in three or four of their original languages. Apart from herself, the only one with any real practical experience was the stage manager (director) William Fay. *The King's Threshold* preceded by Synge's *In The Shadow of the Glen* ran for three nights at the Molesworth Hall from 8th October, 1903. Synge raised a storm of abuse, and *The King's Threshold* was received in more or less complete apathy, but Annie's costumes received universal favour,

"The costumes are classic in the dignity of and beauty of the lines of the draperies...."

Lady Gregory delighted in playing the role of Lady Bountiful, and she patronised the actors in subtle ways. Her famous Gort cake, a rich fruit cake, was always available in the Green Room, and one slice of the confection was enough to assuage the hunger pangs of her supposedly starving actors. Annie's approach was very different. Like her hero Shaw's Professor Higgins she treated everyone in the same manner so that the players warmed to her. Although she had mentioned her plans to Yeats in 1903 who dismissed them as her response to his rhetoric, Annie confided in Willie Fay that she was prepared to invest some money in a proper fully operational theatre for the company. This important confidence shared with Willie Fay, a man whose work and sincere efforts she admired, reveals her absolute trust in him, and his undoubted ability to find an empty theatre or any suitable building that would suit his players and Miss Horniman's pocket.

In 1904 the local fire authorities tightened up their fire regulations following a spate of serious theatre fires in England. Some unimportant back-street halls were forced to close, but the Hibernian Theatre of Varieties, facing on to Lower Abbey Street, was served with similar notice. This was an extremely dirty, run down low music hall which was managed by Mrs Glenville who also rented out costumes and scenery, but whose chief claim to fame was that she was the mother of the famous dame comedian, Shaun Glenville who was married to the incomparable principal boy, Dorothy Ward. The Hibernian had once been known as the National Theatre (in name only) but had become known in Dublin lore as 'The Mechanics' because it was attached to the Mechanics' Institute, which had been built on the site of the Theatre Royal Opera House, built in 1820. Mechanics' Institutes flourished in Britain and the United States between 1820 and 1860; presumably charitably financed, at one time there were over 600 in existence. Their aim was to provide educational, and cultural facilities for craftsmen, skilled workers, and mechanics many of whom were illiterate. Each Institute was to have a library, a museum and a laboratory, and would organise public lectures and courses in various skills, but few branches were able to provide all of these facilities. The Dublin Institute rented out its stage to amateurs and it had the distinction of a stage appearance by Sean O'Casey in a production by his brother of one of Dion Boucicault's melodramas. Round the corner in Marlborough Street was an empty building which had served a number of uses from a savings bank to the City Morgue.

Annie Horniman agreed with Willie Fay to the purchase of the buildings. There appears to be no record as to what she paid for them. Miss Horniman appointed as architect Joseph Holloway, who was a fanatical first nighter of both legitimate and variety theatre; he was a critic and historian and above all a diarist, who later presented his 15 million almost indecipherable words about Dublin's theatres to the National Library. Miss Horniman, Willie Fay and Holloway visited the site and Miss Horniman, on Fay's advice recommended a thorough clean up. Conversion of the old buildings was discussed with a new foyer situated in Marlborough St in order to obliterate any connection with the 'Mechanics' and priority was to be given to a new stage and dressing rooms. Holloway, being aware of the requirements of the fire authorities, put his price at £1,300. Miss Horniman said yes without argument.

Returning to London she wrote a long and business-like letter to Yeats in which she gave notice of her intention of letting the theatre for lectures, concerts etc., when it was not being used by the Society. To this end she made it clear that the seat prices could be

A corner of the foyer with staircase to the Balcony.
Entrance to the Stalls was downstairs on the right

A view from the Balcony of rehearsals in progress

raised, but not lowered which might encourage cheap entertainment. On 11th May her offer was accepted and signed by over twenty members of the Society. One of the original drawbacks which had prevented 'The Mechanics' from operating as a proper theatre was the absence of a Royal Letters Patent in respect of the building, and Dublin's three other theatres amalgamated in their objections to ensure that no Patent would be granted. This was the situation that confronted Miss Horniman when she returned to Dublin in 1904 in order to obtain a licence. She engaged a barrister who had prepared an adequate defence. The opposition were not interested in the literary debate but in drawing up a legal document that would prevent Miss Horniman from letting her theatre to commercial travelling companies, which would lower the tone of the buildings and rental values in the neighbourhood. Miss Horniman made it clear that she had no desire to make any money from her theatre, but at the same time she did not want to waste money. She wanted a patent that would run for twenty one years and she undertook to give the theatre free to the Irish National Theatre Society which produced plays not ordinarily performed in theatres. She simply wanted to make them a present of it. Finally, as Miss Horniman was not resident in the country a patent for six years was granted on 20th August, 1904 to Dame Augusta Gregory. Miss Horniman met the costs of £455.2s.10d (£455.14½p). Lady Gregory stood in for Miss Horniman (as long as she would incur no financial responsibilities) and unfortunately, from the beginning, it somehow created an illusion of ownership that Lady Gregory increasingly claimed as her right.

Work at the theatre was proceeding, but someone was needed to keep an eye on the construction work, especially the requirements of the fire authorities, so Willie Fay was persuaded to abandon his secure trade as an electrician in order to take on the job of overseer.

The new stage had a proscenium opening of 21 feet; curtain line to back wall 16 feet, 4 inches; width of stage from wall to wall 40 feet. There were only two dressing rooms. There was no scene dock and scenery and properties had to be stored underneath the stage. The shallow stage meant that performers wishing to cross the stage out of sight of the audience had to make their way along a small alleyway outside of the theatre at the back of the stage. The theatre, which was otherwise untouched in the auditorium, seated 562 persons with perfect sight lines except for the side balconies upstairs. The balcony was built in a horseshoe style supported by slim graceful, black iron pillars, but this did not compensate the unfortunate patron seated in a side seat known as "the blind men's seats" from which it was possible to see only half the stage. Patrons had been known to pay a second visit to a play and secure a seat on the opposite side to his first visit in order to see what was happening on the other side.

There was an exit at the back of the auditorium into Abbey Street where the original main entrance had been, and since the patent did not permit the sale of drink many patrons slipped down the road to Tommy Lennon's bar during the intervals where the company might be just as distinguished as that to be found on the Abbey stage that evening. There one might find Cyril Cusack, Liam Redmond, Donagh MacDonagh, or Delia Murphy playing chess in the upper room. A fine portrait of Cyril Cusack as Clarence Mangan in Louis Dalton's *The Man In The Cloak* stood for many years on Lennon's bar.

Miss Horniman commissioned Irish workmen to reconstruct the building and to furnish and decorate it. Reconstruction of the theatre was carried out by Farmer Bros. Builders and Contractors, 22 Nottingham St., North Strand, Dublin; the paintwork was executed by Marks Bros. Painting and Contractors, 13 South Anne Street, Dublin. Bill-posting, which was very plentiful around the city, was buff in colour with black lettering and a logo from Elinor Monsell's woodcut with the motif of Queen Maeve, holding in leash an Irish wolfhound. This woodcut was used on posters, display cards, programmes and note paper and became a famous emblem which was slightly reminiscent of the Beleek Pottery china mark. Large copper-framed mirrors like ancient Irish shields came from a metalworks in Youghall and decorated the walls rather sparsely. Miss Horniman gave the Yeats family income an unexpected boost by commissioning W.B.'s father, Jack Yeats to paint portraits of all the leading figures in the Society so that the portraits could hang in the foyer of the new theatre. These were added to from time to time and the last one was described, probably by Cyril Cusack, as a custard trifle of Ernest Blythe. Lennox Robinson wrote a small booklet called "Pictures In A Theatre" in which he used the device of showing a visiting American round the portraits in the Abbey foyer, with appropriate comments on each. "Ah! says the American, "here's your great Mr Singe" "No, no" replies Lennox blearily "You singe a cat but you sing Synge".

Miss Sarah Purser was also contracted to design two stained glass windows and three lunettes for the foyer. In front of one of these windows on the right hand side of the entrance there was a constant issue of steam in the Tea Room under the management of Messrs. Huish, who also announced that Refreshments would be served in the Theatre, if desired. It is strange that this age old custom (still operating today) of eating and drinking in the theatre should have found favour in the Abbey which concentrated on what was happening on the stage. Above the facade and the three windows the legend "Savings Bank" retained the link with bygone days. Nor was the Morgue to be forgotten. Some bones were found during the course of excavation and a story put forward by a former morgue undertaker, in response to the furore raised by the newspapers, has been accepted as authentic. This man remembered that on one occasion just before an inquest a body was lost, but the result was that the Abbey became the home of a very unwelcome ghost which was allegedly seen by reputable actors and officials. It was all very reminiscent of Joseph Holloway's notes written on the day that the Abbey took over 'the Mechanics' –The manager called them "land grabbers!" and shouted as his parting shot "May you and your morgue have luck!"

On Tuesday, 27 December, 1904 the distinguished audience stood in knots on the stairs or congregated beside the box office close to the Stalls outside of which on the left hand side were the toilet facilities where, years later, a mischievous Samuel Beckett expressed the desire to flush someone's ashes down the toilet and pull the chain. An interesting feature of the evening was the gong which was struck thrice as a warning that the play was about to begin. The audience drifted into their seats noting that the ceiling was very high, the walls were painted a dull red although some expressed the opinion that they were the colour of dried mud. The emergency exit was indicated by a painted hand pointing downwards and the inevitable suggestion that the floorboards would have to be pulled up in the event of an unexpected departure. People were distracted by the rich carpeting; the triple electric lamps; the red leather seats individually divided by polished brass fittings. It was reported that the seats were not upholstered but covered with red leather; they were anything but luxurious, but they were comfortable. There was not a vacant place in the theatre when all the audience at last assembled. The theatre is said to have had a superb lighting system, and the front curtain was black with gold stripes.

The plays were *On Baile's Strand* by Yeats with costumes by Miss Horniman and as Cuchullain, F.J. Fay would be the first actor to step on to the new Abbey stage. *Spreading The News* by Lady Gregory, Yeats's *Cathleen Ní Houlihan* and *In The Shadow Of The Glen* by Synge completed the bill. Lady Gregory, despite encouragement from Yeats, was alleged to be ill at Coole Park, and was not present, and despite reports in Irish and British newspapers, Miss Annie Horniman was not present either. Her absence, yet no one described her appearance, was so inexplicable that it was automatically assumed that she was there.

Willie Fay recorded sorrowfully that she had returned to England. He was sincerely distressed that she had missed the first night, as he regarded her affectionately and respectfully as the "real *sage-femme* of the Abbey Theatre, without whose aid it would have been still-born". By this time her relationship with Yeats was stormy and there had been furious scenes between them at rehearsals.

Right from the start of the Abbey Theatre, Annie's responsibilities were concentrated in London and the English provinces where contacts and publicity were needed. About a year after the opening some stables became available in the laneway at the side of the theatre, and Miss Horniman bought them converting them into a green room, wardrobe room, a scene dock, a paint room, a workshop, a small rehearsal stage and six small, but adequate dressing rooms. In 1908 Dr Jack Larchet, later first professor of music at University College, Dublin, was installed with a new trio. He spent ten years trying to leave the Abbey, but he loved the place because it had all a good musician craves – good acoustics. He claimed that the acoustics were so good that a whisper from the stage was as good as a shout elsewhere. He built up an excellent orchestra. He told Sean McCann that he spent seventeen years at the Abbey, but only because he was persuaded to stay on by Lady Gregory. In October 1905, Miss Horniman was virtually ignored when Yeats, Lady Gregory and J.M. Synge decided to turn the Abbey into a private Limited Liability Co. Miss Horniman who had spent £4,000 on the company had put herself in the position of paying the bills and having no authority. Still, she organised very successful tours of England, and incredibly, she undertook to pay quarterly £500 for salaries and £100 to cover administration costs. The money that came from rents would be used to pay the rates and taxes on the theatre; she would also meet any bills for repairs and pay half of the scenery costs. She resolved that she must release Yeats from wasting his time on business matters and she added a further £200 to her Abbey subsidies to pay for a business manager. But this was not enough. Nothing was ever enough. Feeling hurt and outrage over her treatment by the company, she engaged a former contemptuous Abbey manager, Ben Iden Payne to help her organise a new repertory theatre in Manchester. Yeats actually wrote to him warning that his contract should be clear and concise with no room for Miss Horniman to assert her authority. "She is", Yeats explained "a vulgarian". He was obviously smarting from fits of jealousy that agitated him every time he thought of his benefactress starting a new venture without him. Miss Horniman's new company was an outstanding success and produced plays by Shaw, Arnold Bennett, Galsworthy and a very famous Mancunian play *Hindle Wakes*.

The audience which had thronged the Abbey during its first years began to dwindle. A few loyal souls went every week but it was a depressing experience, to recognise the same people every week. A few in the pit, a few in the balcony and a few in the stalls. This was at a time when the theatre was open only three nights a week with a matinee on Saturday. There were many rows and break-aways, sometimes for the most stupid

Production for the first time on any Stage of On Baile's Strand and Spreading the News, on Tuesday, 27th December, 1904, and every evening till Tuesday, 3rd January, 1905.

ON BAILE'S STRAND, A PLAY IN ONE ACT, BY W. B. YEATS.

CUCHULLAIN, the King of Muirthemne	F. J. Fay
CONCOBAR, the High King of Ullad	George Roberts
DAIRE, a King	Arthur Sinclair
FINTAIN, a blind man	Seumas O'Sullivan
BARACH, a fool	W. G. Fay
A YOUNG MAN	P. MacSiubhlaigh
YOUNG KINGS and OLD KINGS	Maire Ni Gharbhaigh, Emma Vernon, Sara Algood, Doreen Gunning, R. Nash, N. Power, U. Wright, E. Keegan.

SCENE—A Great Hall by the Sea close to Dundalgan.

Costumes designed by Miss Horniman.

SPREADING THE NEWS, A COMEDY IN ONE ACT, BY LADY GREGORY.

BARTLEY FALLON	W. G. Fay
Mrs. FALLON	Sara Algood
Mrs. TULLY	Emma Vernon
Mrs. TARPEY	Maire Ni Gharbhaigh
SHAWN EARLY	J. H. Dunne
TIM CASEY	George Roberts
JAMES RYAN	Arthur Sinclair
JACK SMITH	P. MacSuibhlaigh
A POLICEMAN	R. S. Nash
A REMOVABLE MAGISTRATE	F. J. Fay

SCENE—The Outskirts of a Fair.

Programme for the opening performance on Tuesday, 27th December, 1904

On Tuesday, Thursday, and Saturday, 27th, 29th, and 31st December,
On Baile's Strand will be followed by :—

KATHLEEN NI HOULIHAN, A PLAY IN ONE ACT, BY W. B. YEATS.

KATHLEEN NI HOULIHAN	Maire Nic Shiublaigh
PETER GILLANE	W. G. Fay
BRIDGET GILLANE, his Wife	Sara Algood
MICHAEL GILLANE } his Sons	P. MacSiubhlaigh
PATRICK GILLANE }	U. Wright
DELIA CAHEL	Maire Ni Gharbhaigh

SCENE—A Cottage near to Killala, in 1798.

On Wednesday and Friday, 28th and 30th December, and on
Monday and Tuesday, 2nd and 3rd January. On Baile's Strand
will be followed by :—

IN THE SHADOW OF THE GLEN, A PLAY IN ONE ACT, BY J. M. SYNGE.

DAN BURKE, Farmer and Herd	George Roberts
NORA BURKE, his Wife	Maire Nic Shiubhlaigh
MICHAEL DARA, a Young Herd	P. MacSiubhlaigh
A TRAMP	W. G. Fay

SCENE—The last Cottage at the head of a long glen in
County Wicklow.

The next production will be a new play in three acts,
by J. M. Synge.

reasons: the phrase 'God Almighty' might be unacceptable to an actress, so she left with her soul cleansed. The Abbey directors were more attentive to their playwrights than their actors, but more seriously, rows about money were justifiable on the actors' part. W.G. Fay, a recognised genius, was considered to be overpaid at £4 per week. And a receipt for £1 dated 11 January, 1905 was found many years later and signed by Sara Allgood – her salary for a week's acting for the woman who had undoubtedly added to Synge's reputation by creating roles in his plays like *The Playboy of the Western World* and *Riders To The Sea* in particular. This shrine of acting became, in time, grubby and un-attractive to the few Americans who found their way there and stared around them in disbelief. To them this famous temple of art looked more like the foyer to some dis-reputable off-Broadway slum theatre in Greenwich Village. Passing locals occasionally looked in to satisfy themselves that the walls were still the colour of dried mud.

Undoubtedly the Abbey was a strange place, and an enormous amount of the strangeness could be attributed to W.B. Yeats and his later manager, Lennox Robinson. Robinson was, at least, enthusiastic; for some time many Dubliners regarded him as a theatre cleaner; the official cleaner was a Mrs Martin, but very often Lennox would take it into his head that the footpath in front of the foyer was in urgent need of a sweeping. He would emerge with an ordinary house brush and proceed to sweep the footpath with vigorous strokes and in time with a certain degree of professionalism. At the same time the company listed on December 11th 1917 in a play called *Blight* by A.& O (Dr. Oliver St. John Gogarty) included Fred O'Donovan, May Craig, Maureen Delaney, P.J. McDonnell, Barry Fitzgerald, Arthur Shields, Eric Gorman, and a young man newly arrived in Dublin who had introduced himself to W.B. Yeats as Alfred Willmore and now appeared in the programme as "Michael MacNaimmhoir". Later he would arrive at a translation of his name closer to the original, "MacLíammóir". Frank Fay and Yeats did not have a happy relationship. Lady Gregory had been aware of the friction between them and she and Yeats decided that Fay must go. After much political manoeuvring Yeats managed to give the impression that the other members of the company had been responsible for the departure of Fay in 1907. By early February Willie and his wife Brigit O'Dempsey and his brother Frank were sailing to America by courtesy of the playwright James Barrie, who told Fay that he had seen every one of his performances with the Irish players, and organised a contract for him with the great American impresario Charles Frohman. They played New York and Chicago.

Remarkably, Annie was still on good terms with Yeats but in 1910 Lennox Robinson, in the absence of any firm instructions, kept the theatre open on 7th May while the other Dublin theatres closed as a mark of respect on the death of King Edward VII. Miss Horniman took it as a deliberate personal insult and an openly defiant political act. It rankled that she had never been officially informed that Lennox Robinson had been appointed manager of the Abbey and she did not know that he alone was in charge at the time of the King's death. In June, while the Irish players were in London for a season, news broke that Miss Horniman was withdrawing her support for the Abbey Theatre. Annie wrote to Joseph Holloway, one of her few remaining friends in Dublin, telling him exactly how much she had lost over the Abbey venture. She estimated that she had spent £10,350, not including the losses of English tours (according to Ms. Sheila Gooddie, biographer of Annie Horniman). Any profits were always handed to the directors. The shop and house in Abbey Street and the stables behind the theatre had cost £1,428, and she was giving all the contents of the buildings. She told him that it had taken her a long time to realise that Dublin had no use for a middle-class educated woman (as opposed to

Acclaimed as the greatest Abbey Theatre actor, F.J. McCormick as (left) Joxer Daly in O'Casey's "Juno and the Paycock" and (right) Shell in Carol Reed's film "Odd Man Out"

SOME OF THE ABBEY THEATRE COMPANY OF THE MIDDLE TWENTIES

Arthur Shields   Eric Gorman   Maureen Delaney   Gabriel Fallon   F. J. McCormick

Sara Allgood   Ria Mooney   Christine Hayden   Eileen Crowe   Barry Fitzgerald   Michael Dolan

Some of the Abbey Theatre Company of the middle twenties which toured the United Kingdom and the U.S.A. (names as indicated)

one from the landed gentry) with a great love of the arts. On 1st November, Dublin's *Evening Telegraph* noted that it was the day that the Abbey Theatre patent expired and added "Our Drama loses the best friend it ever had in parting with Miss Horniman today". It was quite a reversal from previous press comments such as "Why should an English lady (however estimable) have so administrative a connection with the Irish National Theatre Society? Is not the Society able to manage its own affairs?" It might manage them – barely, but it certainly couldn't finance itself.

Unhappily for Miss Horniman, like George Moore, Edward Martyn, George Russell(AE), and the Fay Brothers, along with many others, not least the countless actors and actresses who had worked for a pittance and then found that, following a more lucrative engagement elsewhere, their services were no longer required, she discovered too late the duplicity of the man to whom she had given so much. Significantly, Yeats's title in the secret, Masonic-like societies of which he was a member was "Demon Est Deus Inversus" (A demon is an inverted god). Miss Horniman's fascination with the Tarot cards should have warned her. At last Yeats was total master of the Abbey. Some very excellent playwrights received much less than their due. George Fitzmaurice for instance, author of *The Country Dressmaker* and the delightful *Magic Glasses* was superior to other more favoured writers. Scripts submitted to the theatre were lost and never seen again. Lennox Robinson is alleged to have 'mislaid' a hand-written copy of O'Casey's *The Shadow Of A Gunman* which the unfortunate author was obliged to rewrite from rough notes and memory.

And so the theatre continued to exist in its usual idiosyncratic way assisted, especially by the contributions of Sean O'Casey and the furious reaction of the normally disinterested Dublin public which filled the theatre for *The Playboy Of The Western World* and *The Plough And The Stars* and developed into riots in the theatre. These were undoubtedly the work of rabid nationalists, fanatical Catholics, hypocrites, and people of such alleged purity that they were unaware of the existence of whores on the streets of Dublin. These were the finest occasions for self-publicity that Yeats had ever stage-managed and slyly exploited. The serious attention given to Yeats, as a person, grew in absurdity. One thing about Yeats impressed Sir Ian Hamilton on a visit to Coole where Yeats was enjoying the comfort of the house and Lady Gregory's cuisine (not Gort cake), although its significance was not apparent at the time. Listening to the insane rantings of Hitler in 1938 he was struck by the expression of over-charged emotion by the dictator, which he distinctly recalled was almost identical with the expression of the poet. In the light of this it is important to remember the fascism of Yeats and hatred of the Republican forces during the Irish Civil War. In 1910 Yeats was given a valuable pension by the British Government, an allowance which he drew even when his cash award from the Nobel prize made him rich. This, of course, became generally known and gave the Dublin caustic wits the opportunity to dub him, 'Pensioner' Yeats. He didn't fool many of them. Yeats kept out of the country during the period of fighting and curfews and returned in 1921. During his absence only the assistance of friends like Bernard Shaw, John Drinkwater, and John Galsworthy among others, enabled Lady Gregory to keep the Abbey going. Against Lady Gregory's wishes in June, 1924, a letter signed by herself and Yeats informed the President of the Executive Council that he could have the theatre for nothing. Since he had won the Nobel Prize (no doubt on his merits) the Abbey was of no further use to him and with a generosity worthy of the seeker of self advancement, he decided to give away what he did not want, although his moral right to do so will always be in serious doubt. The Minister for Finance saw through the alleged gift 'to the nation' and told President Cosgrave that the offer was more tactical than serious, but being an admirer of the Abbey, in particular the clauses in its Patent that it was expected to produce plays in the Irish language, he recommended an annual grant which created the first state-subsidised theatre in the English-speaking world. The future was secure as now the Abbey was a State owned theatre. When O'Casey submitted his *Silver Tassie* and Yeats saw its poetic content in the second act, it warned him that O'Casey was becoming a possible rival and sent O'Casey a megalomanic, insulting letter of rejection. This was his last unscrupulous intrigue.

Some further property had been acquired beside Sean Thompson's yard, and this had been transformed into a tiny experimental theatre downstairs called THE PEACOCK. It was decorated in a peacock colour scheme that was not the most popular of the twenties. The later to be famous Hilton Edwards and Micheál MacLíammóir presented their first Dublin Gate Theatre Production at the Peacock, *Peer Gynt*. There is a story that Denis Johnston submitted a play about Robert Emmett to the Abbey, but Lady Gregory did not think its style was suitable, and she recommended that it should be offered to the Dublin Gate Co. downstairs with a small amount of cash to help defray production costs. Edwards & MacLíammóir accepted and it is said that in view of Lady Gregory's kindly rejection of the play they decided to call it *The Old Lady Says 'No'*. Later an experimental theatre was opened under Ria Mooney, and she produced some interesting plays like *In Sand* by Jack Yeats and from which a new company of players would emerge. Upstairs in a door off the hallway on the right, Lennox Robinson ran a school of acting seated regally in a large throne-like chair from where, in a haze of gin, he encouraged his pupils to repeat "Do You Remember An Inn, Miranda?" or "The Lake Isle Of Inish Free" about which he would question people closely as to whether they had ever heard it before! The only actor known to have emerged from Robinson's school was Alpho O'Reilly and even he displayed a preference for design. Another room was a school of ballet.*

Upstairs in the main theatre the playwright and author, Walter Macken, told Sean McCann that "There was a sort of dirty glamour about the place. I think it was the wardrobe room that gave it this. The costumes seemed to be always old, shabby and dirty –tenement clothes if you like for that was the sort of play we always seemed to be doing. We always seemed to be dirty ... but still the glamour of the place was always there". Some playgoers confined their visits to the works of George Sheils, Brinsley McNamara or Rutherford Mayne merely to observe the sartorial vision of Billy O'Gorman, Harry Brogan, Fred Johnson or M.J. Dolan dressed as 'farmers'. This ensemble consisted of drain-pipe trousers of a very dark and tough almost immobile material with a matching waistcoat and three-quarter length jacket all of which seemed to have been woven from some basic material closely resembling turf. A square shaped hard hat completed the ensemble which lacked a collar and tie. This hat was a curious object and the late Sir Winston Churchill has been seen in something similar, but it is unlikely that the Abbey farmers went to Bond Street for their headgear or that Sir Winston sent to 'little towns in Connaught' for his distinctive bowlers.

All of this was happening at a time when everyone knew that in every house in city and county there was a wardrobe or at least a cupboard which held within a new or at least good, navy blue suit for the owner's weekly visit to Mass, after which it was removed and stored for another Sunday display of respectability and financial rectitude.

Most of the plays which were invariably described as comedies were in fact alien farces set in places that did not exist and peopled by extraordinary characters whom one did not recognise. There can be no doubt some of these characters were the saviours of the Abbey. Patrons went regularly to witness some great acting because the players often raised a decidedly odd character into a believable creation. They could, with a single speech or a few lines, establish the true basics and humanity of a character which were otherwise concealed. George Shiels and the great F.J. McCormick served each well in this respect. 'Professor Tim' was slightly unremarkable, but the poacher 'Rabit Hamil' was a delight; but the masterpiece was 'Marcy' in *The Rugged Path* with McCormick as an oily hypocritical man of the roads gravely offering some pebbles to the woman of the house with great reverence as they had been given to him by "a holy man in slemish". In *Peter* by Rutherford Mayne, F.J. was outstanding as 'Sam Partridge' and there has never been a tailor, complete with cigarette in the corner of his mouth and measuring tape around his neck, quite like that which McCormick played in *Look At The Heffernans*. Who can forget the opening scene of *The Shadow Of A Gunman*? A woman outside the bed-sitting room is shouting "Are you awake, Mr Shields – Mr. Shields are you awake? Are you goin' to get up to-day at all, at all?" There is a movement somewhere in the centre of a pile of rags on the bed, and F.J. McCormick wearing a dirty vest slowly emerges scratching himself. "Oh-h-h. I was fast in the arms of Morpheus – he was one of the infernal deities, son of Somnos, wasn't he?"

Most people hated the Abbey and only supported it for a variety of reasons, some of which are given above. Most agreed that the plays were rubbish and prompted Valentine Iremonger to address a protest to the entire audience from the centre circle. Almost certainly it was the people who were closely associated with it that inspired this love-hate relationship with the building. Or perhaps Dubliners were only too well aware of the great injustices perpetrated there, and of those who were responsible. Still, most of the old school of actors were happy there. McCormick went in for rehearsals happily every morning and gave his usual cheerful hello to his friend Joe, who was a street sweeper who pushed his cart and brush along Marlborough St. A time came when F.J. was aware that Joe's father was seriously ill and he always made a point of asking after him. He expressed his usual solicitude one morning when a tearful Joe leaning on his brush explained to F.J. that on the previous evening his mother had called him to his father's bedside, but he had barely reached the patient when he died. "Dead, gone, Mr. McCormick, I hadn't even time to say a word to him, Mr. McCormick. Gone, Mr. McCormick, like a fuckin' spit off a wet roof". What O'Casey wouldn't have given for that line!

At twenty-five minutes past twelve on the morning of 18th July, 1951 a fire began in one of the dressing rooms and spread to the green room where a cupboard full of lost and mislaid scripts added to the conflagration and in a short time Irelands most famous and controversial theatre was gone. There were some small blessings: the police broke through the front door and rescued the famous paintings in the vestibule. Actors, stage hands and general helpers rushed in to try and save what they could, but historic costumes, records and manuscripts were lost. Lennox Robinson was reported to be seated on the opposite footpath enjoying a drink when he was approached by a reporter. "Go away, young man," Lennox said testily, "can't a man enjoy a drink by his own fireside?" This was either a piece of colour added to the reporter's account or it was a deliberate plagiarism by Robinson of Sir Richard Brinsley Sheridan's remark which was exactly the same when his theatre at Drury Lane, London, was destroyed by fire on February 24th, 1809.

The play in production that week was *The Plough And The Stars* with W. O'Gorman (Billy O'Gorman) as Fluther. Well-wishers brought in old clothing and the Abbey back stage staff worked overtime so the play could go on in the 100-seater Peacock Theatre that night. It is more than likely that thereafter for a time Messrs Guinness came to the rescue by offering the Abbey company their well-appointed Rupert Guinness Hall in James's Gate. Lennox Robinson was one of the last of the band of people who had seen the Abbey through to the end. Most of the others were dead – or in exile forbidden to darken the door because they had once left the theatre voluntarily.

The Abbey tenancy of the Queen's *q.v.* was not a happy one. The theatre was too large and there were nights when twenty people in the stalls was a crowd. There were still some good plays but generally the casual visitor could be forgiven if he thought he was back in the days of the old Queen's Happy Gang. Ernest Blythe, a fanatical Irish language revivalist, presented regular one act plays in Irish as an afterpiece, to which the patrons generally responded by repairing to the bar while Blythe stood at the entrance glowering at them malevolently. He also presented a concoction described as a pantomime in Irish. Blythe sat in the stalls at every performance with his ear cocked, all the better to pick up the Irish blas of the players and to note any inadvertent slips back into the English language, which usually cost the unfortunate thespian a hefty fine. One afternoon Blythe was concentrating on his priceless addition to the theatre when he became aware that a party of mature schoolchildren was laughing loudly at the jokes and generally enjoying the pantomime. He turned on them in fury and informed them that as they were preventing him from hearing the dialogue, they must be disturbing others and if they were not quiet he would have them removed from the theatre. This must be the first occasion anywhere in the world where the audience were threatened with expulsion for laughing at a pantomime. But let it not be forgotten that this was an Abbey pantomime, under the control of one of the biggest despots that ever ran that company.

In February 1961 the bulldozers tore down the remaining walls of the old Abbey in Marlborough St., and the contract for the new theatre was signed with architect Michael Scott in June, 1962. It was rumoured at the time that the outer blocks in the original facade were to be numbered, with a view to re-erecting the walls for the joy and edification of American tourists of the future, but there has been no further news of the scheme.

The President of Ireland, Eamon de Valera, laid the foundation stone on 3rd September, 1963, but even as Mr. deValera was yielding his little silver trowel, allegations were being made that the new theatre was being founded on ignorance. Of course it had to be another Abbey intrigue. The original intention had been to include the names of only Yeats and Lady Gregory on the stone. There was an objection to this because Lady Gregory's correct title was not used. Eventually, on the stone alongside Yeats, Synge and the Fay brothers, she was described as Augusta, Lady Gregory. But the full inscription was in Irish and this provoked another row: it should have been in both Irish and English! But these were mere quibbles compared to the most insulting lack of gratitude omitted from the stone – Miss Horniman was forgotten, her name was eliminated without trace and as *The Irish Times* commented 'the decision must have been a hard one for the chivalrous persons responsible'. One must assume that the name of Miss Horniman, generous benefactress of the Irish National Theatre even before a state existed, whose name should have been included in common gratitude, was deliberately excluded for some unimportant Irish or nationalist reasons.

* The ballet school was run by Dame Ninette de Valois, who would soon find a greater appreciation of her talents than that afforded her in her native land, when she created the Royal Ballet School.

She was foiled in her attempt to nurture an Irish ballet tradition at the Abbey, despite support from Yeats. The following extract from his "Plays for Dancers" suggests that in the prevailing climate at the Abbey, such ambitions were untimely:

> "I desire a mysterious art, always reminding and half-reminding those who understand it of dearly loved things, doing its work by suggestion, not by direct statement, a complexity of rhythm, colour, gesture, not space-pervading like the intellect, but a memory and a prophecy . . . . ."

Yeats went on to recall a mere handful of moments in the Abbey's history which "haunted" him, including "that great artist Ninette de Valois in *Fighting The Waves* . . . . . these things will, it may be, haunt me on my death-bed; what matter if the people prefer another art, I have had my fill".

Sean McCann, in his 1967 book "The Story of the Abbey Theatre", suggested that W.B.'s hope for such expressive theatre at the Abbey was a forlorn one when he wrote those words. "One only has to think of the Abbey Theatre of the 'twenties exhibiting a naturalism which Antoine and Stanislavsky might well have envied to realise that it was incapable of giving Yeats what he now required".

The Coliseum

THE COLISEUM
Opened April, 1915; Destroyed in the Easter Rising 1916

Of the lost theatres of Dublin, The Coliseum suffered the most sudden and tragic fate, This 3000 seat theatre in Henry Street was opened on Easter Monday, 1915, but by the end of the Easter Rising in the following year the Coliseum lay in smouldering ruins, never to be rebuilt. The theatre was situated at the back of the GPO, and therein lay its fate. When the GPO was battered by shellfire and engulfed in flames it was impossible for the fire services or anyone else to even approach and try to save the newly opened theatre.

The front entrance to the Coliseum had a facade in the Grecian style, and stood exactly opposite Moore St, where the GPO Arcade now runs.

It took 12 months to build and it was designed by Mr. Bertie Crewe as a variety theatre. Crewe was a student of the great Frank Matcham. R.F. Bergin, a well-known Dublin architect, was associated with the design which was constructed by Messrs Martin. The Coliseum, it was claimed, 'was the finest theatre in Ireland', planned for luxury, comfort and safety replete with every accommodation and appurtenance. The carpeting was blue, the draperies were old rose, and the decorations cream and gold. Claimed as the last word in theatre construction, a proud boast was that there was not a single column in the auditorium to obstruct the line of vision, a cantilever feature originally introduced into theatre design by Frank Matcham. Four boxes, two on each side of the stage, were surmounted by life-size groups of statuary, symbolising Rome and Greece. In the light of the theatre's tragic fate it is ironic to read the claim that the possibility of fire was almost nonexistent in view of the fact that all the woodwork had been rendered fire resistant.

It had an exceptionally large stage – 80 feet wide and 40 feet deep under which there was a large tank intended for water shows. On the Good Friday, three days before the opening, Joseph Holloway, himself an architect, and his friend W.J. Lawrence inspected the Coliseum. Holloway noted that the colour scheme was the same as that at the Empire – cream and gold. He was very much struck by the size of the stage, and confirmed that a very good view could be obtained from all parts of the house. "The rake of all the seats on the circles is very great" he wrote, "being so near the stage". This gives the impression of almost perpendicular seating which cannot have been very comfortable for patrons, suffering from vertigo. This form of seating is one of the few drawbacks at the Victoria Palace, London.

As Holloway and his companion stepped back on to the street... "The manager, Mr. Marsh, formerly manager of the Empire, drove up in an outside car looking excessively overdressed, as only a theatrical manager can when he tries to look like a gentleman, top-hatted, frockcoated, big cigar in mouth, and self importance oozing out of his whole rigout. My opinion is that there is not room in Dublin for four big music halls". The other three were the Theatre Royal, the Empire and the Tivoli. One suspects that Holloway, who was normally a placid man, and the unfortunate manager, Marsh, who was after all only living up to his image as a showman, must have crossed swords on a previous occasion. "On Holy Saturday" Holloway continues, "Close on 1000 citizens were allowed to view the Coliseum and after some unusual selections from the orchestra and a few vocal items, Mr. Lorcan Sherlock, the Chairman of the company, said they had succeeded in establishing in the city a great and magnificent theatre, at a cost of £40,000". On Easter Monday evening, Holloway went to the first house starting at 6.50. He paid three pence in the gallery. The theatre which gave its address as Henry Street and Prince's Street, and later settled on being "near Nelson's Pillar", had admission prices from 3d to 2/- (1p–10p).

> "There were no programmes sold on tops at the first show, and the gallery filled in well. The band – a very noisy one at full cock played the opening selection, and the curtains were drawn up and 'Idento and May', in an eccentric juggling act, had the honour of being the first turn to appear on the stage. The turn was ordinary. 'Rosie Wylie' then sang a few songs, and the 'New Macs' made good at once and met with a popular ovation on coming out. [The 'New Macs' appear to have been a local act as a newspaper critic commented: "The New Macs were justly popular in their own city" – Author] They, sang, danced, pottered and boxed; some few of the jokes, were vulgar and the gestures of one of them suggestive. Otherwise their turn was excellent of its kind. Signor Jose de Moraes, a Portuguese tenor [who claimed some Royal Patronage – Author] sang three songs – one in Italian and two in English. His singing was well received. Then followed the big turn of the bill 'Zona Vevey and Max Erard' – the latter featuring a big cathedral organ and playing it with great effect and richness of tone. [Mr. Erard claimed to rank very highly among British composers; the organ cost £2000 and with its full range of stops and weights weighed eight tons – Author]. The vocalist's quality of voice was not pleasing, but she sang several songs with some effect and spoke a little piece about an old organ – to organ accompaniment as she sat on the floor, or rather knelt – a man behind me 'hoped she'd say one for him'. They gave a good long, turn, with many seeming endings, but were wooed back by applause. But alas, the turn that was doing so well was completely spoiled by her singing of a recruiting Jingo song, "Your Country Wants You". 'It does, and we intend to stop it' said a man behind me as she sang. "Give us something Irish" shouted another, and then I knew trouble was brewing for her, and sure enough when she had finished, a stream of hissing and booing broke out and the two artists, retired amid a tornado of ugly sounds."

"I wonder" mused Holloway, "Did she attempt to repeat the song at the second show". [She didn't – Author]. The diarist continues: "'Tom E. Deane' an eccentric comedian, followed and sang a medley. 'Darby and Partner' acrobated eccentrically, and the programme concluded with The Bioscope which introduced up-to-date and current events. A bar of England's anthem brought the first show to an inglorious end, amid hissing, which cut short the music, as the imported conductor dropped his baton when he saw the way the land lay". A marginal note by Holloway reads: "This anthem has always been translated, when played in Ireland, into 'To Hell With The Catholics', and will always, I fear until we are allowed to govern ourselves. Therefore, it is better omitted from programmes of a general nature".

This prolonged objection from Irish theatregoers to British 'Jingo' songs and their national anthem is at complete variance with the view of some commentators that the 1916 Rising was not a popular one.

The British anthem was not played at the second house and despite the debacle of the first house, the second house at 9 o'clock was a sell out, and hundreds were turned away.

That same week in Dublin the D'Oyly Carte Company were at the Gaiety; Harry Taft and Cissie Lupino were at the Royal; Tom and Vic Collins were at the Tivoli with their sketch "Buying A Pub"; R.G. Knowles and Leo Dryden were at the Empire; the Queen's had a 'romantic Anglo-American' play *The Indian Scout* and two new plays were being presented at the Abbey, *The Bargain* by William Crone, and *The Philosopher* by Martin J. McHugh. Sean Connolly, the first man to be shot in the Easter Rising, took a role in the McHugh play at short notice.

The second week at the Coliseum saw *Town Topics*, – 'a revue with a reason' starring Arthur Reece and the entire London Beauty Chorus. It was stated to be the 'latest skit on passing events'. *Cheer up* – "a real our times revue" came in May, followed by a bizarre feature called, "Carmo – the one-man revue". Carmo was supported by The Wolkowsky Troupe playing on balalaikas and performing Cossack dances.

Karno's Komedians in two new sketches must have been a relief in June. They were supported by well-known vaudeville acts. The Coliseum management always used the American term "vaudeville", to describe anything resembling "variety". Jean Aylwin starred in a revue called *All Scotch*, announced as the Tartan Revue! Far down the cast list for this show was the name Jack Buchanan; Buchanan first appeared on stage in 1912 and he made a steady upward climb until with his personality and individuality his name was removed from the obscurity among the 'wines and spirits' in touring revues to become at the other extreme the "West End" debonair and sophisticated Londoner. But, in fact, he was born in Scotland and he loved his native land.

In July, after another revue, *'S Only A Rumour* with Arthur Rigby, the Johnson-Willard fight film was a big attraction. Johnson, who had won the world title fight from Tommy Burns in 1908 was floored in the 26th of a 45 round contest by Jess Willard at Havana, Cuba. The crowd jeered at Johnson, who it was said, was beaten by the weight of years. The fight film was, of course, supported by vaudeville acts; in this instance, The Great Leon & Co. – exponents of Hindu magic!

Following the *All French Revue* in July, Stanley Lupino starred in another revue *This Is The Life* before going on later to star in dozens of films.

In August the musical Scena *Symphonia* was greeted as "Truly a concord of sweet sounds" by the *Irish Times* and a "combination of rare talent" by *The Freeman's Journal*.

In August in *Miss Paris In London* the Coliseum offered its one and only water show. In a section of the show called "Tronville On Sea" a chorus of Diving Belles provided a magnificent Water Spectacle utilising the 50,000 gallon water tank underneath the stage. There was vaudeville in support.

In a revue called *Search Me* there was a section called "The Burning Forest" described as a spectacular drama in four scenes depicting the dangers faced by inhabitants of the Wild West. There was a forest fire on stage, with the realistic effects of falling trees. A thrilling climax to the scene was a train rushing through the blazing mass. In lighter vein Horace Wheatley provided some respite from the mayhem. Apart from Veronica Brady, (later a musical comedy star in London), Scott and Whaley – coloured singers, and Albert Whelan, with his famous whistling signature tune, there were few acts worth mentioning that would stir the memory today. The only exception to this was the reserved and intensely private genius, Little Tich (Harry Relph) the great music hall star, who sang and recited and wore boots with soles so long that he when he walked on the toe caps he appeared to be on stilts. Only about two minutes of his act survives on very grainy film stock. He was greatly admired in Paris where Charlie Chaplin used to observe him nightly as he performed his act.

Cross-Channel casts appeared in no less than four pantomimes during the Christmas season of 1915/16: *Sinbad The Sailor*; *Jack and Jill*; *Ali Baba And The Forty Thieves*; and *Robinson Crusoe*.

The new year continued with the familiar diet of touring revues: *Hello, Dublin*, (undoubtedly the name of the city changed according to wherever they were playing); *Mind Your own Business* was a cheeky piece of advice given to prospective patrons. With few exceptions all the bills at the Coliseum were cheap and trite, and there does not appear to be any record of engagements to Irish artists, like Mike Nono or Pat McNamara. The latter was enormously popular in his time and was famous for wearing spats on this tap shoes while he delivered his songs in a half singing, half speaking voice. (perhaps he could have played Prof. Higgins in *My Fair Lady*). The last recorded Dublin appearance of Pat McNamara was at a *Herald* Boot Fund Concert at the Theatre Royal in 1940. A few years later Dick Forbes offered him a role in a sketch in one of the Royal revues, but Pat never appeared for rehearsals.

The Coliseum bill for Easter Week, 1916 included: 'The Trombettas' – continental comedians; 'Tom Start' – impressionist; 'Monsieur Foo-Gers' – an Anglo-French entertainer; and Fred Barnes who was famous for his song "Black Sheep of the Family". The show, of course, never went on. Neither did John McNally & Co appear in their sketch, *The Borstal Boy* at the Tivoli; the D'Oyly Carte Co. at the Gaiety, (P.J. Bourke's No. 1 Company is reputed to have replaced them); nor Kitty Francis, the Irish-American comedienne at the Royal. The Abbey's new play *The Spancel Of Death* by T.H. Nally disappeared forever without trace.

The only photograph known to exist of the Coliseum was taken after its destruction. It is a sad thing to look upon but it wasn't to be the last theatre built in Dublin.

(Mr Joseph Holloway is quoted from his manuscript diaries on the Dublin Theatre. 200 volumes are held in the National Library of Ireland to whom the author expresses grateful thanks).

The Capitol Theatre

Exterior of the Capitol Theatre (1920–1972). The original name the La Scala Theatre was carved into the facade and visible behind the neon sign

THE CAPITOL THEATRE

Formerly LA SCALA THEATRE & OPERA HOUSE
– August 10, 1920
Renamed THE CAPITOL in 1927
Demolished in March, 1972

The pit, gallery and stage-door entrances to the Coliseum were situated at the other side of the GPO in Prince's Street, and the stage was also at this end of the building. Prince's Street runs parallel with Henry Street with the GPO in between. The main feature of Prince's St. at that time was the side of the Metropole Hotel; the main entrance was from Sackville Street, which with its balconied windows looked vaguely like a building that might be seen in New Orleans. The Metropole Hotel was another casualty of the Rising, and was eventually rebuilt as the Metropole Ballroom, Cinema and Bars, and the complex also included two restaurants and a high class grill room.

In 1972 both the Metropole and the Capitol were acquired for redevelopment as a British Home Stores outlet (which itself did not find favour with the citizenry), but during negotiations the developers had a hard battle with a lady who owned the Princes Bar which was situated between the Metropole and Capitol properties. The Princes Bar was a Dublin landmark and genuinely Joycean in character. It had marble and glass, mahogany and pewter; its long bar was divided into private little snugs at the front of the house and at the back of a swing door decorated with a stained glass representation of Bacchus there was a large room much favoured by regular clients because they couldn't be seen from the street, and since many of these clients were employees of both the Capitol and the Metropole they were wise to conceal themselves from the prying eyes of alert managers from both establishments. The proprietress held out against the developers for a fantastic sum of money, which she eventually wrung from them to the great delight of the enemies of cement and glass. During the reconstruction of the Metropole, Dublin's first and only theatre specifically designed as an opera house by the architect, T.F. McNamara at a cost of £120,000 with seating to accommodate 1900 people, was opened in Prince's Street on August 10, 1920 as La Scala Theatre and Opera House. The owners of the theatre, F.W. Chambers and George P. Fleming, provided the additional facilities of a restaurant (which was supposed to have been panelled with the timber from the lounge of some famous liner) a cafe, a bar and a ballroom. Close down by the stage door Billy Willis soon established a little cafe/snack bar from which he graduated years later to Dublin's first late-night restaurant The Green Rooster on O'Connell St.

In the week that La Scala opened, the GPO was still in ruins and the country was living through the chaos of the War of Independence, and people queuing for the second house at the Empire Theatre were fired on by the military who broke out of the Castle and ran amok as the variety-patrons took to their heels. Theatregoing was a hazardous past-time in those days and the newspapers reported inquests on civilians, shootings and reprisals. Although La Scala was designed as an opera house, between the drawing board and the opening night there were second thoughts, or perhaps a dearth of opera companies willing to risk life and limb in the Dublin of the times, so the theatre opened as a cinema with a brief stage show under the management of T.A. Senior who was assisted in his managerial role by the mother of the late Joe Kearns, manager and director of the Gaiety Theatre. It was not until the early 1940s that in this theatre, built as an opera house, the Dublin Operatic Society presented a few seasons of Grand Opera organised by George Sleator.

The opening film, *Parentage* was described as "a six-part selected masterpiece"; the cast is unknown and it was not very well received. The evening was rescued by the short but enjoyable stage show which included John Clarke, a tenor who sang "Eileen Mavourneen" and "Dear old pal o' mine". The 23 piece orchestra under the direction of W.T. Mortimer with Robert (Bobbie) Bolton (later conductor at the second theatre Royal and the Olympia) as leader was a big success. The proprietors appear also to have had their own problems as is evidenced by the following newspaper announcement:

> "The proprietors respectfully apologise to their friends and patrons to whom they had promised invitations, but owing to an unfortunate trade dispute, all arrangements (notwithstanding that tickets were printed) for the opening night had to be cancelled".

The Scala had greater success with the Chaplin film *The Kid* but it was Rudolph Valentino, heart throb of the twenties, in *The Four Horsemen of the Apocalypse*, directed by the Irishman, Rex Ingram, which caused Dubliners to pack the new theatre. The realistic sound effects of the battlefields of World War One were the talk of the town, and a young man who had joined the La Scala staff to help out with the sound effects was Barney Markey, who would much later become manager of the theatre and hold that post for 33 years.

Other notable La Scala films of the early twenties were:

The Prisoner of Zenda; *Scaramouche* with Ramon Novarro (who would be a later visitor to the Theatre Royal); the Gish Sisters in *Orphans of the Storm*; Douglas Fairbanks in *Robin Hood*. Huge crowds attended *Ireland A Nation* which was "a truly remarkable film – a picture of unusual, and incidentally, topical interest" according to the *Dublin Evening Mail*, which was ironic since it was the Unionist publishers of that paper who had been responsible for the banning of the film in 1917.

La Scala specialised in spectacular stage prologues (for want of a better description) to their most important films, and Frank Fay, the famous Abbey co-founder and actor, was engaged for the majority of them.

On March 17, 1923 world interest was focused on the theatre when Mike McTeague beat Battling Siki (who had roamed the streets of Dublin with a leopard on a leash) for the world light heavyweight championship. The ring was set up on the stage and amongst the many distinguished ringsiders was the debonair Georges Carpentier who had lost the title to Siki the previous year in Paris. In the streets outside the Civil War was now running its tragic course, and the Free State military patrolled outside the theatre, but during the fight a landmine exploded in Moore St. with the apparent objective of cutting the power line to La Scala. For many years the policy was to show films only, but in the twenties, Joseph P. Sandes organised several Sunday afternoon celebrity concerts in aid of the Mater Misericordiae Hospital. One of his stars was Lauritz Melchior, the Wagnerian singer, and later Harold Holt ran celebrity concerts featuring John Count McCormack, Paul Robeson, Conchit Supervia, Beniamino Gigli, Heifeti and Horowitz.

There is a story that Gigli returned to the theatre following his afternoon concert, and nearly fell out of his box laughing at W.C. Fields in *You're Telling Me*.

At what the Earl of Longford and Thomas P. O'Neill describe as "a large meeting" in April, 1926 in the La Scala Theatre in Dublin, beside the General Post Office – which ten years before had been the scene of the reading of the Proclamation of the Republic by P.H. Pearse – de Valera publicly launched his new party. (Fianna Fáil).

In the same year the man with the homespun humour, star of the *Ziegfeld Follies* and the movies, Will Rogers, gave his services free in a concert in aid of the Drumcollogher disaster fund; forty eight people had died in a cinema fire in the Co. Limerick village on September 5, while they were watching *The Ten Commandments*. Rogers displayed his agility at rope spinning, all the time talking "sense" in a nasal Texan drawl:

> "Women is just like elephants; I like to look at 'em, but I'd sure hate to own one"
> "I'm not a real movie star – I still got the same wife I started with nearly twenty-eight years ago"
> "Shakespeare is the only author that can play to losing business for hundreds of years and still be known as an author"
> "There is only one thing that can kill the movies, and that is education"

He was deservedly known as "America's Ambassador of Mirth", but he had also been known to engage in serious private conversations with the President of the United States.

In the following year, 1927, the Hollywood film company, Paramount, which favoured a policy of having its own film release outlets, took over the lease of the theatre, and made some significant changes. The name La Scala Theatre and Opera House, which was embossed in white marble high on the facade, was covered though not completely concealed from the madly curious, by an elaborate neon sign reading "Capitol", with elaborate 'sunbursts' of neon tubing to add glamour to the theatre's new name. Alec C. Fryer from the Rialto Cinema, London was appointed musical director, and a troupe of the John Tiller Girls (who were resident in theatres all over Europe) were introduced to Dublin. The son of a Dublin civil servant and ex pupil of Blackrock College, the legendary Tony Reddin, was appointed manager and stage producer. The policy of the parent Paramount company in America was to devise what were called 'unit stage shows' for each important film that was released, and this show travelled with the film wherever it was screened, thus guaranteeing artists at least forty weeks work each year. But there was only one outlet in Ireland so Tony Reddin had the task of producing a new stage show practically every week. His shows were so successful that the theatre earned the slogan "The Mecca Of Entertainment In Dublin". A weekly visit there became the vogue, and its famous intimate boxes at the back of the Dress Circle were extremely popular.

In the first year of Reddin's management Hilton Edwards, who was planning the opening of the Gate Theatre with his partner Micheál MacLíammóir, appeared at the Capitol as a singer. He is reputed to have delivered "The Road To Mandalay" in a rich baritone and to have appeared in a gypsy encampment scena wearing large curtain ring props as earrings. Clearly this was a quick method of making a few badly needed pounds for Hilton, and Phil Murtagh who was then playing in the pit at the Capitol, before he became the Irish premier orchestra leader at the Metropole Ballroom, had a few drinks with Hilton in the Princes bar which he remembered mainly because to his astonishment: "Hilton had barely a boot on his foot!"

In 1929 the Capitol screened the first talking picture, *The Jazz Singer* with Al Jolson.

In April of the following year, Sophie Tucker, "the last of the red hot Mommas" played the theatre to a packed audience for a week. Jack Hylton and Geraldo presented their band shows, and in 1932 the superb Abbey actress Sara Allgood gave a recital there. A firm local favourite was young Peg Tisdell who was billed as "the pocket Sophie Tucker" and went on to win international fame as Peggy Dell, a name that looked better than her own on the bills.

PEGGY DELL was a Dubliner whose father was a professional piccolo and flute player in the orchestra at the Empire Palace, and at the age of three she started to learn the piano from him. Her first stage appearance was at the Empire as a child of nine doing a double act with another small girl, who would become the future opera star, May Devitt. They called themselves the Harmony Juveniles. Peggy's first regular job was playing sheet music for prospective customers in Woolworths' of Grafton St, and later, in the same street, she played background music for diners in Fullers' posh restaurant. Soon she formed her own little five piece band, and it wasn't unusual to read a newspaper announcement like:

CLARIBELLE DANCE, EASTER MONDAY (1930)
Dancing 8p.m. – 2a.m.
LEGGET-BYRNES, 27 Adelaide Rd.
PEG. TISDELL and HER BAND
Spot Prizes – Tickets 3/-

Charlie Harvey, who had been orchestra leader under Alec Fryer (who had now transferred to the Queen's), took over as conductor of the orchestra, which was now known as The Capitolians. A sample bill for "Dublins Mecca" the Capitol in April, 1930 read as follows: The film was *The Mysterious Dr. Fu Manchu*, Paramount's all-talking Dramatic Masterpiece. The stage presentation featured: Charlie Harvey and the Capitolians introducing Capitol Tiller Girls in Capitol Extravaganza. Also Irish Traditional Dancing by Miss Medlar's Pupils.

After Peggy's outstanding success at the Capitol, Tony Reddin recommended her to the large Paramount circuit of theatres in Britain. In December, 1932, Roy Fox the London band leader engaged her as vocalist with his band at the Cafe Anglais, and it was at this time that she changed her name to Peggy Dell. Roy Fox and Peggy moved to the famous Kit-Kat Club, the mecca for high-society in London, where a promising young man called Joe Loss led the relief band at the venue. There were broadcasts and gramophone records to be made, but when Jack Hylton invited her to tour America in 1935 she accepted, and enjoyed travelling America for nine months. She returned to England in 1936 and stayed with Hylton until the outbreak of war in 1939 when Hylton advised her to return to Ireland. Peggy regarded Jack Hylton as a marvellous man and a great professional and showman. She said: "He presented fabulous band shows. I mean if we were doing a number like say "Horsey-Horsey" he'd have two real horses at the back of the stage running on rollers".

Back in Dublin she was a regular performer in all the Dublin theatres, where she was greatly respected by her fellow artists. Noel Purcell, one of her most sincere admirers said that she had "amazing qualities as a singer and performer". She was resident pianist in the Metropole Georgian Room for eleven years, and she had her own television programme "Peg O' My Heart". She died following a stroke on April 30, 1979, aged 73. The many tributes that were paid to her were summed up by Cecil Nash, a man who could instantly detect the phoney, who said:

> "I have been privileged to work with this lively lady. I have had the thrill of standing beside her, and it was the power behind the piano that brought out any talent I had in me. Working with Peggy Dell was working with an international artist, you instantly knew you were in the presence of a brilliant star. Her music was magic, her advice to you was worth a fortune because this wonderful woman claimed the friendship of Benny Goodman, 'Fats' Domino, "Satchmo" and many more".

Whereas Peggy's talent had been exploited to the full, the manager/producer Tony Reddin never allowed his gift for comedy to develop. He made occasional appearances on the Capitol stage singing comic songs, some of which he recorded, including: "Mick McGilligan's Daughter, Mary Ann"; "The Fighting Kalilbar"; "The Bugaboo"; "Dangerous Dan McHugh". More importantly, Tony Reddin is credited with introducing "Biddy Mulligan the Pride of the Coombe" for the first time to Dublin audiences of his generation. Billy Carter, whose Selma Follies Dance Band was appearing on the Capitol stage related that he overheard Tony vamping this song, which he had never heard before, at the side of the stage one morning, and when he had heard Reddin sing the verse and chorus he tried to convince him that he should sing the number dressed 'in character' in the following week's show but Tony was reluctant, never having appeared as a Dame before. A suitable 'shawlie' outfit was obtained from Bourkes' of North Frederick St. but on the Monday night when the orchestra played his introductory music, Tony got cold feet and didn't go on. On the following night he summoned up the courage and sang the song for the first time since it had been sung in a Gaiety pantomime in 1889 as "The Widow Twankey, the Pride of the Coombe". As Tony sang the song he began to sense that the audience was enjoying his performance as the goodhearted, good humoured and brave little Dublin street-seller, so he raised his long black skirt and performed a little dance as he sang:

BIDDY MULLIGAN THE PRIDE OF THE COOMBE
(Tony Reddin Version)

> "I'm a dacent aul' widdah, I come from a spot, and in Dublin it's known as the Coombe,
> I've got comfort and ease which no one can excel, sure me palace consists of one room.
> And at Patrick Street corner for forty five years I've stood on me tod, it's no lie,
> Aye, and no one in Dublin would dare for to say that black was the white of me eye.
> You may ramble from Clare to the County Kildare, or from Drogheda down to Macroom,
> Aye, and where would you see such a widdah like me, Biddy Mulligan the Pride of the Coombe".

Tony stopped the show that night. It is impossible now to say if these were Tony's own lyrics or from whence he obtained them, but they are certainly different in many respects not only from the 1889 original but also from the version attributed to a Seamus Kavanagh which was subsequently published by Waltons.

In the audience that night was another famous Blackrock College boy, Jimmy O'Dea, who upon witnessing Reddin's performance decided that he could do better, and had a serious discussion with his script-writer, Harry O'Donovan, with the result that they created the character of Biddy Mulligan, first for gramophone records and finally for the stage, but her exploits were often at variance with the words of the song which O'Dea used mainly as his theme music. Phil Murtagh, who played the sax in the Capitol orchestra, regarded Tony Reddin as an outstanding, innovative producer who had really been ahead of his time. Phil claimed that Tony could take a very ordinary act, groom it, change its routine, advise it until finally it could almost take its place at the top of the bill. Phil also confided that the usual crop of Dublin "knockers" spread the rumour that Reddin was a member of both the Knights of Columbanus and a Masonic Lodge. Who was to say that "black was the white of me eye!"

When Tony wanted a particular stage effect he would go to the most extraordinary lengths to achieve it. In one show he wanted a gas street lamp effect and was dissatisfied with everything rigged up by his stage staff. Eventually, Tony had them run a thick rubber tube from a gas point in one of the dressing rooms and attach it to a gas mantle on a fake lamp post which was duly lit successfully, all in the name of realism. Tony left Ireland in 1934 to become Director of Theatres and Publicity for Paramount in Britain, but on occasional visits home, in the exotic company of at least two London show-girls, he would visit the Metropole Ballroom to hear Phil Murtagh's Orchestra and Phil, who never under any circumstances sang with the band, made one exception for his old boss sitting in the mezzanine balcony and sang an old favourite of theirs from the Capitol days:

> "Beautiful were her lips, her eyes, her nose;
> Each tooth a perfect pearl.
> Soon we were walking down the aisle,
> For I married that girl".

The lease of the Capitol again changed hands to the Capitol Theatre Company Ltd. whose directors included Walter McNally, the baritone who had sung in *Madame Butterfly* with Margaret Burke Sheridan in the San Carlo Opera House, Naples, and Barney Markey was appointed resident manager. The policy of the new company was to present only films which, in retrospect, seems to been shortsighted because in the same year (1934), the second Theatre Royal was demolished, so that the Capitol, with a firm reputation for good class stage shows, at least as good as the Royal had been presenting, would have had the advantage. The theatre's fortunes during its exclusively cinematic spell are unknown, but possibly in a back-water.

In 1941 there was yet another change when the lease went into the hands of G.P. Fleming, one of the original owners, and members of the Farrell family, of whom Peter was the best known. The production of only one legitimate three act play can be traced at the Capitol, and this was in 1942 when the Anew McMaster Company appeared in *The Scarlet Pimpernel* with Mac, naturally, in the name part supported by Ronald Ibbs. The following year had Michael Bowles conducting the newly formed Radio Éireann Symphony Orchestra on Sunday afternoons at the Capitol, when the orchestra transferred from the acoustically unsuitable Mansion House. Delighted concert goers were heard to comment on the excellence of the sound in the Capitol and compare it to the atmosphere of a Continental opera house.

In 1943 the La Scala Ballroom was closed down to make room for more much needed dressing rooms in the theatre, and Dubliners were fascinated to read large display advertisements in the papers announcing the forthcoming production at the Capitol of a show of previously undreamt of spectacle called *Hello, Wonderful*, which seems to have been the inspiration of some independent production company. It got a bad press. No one has ever admitted to having seen it, and there appears to be little on record about it except for the valuable recollections of Roy Croft, who was in the show:

> "I was invited to audition [Roy had been in a group called "The White Blackbirds"], for this extravaganza, *Hello Wonderful* which was to be a very big affair, beautifully mounted and costumed. So we went into production and it looked good on paper. The musical director was Oliver O'Brien, but the show was a monumental flop. I remember leaving the stage door that night and the bouquets of flowers that had been in readiness for presentation to leading ladies in the cast were pushed into dustbins because, of course, they couldn't be presented".

Shortly afterwards Roy received a telegram asking him to be at the Capitol at 10a.m. on the following morning. Peter Farrell asked him what he did apart from his appearance in the recent flop, and Roy replied that he did impersonations. "Right" said Farrell, "get up there on the stage and impress me!" Roy was engaged to participate in what was virtually a revival of stage shows at the Capitol in the Cine-Variety format, and he was to remain there for the next four years. Frank Doherty was musical director of a full (and excellent) theatre orchestra which included many well-known Dublin musicians: Jimmy Banks the pianist and drummer Joe Bonnie, whose daughter Monica appeared later as a solo act at the theatre playing the xylophone, singing and dancing. Her act was not unlike that of another juvenile, Kay Maloney.

Tommy Rogers was stage manager like his brother Hughie, in a similar position at the Theatre Royal, and there was a full troupe of dancers – The Capitol Girls who offered no competition to the Royalettes although the dance directors, two brunettes from Dublin, were Dolly Sparkes and Nora Flanagan who, as youngsters, had been rivals in Irish dancing competitions, but who became firm friends when they joined the Queen's Moonbeams. They left the Queen's to form the Capitol Girls and in the course of time their routines became increasingly ambitious. One of their most memorable presentations was in a Christmas show called *Snowflakes* in which the closing dance routine "Dancing in the Winter Wonderland" was light and joyous.

The comedy team in the early days was Mike Nolan, Roy Croft and Freddie Doyle. Much of the comedy material was written by Paddy Crosbie (of Radio Éireann's "School Around The Corner" fame), and whose brother Martin Crosbie, the popular tenor, could never leave the Capitol stage without singing "The Miller's Daughter". Freddie Doyle, apart from sketch work, usually contributed a top hat and tails routine. Freddie was no stranger to the Capitol stage as he had appeared there in the 1920s. He was 14 in 1916 when Louis O'Brien picked him from a choir at St. Andrews' Church, Westland Row, to be one of the glee boys in a scene at the Tivoli music hall. Barney Armstrong of the Empire Palace looked in one night and was so impressed by Freddie's voice that he offered him an engagement at the Empire billed as a boy soprano. Later he appeared at the second Royal where his singing and dancing with Connie Ryan so impressed the lovely Dorothy Ward that she took him on tour of Great Britain. His most memorable performance at the Capitol was when, dressed as an old style Principal boy like Florrie

Mike Nolan, Popular resident comedian at the Capitol for many years

The wedding of Martin Crosbie and Thelma Ramsey. Thelma later became Musical Director of the Gaiety's pantos and summer shows in which, with unerringly sound instinct, she introduced the latest and best Broadway showtunes to Dublin audiences for the first time

Forde, complete with staff, he sang "I'm the Last Of the Principal Boys". His last appearance was as Dame in *Dick Whittington*, at the Pavilion, Dun Laoghaire. He died in July 1972 after more than fifty years in show business.

Mike Nolan was the outstanding comedy performer at the Capitol. He was a sketch comedian who frequently appeared as a Dame, but he also did a stand-up comedy routine. Mike was painfully thin and when he stood in front of a microphone he would say: "Look, two mikes for the price of one". Then he would stand aside and claim that he was making a short personal appearance before retreating back behind the microphone remarking as he went: "They didn't throw confetti at my wedding – they threw vitamin pills!"

Unfortunately, Mike Nolan never created his own character or persona by which he would be readily identified, but he was nevertheless a first rate comedian whose talents raised the standards of many variety shows and even straight plays in Dublin. One Dublin critic noted:

> "Mike Nolan created no easily remembered character like Jimmy O'Dea's Mrs. Mulligan, Jack Cruise's John Joe Mahockey, or Cecil Sheridan's Martha Mary Ann Magee, but in his most notable years he had the readiest of wit and an enviable flow of authentic Dublin wise-cracks. He was a great soul, great in his simplicity of manner, his total absence of pretentiousness".

The stage shows at the Capitol, despite an effort by Jack Cruise to inject some life, had grown increasingly lack-lustre. The shows lacked speed and were predictable. No one would seriously dispute the mastery of Leo Rowsome on the Uilleann Pipes, but 15 minutes of Mr Rowsome over a period of several weeks, playing seated on a kitchen chair was not the stuff of fast moving variety. Sean Mooney came over from the Royal and selected his programmes carefully; he was the first performer to sing "How are things In Gloccamorra" from *Finian's Rainbow* in Ireland (he had obtained the sheet music from his old pal, Albert Sharpe who was starring in the show on Broadway) but he was subjected to considerable hassle from the publishers, which he ignored. Cecil Nash joined the company from the Queen's and Jack Kirwan, who had been a barber or "tonsorial artist" as he described himself, favoured a very long hair style which gave rise to his catch-phrase:

"Me hair is killin' me!". He had another stock complaint – "I'M JADED".

But the die was cast and the last show was performed on October 29, 1953. The theatre was completely crowded out for the final performance by an audience which valued flesh-and-blood performers in preference to the flicker of shadows on a screen; there was regret too that so many people who had given pleasure in the past should now be facing a bleak future. Johnny Keyes, an old Capitol favourite came over especially from England to sing, "To-night's the Night" and "Eternally" was the choice of Phyllis Power; Sean Mooney sang "I'm off to Philadelphia In the Morning" (he wasn't actually, he joined the Jack Cruise Company instead!). In the final scene, many former Capitol Girls joined their old colleagues and danced with them in their final routine while Jack Kirwan cracked his last Capitol gags and Cecil Nash mused upon the fact that "It's A Funny Old World That We Live In...." At the closing moments the performers and audience sang "Auld Lang Syne" and the company on stage leant over the footlights to shake hands with Frank Doherty the conductor, and members of the band. Many gifts were handed up before the great maroon curtain fell on the last Capitol show at 9.15 exactly.

Principals of the pantomime "Babes In The Wood" (1950/51).
Patty Ryan (Principal Boy), Phyllis Power (Principal Girl), O'Keeffe Bros. and Annette
(acrobats), Jack Kirwan (Comic), Teddy Ahearn (Dame), Sean Mooney (Baron),
Johnny Keyes (vocals)

The Capitol pantomime 1949/50. Sean Mooney and Jack Kirwan backstage at
"Jack and the Beanstalk"

The theatre critic of *The Evening Herald*, John J. Finegan wrote:

"The last Capitol stage show? With a theatre so well equipped as that – I wonder".

But there was to be no reprieve; the Capitol concentrated on showing films until 1972 at which time it was decided that the site upon which it stood was more valuable than the theatre itself so the Capitol was demolished in March, 1972.

In the weeks that followed, the demolition squad had difficulty pulling down the Capitol. The site foreman said: "It is one of the toughest jobs we have had – it is all solid concrete, they don't build them like that nowadays".

"Graveyard of the Capitol". Only one of hundreds of similar scenes all over the U.K. and Ireland. Former resident performers Martin Crosbie and Sean Mooney lay a symbolic wreath in 1972

The Torch Theatre

THE TORCH THEATRE
Opened February 27, 1935; Closed 1941.

There have been many small, little known, uncommercial, uneconomical, badly managed or semi-professional theatres in Dublin down the years, among them the Grafton Theatre and The Harp (which was run by Pat Kinsella). The Mechanics in Abbey St. (opened in 1874 and closed in 1902) was a place of Dickensian squalor where the rats from the city morgue next door developed a taste for the artists' greasepaint.* Madame Rocks was situated over a piano shop opposite the Gresham Hotel; the Hardwick Hall** was a cold, miserable place where Edward Martyn presented European drama, and where Jimmy O'Dea and Noel Purcell made early appearances, and where Micheál Mac Líammóir painted the scenery for one production. To its credit it must be recorded that it was the forerunner to the the Gate Theatre. In relatively recent times we had Barry Cassin's and Nora Lever's 37 Theatre Company at at least two different venues, The Globe Theatre, Dun Laoghaire which produced many of our best contemporary actors, and the Pike Theatre, famous for its first productions of Brendan Behan and Beckett and the farcical interference by the 'authorities' in a production of *The Rose Tattoo*. In addition there were the Studio, the Lantern, the Eagle, the Pocket, the National Arts, the Garrick, the New Theatre and the Pilgrim Players.

There were others, of course, both in the distant past and in the planning stages at this very moment. As a reminder of their very unprofitable endeavours there follows a reasonably detailed account of the Torch Theatre in Capel Street in tribute to the dedicated people who contributed talent, dedication and time in abundance to all the other 'little theatres' and laboured under the decided disadvantage of an absence of atmosphere, gilt and red plush which they must have been aware is where real theatre begins before the curtain rises.

THE TORCH THEATRE

The Torch Theatre was situated at 114-116 Capel Street (at the Bolton St. end) in a large and dignified building which was the headquarters of the United Trades Council and Labour League. The theatre, with the auditorium at street level, was only slightly larger than the Gate and over the proscenium arch the city arms were displayed. It was opened on Februrary 27, 1935 by the founders Charles L. Keogh, actor and director, and his wife, Evelyn Lund, a well-known actress. Keogh was a brother of J. Augustus Keogh who was manager of the Abbey in 1916-17.

Charles L. Keogh had appeared with William Macready in a season of melodrama at the Queen's in 1923 and in the same year he had appeared in the same theatre with Jimmy O'Dea and May Craig in a sentimental melodrama. But when he joined the O'Dea/O'Donovan revue company in 1930 he changed his name to Charles O'Reilly. Perhaps he thought it below his dignity to appear under his own name in the London Coliseum, then the greatest music hall in the world. His wife, Evelyn Lund, had appeared at the Queen's in *Arrah-na-Pogue* in 1925, and she had co-starred with Pearl O'Donnell, a very versatile Scottish lady (who was the wife of Val Vousden) in *The Two Little Vaga-bonds*, in which they appeared as two boys, which was customary casting at the time. Miss Lund is reputed to have acted later at the Gate.

The policy of the theatre was to present a repertoire containing a high quota of melodrama, and the opening production at the Torch was *The Colleen Bawn*. Admission prices ranged from 6d. – 2/- (2½ – 10p). The Boucicault melodrama was followed by Ira Allen's *The Boys Of Wexford* and *East Lynne* (of which there are many versions) then by some abberation *The Anatomist* by James Bridie, and *Witness for the Prosecution* by A.E.W. Mason. There was a hasty return to melodrama with *The Shaughraun*, *Wolfe Tone* and J.W. Whitbread's *The Insurgent Chief* which was about bold Michael Dwyer.

The theatre closed during the summer months of 1935 and reopened on September 2, with *A Royal Divorce*, followed by *The Speckled Band*, (which may have been a stage version of the Arthur Conan Doyle story), *A Tale Of Two Cities*, *The Face At The Window*, *Sweet Nell Of Old Drury*, P.J. Bourke's *Kathleen Mavourneen* described as a Domestic Irish Drama with Music, and Ira Allen's *Father Murphy* in which F.J. McCormick had appeared under his own name, Peter Judge, at the Queen's in June, 1912.

Some of the actors in that year included: Harry Brogan (using the name, H.M. Emmett); Alex Dignam; James Henry (could this have been J.J. Henry of the Father Matthew Hall?); Denis Franks etc. Interval music was played by Madame Van Aalst who also provided music in restaurants all over the city.

The year ended with a three night engagement in December by An Comhar Dramaíochta and finally, a pantomime called *Irelands Own*. Henry Irving's pot boiler *The Bells* came in 1936, then a revival of *East Lynne* (It is an old showman's secret – when things are going badly, revive *East Lynne*!). Next came *In Memory Of The Dead*, surprisingly by Count Casimir Markievicz, and a dramatisation of the novel *Under Two Flags*. The first anniversary of the opening in February was marked by a revival of *The Colleen Bawn* followed by *Uncle Tom's Cabin*, *True Irish Hearts* – an Irish-Canadian comedy, and *Patrick Sarsfield* by Miss L. MacManus, the novelist – P.J. Bourke's play on the subject in 1917 must have been considered by Miss MacManus as being inadequate!

Cyril Cusack directed a play in Irish for An Comhar Dramaíochta called *An Gaducthe*, (The Robbers), and also designed the setting. *The Sign Of The Cross*, *Trilby*, *Arrah-na-Pogue*, and Galsworthy's *Silver Box* completed the early season of 1936. Performances were given on Sundays and the theatre was closed on Mondays.

The Torch reopened in September with two new directors, Lilian Davidson (stage name Jennifer Maude) and Hugh H. Hyland, a former manager of the Gaiety. There was also a new policy which laid less emphasis on melodrama, with the type of play being presented at the Gate receiving favourable consideration.

The opening play was *Queen of Scots* followed by Alfred Sanger's *The Brontes*, and *Charley's Aunt* was brought from Brazil to relieve the literary gloom for more light-minded patrons. *David Garrick* who had walked the streets of Dublin in his time was duly remembered, and Lennox Robinson's *Harvest* and *Crabbed Youth And Age* reflected this author's London rather than his Abbey success. *Peg o'my Heart*, and *A Royal Divorce* were seen before J.B. Fagan's comedy about Samuel Pepys *And So To Bed*.

The thriller, *The Two Mrs. Carrolls* by Martin Vale, had its Dublin premiere at the Torch. *Nell Gwynn* followed it and then a comedy *Facing The Music* and Norman Gins-bury's *Viceroy Sarah* and before pantomime time, *Rose Without A Thorn* by Clifford Bax. The pantomime was based on Thackery's *Rose And The Ring*. Eve Panton (Eve Watkinson, later a leading lady at the Gate) appeared in some productions.

The Torch had the distinction of giving both the Irish and English premiere of Oscar Wilde's tragedy in blank verse, *The Duchess of Padua*. The *Evening Herald* drama critic, David Sears asked why the play had been ignored for so long by theatre managements. The answer may have lain in the Torch experience of the play; attendances were not up to expectations in the Spring of 1937, and during the second week of the Wilde play two seats were being offered for the price of one.

The Tudor Wench followed and the Irish premiere of *Parnell*, by the American writer, Elsie T. Schauffler. Noel Dalton was Parnell and Evelyn Lund was Kitty O'Shea which is a matter of only passing interest when it is discovered that Jack Plant, of pious and immortal memory, was also in the cast. This proved to be the last production by the Keogh-Davidson company, which, after the final performance on March 15, 1937 went on tour and never returned to the Torch.

It is probable that there were no further shows until February 12, 1938, when the New Ireland Musical and Dramatic Society staged revues, variety shows and were followed by other groups. On March 21 of that year Lorcan Bourke presented a revue, *Good Times Coming* devised by himself and with Jimmy Harvey, Jimmie O'Brien and the Moonbeam Ladies (borrowed from the Queen's?) in the cast. Other revues followed and at Easter 1938, Lorcan presented a pageant *The March Of Freedom*, in co-operation with the Collins Barracks Dramatic Society. It was written by his brother, Jimmy, (Seamus de Burca) with music by their uncle, Peadar O'Cearnaigh (Peadar Kearney). Lorcan revived this show in the Olympia Theatre in April 1941.

On this second occasion he had the assistance of the 36th Battallion. In May Lorcan and Billy Bourke directed *Arrah-na-Pogue*, and then came Jack Randal's road show, with Mlle. Yvonne, Continental fan dancer. In the same month, May, Dot Productions were a little out of season with their pantomime *Aladdin*. That seemed to be the end of all activity until the theatre reopened on February 18, 1940 with a revue *Sensations of 1940* directed by Dan Rockford. Apart from a few film shows this appears to have been the last show at the Torch.

There is now a preservation order on the facade of what must have been the most erratically managed theatre Dublin has ever known.

(The author is indebted to the theatre correspondent, J.J. Finegan for much of the information contained in the Torch Theatre section).

---

* "The Mechanics Theatre" was in fact properly known as the Hibernian Theatre of Varieties, but became known as 'The Mechanics' because it was built on the site of the Mechanics Institute which in turn had been built on the demolished site of the old Theatre Royal Opera House. Just around the corner in Marlborough St., was the city morgue. The aim of the Mechanics Institutes, of which there were 600 in existence in Great Britain and the United States was to provide educational and cultural facilities for craftsmen, skilled workers and mechanics, many of whom were then illiterate. The Mechanics Institute in Abbey Street was probably closed around 1860 and then housed what was once known as the National Theatre and finally the Hibernian Theatre of Varieties until in 1902 it was closed because it could not meet the requirements of the local authorities in the matter of safety regarding fire regulations.

** Denis Keogh, Manager and Producer of the Rocklin Players, an amateur group, whose members included Arthur (Archie) O'Sullivan and P.J. O'Donnell and Mick Eustace, hired the Hardwick Hall for his activities in the 1940s and always claimed that mortally wounded volunteers and citizen army men were laid out in rows in the Hardwick hall because many churches would not accept their bodies. The Hardwick hall location makes sense as the owners of the property, which had a very extensive library upstairs in the forties, were the family of Joseph Plunkett who was himself executed in Kilmainham Jail.

Dan Lowrey's Music Hall
(The Olympia Theatre)

Programme cover illustrating the architectural progress of the original "Star of Erin"

DAN LOWREY'S MUSIC HALL
(The present-day Olympia Theatre)
Opened in December, 1879 as "THE STAR OF ERIN"
Renamed: DAN LOWREY'S MUSIC HALL in August, 1881
DAN LOWREY'S PALACE OF VARIETIES in 1889
Capacity doubled to 1, 600 in 1892
CLOSED IN FEBRUARY, 1897 and completely redesigned
OPENED AS THE EMPIRE PALACE IN NOVEMBER, 1897
Renamed THE OLYMPIA THEATRE in JANUARY, 1923

THE PRESENT THEATRE DATES FROM NOVEMBER, 1897

When a patron took his seat in the Orchestra Stalls at the Olympia Theatre and the iron safety curtain covered with advertisements for all sorts of products and services was raised he would be struck by a peculiar aroma of which there was the merest suspicion in other theatres, but was particularly pungent in the Olympia. The overpowering though not unpleasant smell was that of size which is a gelatinous solution used in stiffening stage canvas before the scenery is painted on. The heady aroma is an intoxicant to the dedicated theatregoer, and is an embellishment to the vibrancy of the music as the orchestra plays the overture, just as a rich brown gravy is to a joint of meat out of the oven.

The elegance of the Circles, Boxes and decorative plaster-work, prompted Noel Coward to describe the Olympia as "this lovely baroque theatre". Leo McCabe, who purchased the theatre after the second world war, described his playhouse sorrowfully as "a theatre within a bar". And there are, in fact, two very spacious bars at the back of the parterre (apart from those in the Circles and gallery). Variety patrons were notorious for spending a noisy evening in the bars, emerging to take their seats only when the top of the bill made an appearance. This was a legacy from the days of Dan Lowrey who built the first theatre on the Olympia site. In the 1990s, the practice has had a revival as rock music acts have come to dominate the theatre's booking policy.

Dan Lowrey was born in Roscrea in 1823. He was taken by his parents to Leeds and by the time he was 30 he owned a tavern in Liverpool where in addition to serving the usual food and drinks he also entertained his patrons with songs and stories; this would have been a fore-runner to what became known as the Free and Easies. Music hall was to be in the near future. A near replica of Dan's establishment still exists today in Nottingham. This is the Old Malt Cross Music Hall (1877 – 1914), at 16, St. James St, recently restored (1997) as an entertainment venue after many years as the Potter's House Tea Rooms. The small stage is preserved and its horse shoe shaped balcony supported on cast iron columns decorated with replicas of leaves and bunches of grapes is a unique example of this type of early entertainment venue.

Lowrey returned to Ireland and opened the Alhambra in Belfast which was a great success. He came to Dublin in 1878 and examined the site of an old military barracks in

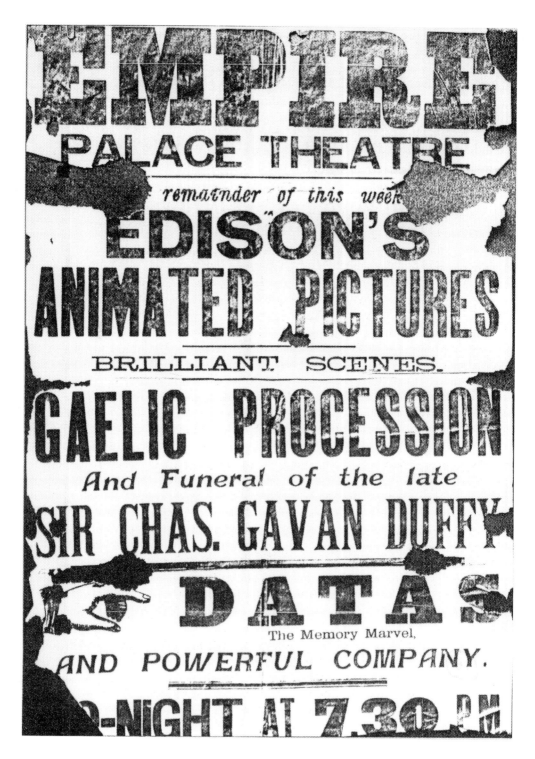

Dan Lowrey's featured films when they were first invented in 1896 but they were technically flawed and unpopular. As this old poster dated 1904 illustrates, films would eventually claim a place on every music hall bill

Crampton Court (off Dame Street) which had also been the site of a tavern known as Widow Quinlan's Free and Easy where Peg Woffington sang as a child early in the 18th century, and in 1855 it opened as the Monster Saloon Music Hall. Dan acquired this site and on Monday December 22, 1879, Dan Lowrey's "Star of Erin" opened its doors to the public. It was a genuine music hall in so far as there was a definite admission charge to defray the costs of the entertainment. Previously, admission to similar establishments, such as the hall in Nottingham mentioned above, was free, and management relied for their income on the sale of food and drinks. The Star of Erin was a long narrow building with a long balcony on each side, unimpeded by boxes extending down to the stage. Tables and chairs were provided on the ground floor. The Star of Erin was not a legitimate theatre, but what could be termed as a "people's theatre" as it hadn't the necessary licence or patent to perform plays, or even sketches involving two people, but it could supply music. The Star was patronised by men only, as ladies protected their reputations by avoiding music halls, which it must be admitted could be rough establishments. But Dan Lowrey had a hand-picked staff of pretty barmaids who were very civil, courteous, and good-humoured and were consequently very popular with the male patrons who were not reluctant to hand their cash over to the delightful dispensers of beer and cheap cigars.

In 1881 Dan entrusted the running of the Star of Erin to his son, Dan Junior, who changed the name of the establishment to Dan Lowrey's Music Hall in August of that year. Later, in 1889 the name was changed once more to Dan Lowrey's Palace of Varieties. A year later old Dan was dead. He died on July 3, at his residence, Wentworth Cottage, Terenure, aged sixty six, and was buried in Glasnevin Cemetery. He had become increasingly less active in the management of his theatre in his declining years, and his passing was scarcely noticed or reported in the Press of the time.

His son doubled the capacity of the theatre to 1,600 in 1892, but he closed the doors again in February 1897 and reopened, completely redesigned, in the following November as the Empire Palace, and as part of the influential Moss circuit, which would guarantee regular appearances by top class artists. The Empire Palace had a new frontage facing on to Dame Street where the main entrance and cash boxes were situated. The name Empire Palace may still be seen over the canopy above the portico of the present Olympia Theatre. Old Dan Lowrey had presented some of the greatest names in the fledgling music halls of his time. Bessie Bellwood, a Cockney rabbit skinner of irish descent brought all the vulgarity of the slums to her art as a low comedienne. Marie Lloyd achieved the same effect as Bessie, but in a quieter manner of sly innuendo, deliberate and pointed pauses accompanied by suggestive glances and an almost imperceptible turn of the head. G.H. Chirgwin – the White Eyed Kaffir, so called because one night when he was making up in black face without the aid of a mirror, he inadvertently left the area around his right eye white which had a stunning effect upon his audience. Bernard Shaw said of him – "Chirgwin earned his salary, not for his make-up as the White Eyed Kaffir or his substitution of a petrol tin with one string for a Stradivarius, but for his infallible musical ear, which kept him always exactly in tune". George Leybourne, in his song "Champagne Charlie", voiced sentiments agreeable to the rebels in his audience against Victorian respectability, and made them wish that they had his lifestyle. Leybourne's outlook on life was that "it was the duty of man to earn all he can in order to spend all he can!". It is not surprising that the wine companies kept him supplied with free cases of champagne. Vesta Tilley, who dressed in her usual male evening dress attire as "Algy, the Piccadilly Johnnie" was to shock Queen Mary at the first (of only two) genuine Royal Command Performance at the Palace Theatre in 1912.

Interior of the present Olympia. No trace remains of the original "Star of Erin"

*England's greatest comedian
Dan Leno with Herbert Campbell*

*Another star of the 'real' music halls,
Vesta Tilley*

The Queen obviously didn't like Miss Tilley in her male attire and consulted her programme studiously throughout her performance. Johnny Patterson, the rambler from Clare who appeared in 1886, and Pat Kinsella, were representative of Irish performers amongst the endless stream of comic acrobats, jugglers, sister acts, singers, and troupes of dancing girls who were guaranteed to empty the bars. The diminutive Dan Leno – "the funniest man in the world", was of Irish descent and started as a champion clog dancer. There is a persistent story that as a schoolboy, Leno appeared in Belfast and that a bearded distinguished looking man made his way backstage and laid his band on the boy's shoulder saying: "My boy you are going to be a great artist", and that the bearded man was Charles Dickens. How Dickens could make such a prophesy on the strength of a clog dance has never been questioned. The true story of Leno's unremarkable meeting with Dickens was related by Bransby Williams, the contemporary of both men, as follows:

> "In his boyhood Dan Leno appeared as a monkey in a sketch with his father and mother. One night in Belfast, his parents took him to see Charles Dickens come out of the hall after one of his famous readings. As Dickens passed through the crowd, little Dan pressed forward, and Dickens patted his head and said. 'Good night, my little man, and God bless you'. Dan never forgot the incident and was proud to relate it, but he never laid claim to Dickens' alleged prediction that he was going to be "a great artist"."

Dan had spent some time in Dublin as a boy and he apparently retained something of a Dublin accent. Dan Lowrey's audience was slightly confused when Leno appeared at the Star of Erin for the huge fee of £100. Was he a Cockney?...No; Was he Irish?...Dublin?...No. Listening to him talk about Mrs. Kelly on an old 78rpm gramophone record and one might think that the material was written for Jimmy O'Dea:

> "But you know Jim's a totally different man – Jim does love me you know, and he's lodging now with Mrs. Kelly. You know Mrs. Kelly?...*You* know Mrs. Kelly....don't you know Mrs. Kelly? Her husband's that stout little man, always at the corner of the street in a greasy waistcoat.....good life, don't look so stupid, don't....you must know Mrs Kelly! *Don't* you know Mrs. Kelly??...Well of course, if you don't, you don't – but I thought you *did* because I thought everybody knew Mrs. Kelly. Oh, and what a woman – perhaps it's as well you *don't* know her...oh, she's a mean woman. Greedy. I know for a fact – her little boy, who's got the sore eyes, he came over and told me – she had half a dozen oysters, and she ate them in front of a looking glass, to make them look a dozen. Now that'll give you an idea what *she* is".

In time Dan Junior's finances were in a mess although he had designed the new Empire Palace, and chairman of the new board was Adam Findlater. The new theatre opened with Charles Coburn as top of the bill. He had two hit songs which kept him on the halls for years and well into his nineties until he died in 1945. "Two Lovely Black Eyes" was really a political song but he bought his greatest hit in 1891 from its composer, Fred Gilbert, for £10 outright with no further royalties. This was "The Man Who Broke The Bank At Monte Carlo".

> "As I walk along the Bois de Boulonge with an independent air,
> You can hear the girls declare, 'he must be a millionaire'

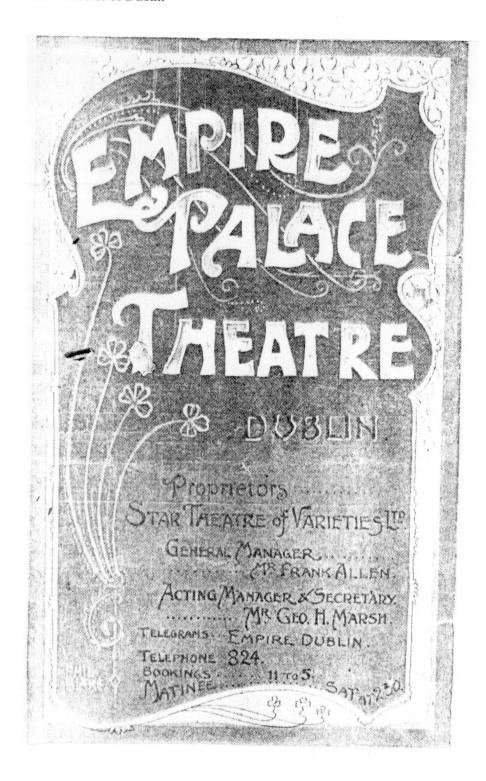

Programme cover from the Empire Palace Theatre

You can hear them cry and wish to die, and you see them wink the other
eye,
At the man who broke the bank at Monte Carlo".

This song was based on fact. Fred Gilbert saw a newspaper seller displaying a placard
which bore the legend MAN BREAKS BANK AT MONTE CARLO. He turned on his
heel and went home to compose his song. Coburn refused to buy it at first, but later
relented and in the effort to make it popular he became what was possibly the first song
plugger. Audiences hated it because they found the words quite intricate but Coburn
kept thinking 'It's a good song...I like it...and they'll have to like it too'. He sang it
relentlessly giving the chorus of the last verse at least ten times each night until his
audiences capitulated and eventually it became one of the most famous music hall songs
of all time.

By the beginning of the new century Dubliners were less than happy with the regular
bills being presented at the Empire. A very critical but extremely ill informed comment
appeared in *The Irish Playgoer* of May, 1900:

"Has anybody noticed (1) That the following artistes' songs are being
sung everywhere at present save in the Empire, Dublin; (2) That we have
not yet had the pleasure of seeing or hearing any of the said artists in the
Empire during its existence? From a host of talent I select the following
from recollection: Eugene Stratton; Vesta Tilley; Peggy Pryde; Marie
Lloyd; Dan Leno; Little Tich; George Robey etc., etc., to say nothing of
old favourite sketch combinations, such as: The Brothers Horn, Dr.
Wallop's Academy etc. Is there the slightest chance of seeing any of the
above on the Empire in the near or distant future? [The writer fails to
mention that most of these performers had appeared in The Star Of Erin
under old Dan's management – Author] There are plenty of talented
newcomers in the variety halls across the water, but, alas, they, are
seldom seen in Dublin, and when they do appear in the Empire the
sapient management, in their unswerving fidelity to the circus class of
entertainment, think that the audience get quite enough of them by
seeing them as a "last turn". This was my experience a few weeks ago
when I went to a matinee in the Empire specially to hear a rising comedian (Mr. Mark Milton), whose songs: 'I'll pay you when my ship
comes home' and 'Have A Game', have become so popular, but he was
generously allowed to sing one song, and was then extinguished by the
curtain, regardless of the wishes of the audience. I think that if it is at any
time necessary to curtail the performance the management should do so
at the expense of a dog trainer, handbalancer, juggler, or some such
entertainer, instead of at the expense of an actor-singer whose "show" is
necessarily of a far higher and more entertaining nature. I recently
visited the Empire to see Chirgwin, he being the star turn, and I,
naturally, looked for his appearance at latest, immediately after the
interval. But no! It was close to ten o'clock before he came on to a house
worn out by hope deferred, and the heat attendant on a packed theatre.
Why cannot the Empire gentlemen make it a rule for the "star" to appear
immediately after the interval? It was the system adopted by the late Mr.
Dan Lowrey, and it worked admirably."

In the following issue of the magazine the onslaught on the Empire continued:

> "The only first-class artists we have ever had at the Empire were: R.G. Knowles, G.H. Chirgwin and T.E. Dunville. It is all very well to have the "circus form of entertainment" on all the time at such halls as the Alhambra, or the Empire, London, where they make a speciality of such turns, but what we want here is variety, and we have not been getting it. I would respectfully suggest that our principal "hall" be re-named "The Empire Theatre of Monotonies" – it would be more appropriate."

The Playgoer campaign seems to have had some effect or it may be that the Moss Circuit took an interest at that time because the Empire Palace began to engage top-ranking performers like Florrie Forde ('Has Anybody Here Seen Kelly'), who was an Australian and who's true name was Flanagan; Vesta Victoria ('Waiting At The Church') who had been given her first professional engagement at the age of five in 1882 billed as "Baby Victoria" by old Dan Lowrey in his Star Of Erin; Harry Lauder, who was paid £20 per week at the Empire, but the canny Scot held out for £40 on his next visit to Dublin at the rival Tivoli music hall; G.H. Elliot – The Chocolate Coloured Coon who was always a firm favourite in Dublin where he continued to perform his amazingly nimble soft shoe dance well into the 1950's; Ella Shields, a Philadelphian who was a bit of an intellectual – and it showed – was renowned for her interpretation of "Burlington Bertie From Bow' performed in tattered male evening dress. Surviving recordings and other performers have given the impression that this is merely an amusing catchy tramp routine. When Ella Shields sang it she gave it a tragic near harrowing interpretation, because the song is in fact, a commentary on the final descent into abject poverty...and possible schizophrenia, of an earlier Burlington Bertie as sung by Vesta Tilley, who wouldn't be seen dead in Bow as he was a masher, a toff or to use an outdated term of the period, a knut. A man who'd "fight and die like an Englishman". These are two different songs about the same character, which were performed by two different artists, although Ella Shield's "Bertie" is the one that passed into legend.

Comedians then were almost invariably singers of comic songs although it is claimed that Charlie Chaplin and W.C. Fields, with his comedy juggling act, appeared at the Empire Palace. The incomparable Gus Elen gave portraits in song, in a genuine Dickensian Samuel Weller accent, of the East End and Covent Garden and their fascinating characters. He could be a sarcastic, leg puller too with songs like 'If It Wasn't For the 'ouses In Between'. Albert Chevalier was an actor who played the role of a Cockney and was very successful with a song which echoed social conditions of the time; this was 'My Old Dutch' which tells the story of an old couple who are separated forever at the gates of the workhouse. It was heart rending in its time but today it is nauseous and cloying. On the other hand George Bastow's 'Captain Gingah' was a portrait of the silly ass army officer type.

Harry Champion was a Cockney who sang comedy songs with tremendous energy and clarity at breakneck speed which would have rendered them unintelligible by any other performer. George Formby Senior would deliberately delay his entrance in order to create an atmosphere before he appeared. Between introductions played by the band he could be heard to shout plaintively off-stage – "I'll be ready in a minute". Then he would come on dressed in a bizarre outfit which was said to have inspired Chaplin's costume for his little tramp, and sing a song conveying to the disbelief of his audience that 'I'm One Of The Boys' and between hacking coughs that he was the Wigan nightingale.

*TWO BERTIES — "Burlington Bertie" (Sung by Miss Vesta Tilley) and
"Burlington Bertie from Bow" (Sung by Miss Ella Shields)*

Bob Konyot, another performer said of Harry Champion "He couldn't sing, he couldn't dance, he looked like a cabbie and danced like Donald Duck...he couldn't do anything, but he had the audience in the palm of his hand and when he sang 'Boiled Beef and Carrots' or 'Any old Iron' they loved every minute of his act. He didn't do anything but he was one of the greatest performers I have ever seen". And there lay the secret, those words "I've ever seen". The great music hall performers had presence and charisma, an indefinable quality without which scores of hopeful acts stayed at the bottom of the bill. They established a rapport with their audiences which is why most of their old gramophone recordings are pale reproductions of the real performance; some are preserved on grainy old film stock and are dismal disappointments. Their acts had the sort of technique and polish that could be obtained only after years of performance, improving it, tightening it up, and assuming suitable visual action and facial expressions to accompany every line. Gus Elen had a notebook which contained a reminder to himself of every move and expression appropriate to the words of all his songs.

In April, 1950 Don Ross presented his show, *Thanks For The Memory* at the Olympia Theatre (formerly the Empire) with a cast of old-timers making their farewell appearances – Randolph Sutton; Talbot O'Farrell (once described as an absurdity singing 'Mother Machree' and 'When Irish Eyes Are Smiling', to enrapture English audiences, despite his name not being O'Farrell, and his birthplace being far from the Emerald Isle); Ella Shields; Gertie Gitana; Billy Danvers and G.H. Elliott. The wonderfully eccentric Nellie Wallace who had been part of the company, died, unfortunately before the show reached Dublin. The house was completely booked out, but the lucky ones were those who had to settle for a seat in the 'gods' where the seating consisted of long and hard wooden tiers of stair-like construction where the feet of the person seated behind dug into one's back. Yet, this high vantage point under the theatre roof had an other-worldly atmosphere likely to be remembered long after. The gods were resorted to by an older generation of theatregoers who had not forgotten the old performers on the stage that night, and the atmosphere was such as must have prevailed in the far off days of old Dan Lowrey himself. The place was really alive in a delightful unison of communal enjoyment. They joined in the chorus of 'Nellie Dean' with Gertie Gitana and 'On Mother Kelly's Doorstep' with Randolph Sutton. Shouts of encouragement greeted G.H. Elliot when he sang 'Lily of Laguna' and performed a strenuous soft-shoe dance with great aplomb, and one youngster who received a vicious dig in the ribs from a large and robust descendant of Molly Malone was asked excitedly "Jasus, isn't it wonderful son, doesn't it take you back?". This was very probably the last memory of a genuine night at a music hall in Dublin. When Randolph Sutton ended his act, he returned after a brief interval to acknowledge the applause, not as it is done nowadays with a jerky wave, but with a graceful bow holding his top hat at his side – a beautiful gesture that spoke volumes – "Your humble servant!"

Madge Clifton, described as the very personification of a Principal Boy, appeared in the Empire's first pantomime *Cinderella*, in 1915, which ran for six weeks under the management of Barney Armstrong. In 1917 the management turned its attention to the legitimate theatre and presented the first play at the theatre, '*Oh, Lawsey Me*' by Thomas King Moylan, and it was the forerunner of many serious productions. Walter McNally, who was to sing with the Irish prima donna, Margaret Burke Sheridan in Italy, presented the McNally Grand Opera Company in 1919, and in the same year Harry Kildare staged his own show *Top O' The Morning*! Harry Kildare reverted to his true name, Harry

Exterior of the Olympia Theatre with the older name Empire Palace visible on the facade

O'Donovan in the 1920s and formed a partnership with Jimmy O'Dea as script writer for their many revues and films. John MacDonagh featured Jimmy O'Dea in his play *The Irish Jew* at the Empire in 1921 and it was so successful that it was revived many times. MacDonagh recognised O'Dea's potential as a comedy actor who had turned his attention to revue, which was unknown to Irish audiences at that time. O'Dea established his professional reputation in these shows when the Empire was renamed the Olympia. The new proprietors, Bob Morrison and Issac Bradshaw, decided upon a broad policy of presenting plays, opera, ballet, variety and pantomime although variety shows took precedence, and when the O'Dea/O'Donovan company was formed in 1927 they were the backbone of the repertoire until in 1937 they transferred their shows to the Gaiety on the invitation of the impresario Louis Elliman.

Cross channel acts continued to appear regularly at the Olympia until the outbreak of war and acts of the calibre of Flanagan & Allen delighted Dublin audiences. The last pre-war pantomime in 1939/40 was *Cinderella* with an English cast which starred Jerry Verno, and Noel Purcell, who had left the O'D company, was one of the Ugly Sisters. In the New Year, Bob Morrison appointed Lorcan Bourke as resident stage director. Lorcan had for many years been lessee and manager of the Queen's until it was taken over by the Elliman family in 1936. He was a well respected man, but some of the stories about him rival the alleged utterances of Samuel Goldwyn. Lorcan had a very broad and distinctive Dublin accent, and when in August 1943 he embarked on a production of *Arrah-na-Pogue* he warned his cast of Shakespearean actors from Edwards/ MacLíammóir's Gate Theatre company that "Der was goin' ta be no Dubbelin accents in dis production". He referred to *One Flew Over The Cuckoo's Nest* as *The Hen flew Over The Chicken Coop*. He also had a mania for movement on the stage, especially in pantomime. So far as he was concerned, everybody standing on his stage should be seen to be engaged in some activity, and from his vantage point in the stalls, taking the final dress rehearsal of a panto, he scrutinised the entire cast in the opening village green scene. He urged them on to even more frenzied enthusiasm when out of the corner of his eye he noticed that the drummer in the pit was sitting with his arms folded. He approached the man furiously, "Why the hell aren't you playing the drums?" The man replied triumphantly, "I'm tacet". "Well play the fuckin' thing" commanded the musical innovator.

With few exceptions most of the wartime shows at the Olympia were straightforward variety. The play *Damaged Goods* achieved some notoriety and a production of *The Strings Are False* broke all existing records at the theatre, and caused Bob Morrison to admit that with such a show he did not have to depend upon the bar receipts in order to make a profit. Incidentally, there was a theory at the Olympia that if drink was seen to be displayed on the stage, or someone had a drink during the course of a show, it invariably resulted in higher bar receipts from patrons who had been subtly and unconsciously tempted to whet their whistles.

During the war years, apart from the occasional plays like *Marrowbone Lane* (a drama in the O'Casey mould by Dr. Robert Collis) Lorcan's elder brother, Seamus de Burca, wrote a musical comedy, *After The Ball* and adapted Kickham's *Knocknagow* for stage production. Ronald MacDonald Douglas also appeared in *The Father* by Strindberg. There were also a few seasons of Grand Opera, but the theatre was kept open due to the efforts of touring companies which in normal times would have been forced to exist in the Irish fit-ups. Lorcan Bourke and Louis Elliman also made determined efforts to foster the talent of outstanding people then performing with amateur groups in the city.

Cecil Sheridan as Dame in "Jack & the Beanstalk" (with Judy Kemp as Principal Boy)

Stalwarts who kept the theatre alive included: Jack Cruise, Cecil Sheridan & Co; Frank O'Donovan & Co; Harry Bailey & Co; Percy Holmshaw & Co; and Edgar Benyon – The Great Bamboozalem; Most of these companies became well-known in Britain after the war and usually started their tours at the greatly-missed Metropolitan in the Edgware Road.

The Olympia Theatre was a happy house; Cecil Sheridan said of it:

> "It was a marvellous place. The audiences there were great, you could get your arms around them because the auditorium was shaped like a horse shoe. The top seats were great, once you got the top gallery with you, they were the ones that made you".

Stanley Illsley and Leo McCabe, who had formed a partnership in Cork in 1938 took over the Olympia in 1953 and announced their policy of presenting world theatre which they did until the early 1960s. Early on in their tenure they continued to present first class cross channel variety acts like – Arthur Askey, Donald Peers, Charlie Kunz, Tessie O'Shea, Ronald Frankau, Turner Layton, Evelyn Laye, Anne Shelton, Frankie Howerd, a 16-year old Shirley Bassey, an even younger Julie Andrews and her family, and Laurel and Hardy etc; but gradually they introduced ballet companies, Spanish dance companies, and straight dramas starring players of the calibre of John Gielgud; Paul Scofield; Tyrone Power (in *The Devil's Disciple*); Emlyn Williams as Dickens; Peter O'Toole; Peggy Ashcroft; Sybil Thorndike; Ruth Draper; Beatrice Lille; Alfred Lunt and Lynn Fontanne; Gladys Cooper; Vanessa Redgrave. Noel Coward was a frequent visitor supervising a pre London tryout of his latest play. But the Olympia was feeling the effects of a world wide rejection of live theatre due mainly to the advent of TV. In 1964 Brendan Smith (Director of the Dublin Theatre Festival), Jack Cruise (who was by now an impresario in his own right), Lorcan Bourke and Richard Hallinan were the new directors when they risked their own savings to take a lease on the theatre from the new owners, a London based syndicate which planned to turn the theatre into a ballroom. Were it not for the faith of these four Irishmen there would be no Olympia standing today.

"The Star Of Erin" and "Dan Lowrey's Palace of Varieties" had disappeared forever so it would be logical to follow the purpose of this book and end the story at this point because the Olympia still stands on the site. Still, it is worthwhile to tell the story of how the Olympia itself escaped, and but for the efforts of the directors, variety and legitimate performers and the general public, would almost certainly have been demolished. It is a heartening story and one wishes that it could have applied to hundreds of beautiful theatres in Ireland and Britain with a particular reference to the St. James Theatre, London. On the afternoon of a day in November, 1974 the cast of *West Side Story* which was to open on that evening, returned to the theatre after a lunch break to find that disaster had struck. In a cloud of dust they found that a section above the proscenium arch which was connected with part of the ceiling (not the roof) had collapsed bringing down heavy ventilator shafts into the front stalls, and a girder from the proscenium arch collapsed into the stage boxes. There would have been certain deaths if this had happened a short time later during the opening performance. It would certainly have spelt certain death for the theatre itself whose future was to hang by a thread for months.

The four directors opened an Olympia Theatre Restoration Fund which, in the beginning received no support from the City Manager, who had the backing of a certain misguided section of the city councillors. Brendan Smith, chairman of the Olympia board, used all his powers of persuasion to convince the Corporation that the loss of what was now Dublin's largest theatre (since the demolition of the Theatre Royal) would be catastrophic, but his appeals were pointedly ignored. The greatest practical support came from performers in every theatre, radio station and television station in the city. A small theatre was hastily fitted out in the Stalls bar of the theatre where artists from every branch of the arts performed nightly in order to swell the coffers of the Restoration Fund. The Olympia bars and front and back of house staff worked tirelessly with the professionals to raise funds by organising sponsored walks and raffles. In May, 1975 Siobhan McKenna laid a wreath on the site of the former Queen's Theatre which received press coverage and drew attention to the plight of the Olympia. This simple ceremony was watched by an estimated 70% of the acting and allied professions who then embarked on the Olympia Walk. The Walk was led by Maureen Potter who said "It was the greatest collection of streetwalkers Dublin had ever seen!". Noel Purcell collected pound notes for the theatre from sympathetic bystanders as he made his Dublin saunter. At the end of the walk, people queued at the theatre box office to hand in donations. The consortium of Irish publicans in London which owned the theatre and had been refused permission in 1964 by the Corporation to demolish the old theatre, must now have looked upon the collapse of the proscenium arch as a blessing in disguise, and the best thing that ever happened, but they hadn't anticipated the popular movement to save the theatre, which nobody except Messrs. Smith, Cruise, Bourke and Hallinan had attempted in 1964. The City Manager and his Councillors changed their attitudes in response to such valiant efforts and dug into the city coffers. They also placed a preservation order on the theatre which is now safe for the foreseeable future.

The Olympia Theatre re-opened splendidly restored and redecorated at a cost of more than a quarter of a million pounds on 14th March, 1977. But for the universal goodwill it would have qualified for inclusion as "a lost theatre of Dublin", but the theatre has a way, on some occasions, of presenting a happy ending. Most theatres today carry a preservation order, so all is not lost, but there must be vigilance; ignorance, greed and disinterest has no regard for the rights of others, nostalgia, tradition or even an architectural masterpiece by Frank Matcham.

Cecil Sheridan: The Parody King
"Now to look at me you'd think I was an independent man......"

Afterword
"The Head"
A memoir of my father, Cecil Sheridan,
by Professor Noel Sheridan

The man in in the heavy lipstick, false eyelashes, ladies stockings, and high heel shoes is earnestly explaining to me how upset my mother is that I have been playing snooker instead of going to school. The man, who is my father, stammers badly.

He is a professional actor so it is difficult to gauge the true depth of his concern. I remind myself that it was himself and a three foot high friend of his who taught me to play snooker in the first place. The tiny friend is also in the room, dressed as a policeman. He nods in agreement with everything my father is saying.

'It's wrong to upset your mother' says the minature policeman in a high voice.

'This is serious' says my father, putting on a blonde wig, adjusting his bra and dress as he follows the tiny policeman out of the room.

I follow them and watch from the side of the stage as they chase each other around a table that is out of all proportion to the gigantic painting of a kitchen that hangs behind it. My father no longer stammers, he now speaks fluently and rapidly to the four thousand people who have come to see this. I can see him adjust his breathing, waiting for the wave of laughter to subside, then, before it dies, he says something which lifts the laughter in an unbroken rhythm as he turns it back to rest in the darkness until he entices it forward again.

For the next eight minutes he encourages and nurses this huge, full throated, choir of an audience to madness and anarchy. All of his intelligence and energy is devoted to this; women are abused, babies are thrown off stage, the handicapped are mocked, sex is trivialised, marriage is destroyed, important people and ideas are ridiculed. This is great. Everybody loves this. (Later, some will complain that he goes too far; but in the darkness of their desire for convocation he confesses for them and he absolves them, all in one fiercely illuminated public ritual).

I smile at him as he leaves the stage, hoping he will continue the mood of euphoria, but he is already in serious conversation with another man, also dressed as a woman, who was his dying daughter just moments ago.

'Feed with the ear! *Feed with the ear!*' he is telling the man.

The first sentence he says loudly, the second is an octave lower and quieter. He is trying to explain pitch and timing, how you must listen to catch the subsiding laughter and feed the straight line into the sound so that the comedian has the correct platform from which to launch the next line.

'I was back-feeding myself half the time. He can't hear the silences' my father complains as I follow him to the dressing room.

'What's back-feeding?' I ask him.

'When you have to repeat the straight line yourself to start the movement and....
Never mind about that. We have to.... talk'. He is now stammering again. As he changes
from women's clothes into a hearseman's claw-hammer coat he continues to give me
advice. He removes his wig and false eyelashes then he pulls a cloth cap on his head.
Finally he is dressed in the coat, the cap, a string vest, baggy trousers and a tie, but no shirt.

'You'll amount to nothing' he warns me.

I follow him from the room and down the stairs to the side of the gigantic stage. It is
terrifying and he is terrified. He clasps his hands across his stomach to stop them shaking.
The titles of the popular songs he will parody are written on the back of his hand and he
checks and rechecks them. His entire nervous system is tuning up to meet the impact of
lights and noise. The sense of communal expectation sharpens as the orchestra plays his
introduction. He shuffles forward to encounter it.

I notice that the man conducting the orchestra is beautifully dressed. He understands
scale and perspective and sight lines; he looks great from everywhere. He is Jimmy
Campbell and he is the tuning fork of this entire theatre and all the people in the
audience know that they could never reach his perfect pitch of eerie, satanic elegance.
Their consolation is that they don't have to; they have paid for him to do this for them.
He is English; he is respected. Grand. Because of him there will be a centre of order and
control; the red artificial carnation, the patent leather hair, the pencil line moustache,
guarantee it. This man is a 'pro'. To the audience, and everyone outside 'the profession',
a 'pro' is a travesty of the class system; to a 'pro' being a 'pro' *is* class. Not high or low;
simply transcendent.

The immaculate conductor smiles secretly up at my father who makes his slow walk to
the centre of the stage. Off stage these men lead very different lives, but here, as 'pros',
they work closely together to tell all the people in this huge auditorium that my mother
is a shrew who drinks the children's allowances, pawns the furniture, persecutes my
father and goes on the town with my slut of a sister, leaving twelve younger children at
home for my father to mind. Each song is introduced by an arpeggio on the piano. In the
pause, before the orchestra enters, the conductor leers up at my father; encouraging him
to ever deeper blasphemy. Nice. The entire orchestra 'feeds with the ear' through him.
He sources the rolling laughter through his shoulders and arms to my father, who
faultlessly cues into the black.

⚙

'What, in God's name, do you see in snooker?', my father wants to know. 'It's a
waster's game. Are you listening to me?'

We are back in the dressing room and my attention is disappearing into the small dots
of red greasepaint that my father has placed with a matchstick in the corners of his eyes.
He uses these to give 'life to the eye' at great distances. Close up the dual vanishing points
confuse perspective. There is no focus to seeing and I am wondering why this happens.

'I'm telling you now. Look at me. If you upset your mother again, I'll fuckin' kill you.'

I stare at him in amazement. Not because he is going to kill me, but because he is using 'bad language'. 'Bad language' has never been in our house. My father is a madman about this. Why is he saying it to me now? He says it again. The other actors in the room listen. My father looks at me through the language and I sense that I'm supposed to say something.

My father turns from me and back feeds the little policeman; saying the word. Right on the beat the little policeman says it. Fuck! Now everyone is saying it. They're saying it to each other, to me. It is dropped casually into the general conversation.

My father has given a new permission for me among these men. I'm supposed to be a man now on this potent sign. I know better than to say the word myself, but I know that he has upped the ante on our relationship. We must now be serious. Men!

Now he begins talking about *our* responsibility to my mother. It is clear that he is utterly dependent on my mother; it is the opposite to everything he was saying on the stage. Only she knows the truth of this man behind his language, fluent or halting; only she can mother his disastrous extended childhood. What she does is harder than focusing the latent uproar of four thousand people. He knows this well, and I am to know it.

I hear his halting speech stitch and nail the details of my new life into place. He is angry and I think of how easily he could destroy me with the power he has developed in his hands and shoulders as an upholsterer; stretching wet leather across wooden frames packed with horse hair. As a child I can remember the beautiful precision of his doing this; rapidly spitting tacks from his mouth into the stretched webbing and then tap, tapping them home with perfectly weighted, timed blows of the claw hammer. My grandfather, who was also an upholsterer, told me my father was a master craftsman. My grandfather's skills had become redundant but my father was the new generation, dealing easily with the new styles. There was little demand for the plush, Victorian pleated, button-back, velvet outrages that were grandfather's style. This thought sometimes made my grandfather sad, as changing styles were later to sadden my father.

In Ireland, at the turn of the century my grandfather was considered strange. Aloof. He had a subscription to John O' London and was always going on about Charles Darwin and how we came from monkeys. He would not pray for his wife who was dying of T.B. but kept talking about invisible germs and how his daughter should not nurse her mother or be in the same room with her because she would get these germs. Heartless. *'Imagine dividing the natural bond between mother and daughter'*. The relations whispered as the disease ran wild through the rooms. Both young women died among much prayer. My grandfather sent his remaining daughter to Sion Hill and set up house with my father who was seven years old. My grandfather retreated to his books, weekend pints of porter, singing in pubs and knowing the answers to difficult question in general knowledge to the amazement and annoyance of the inhabitants of the Clanbrassil St. public houses.

Grandfather used to get barred for not ceasing to sing or for not stopping explaining, with that sharp double intake of breath with which he marked his superiority, the vagaries of the English language. 'Cleave' means 'to split', 'to separate' and yet we say 'cleave to your wife'. 'See it's here in the dictionary'. He sometimes had to walk as far as Emmett Bridge in Harold's Cross to get served.

Without women my grandfather and his young son made a shambles of home life. Some awful thing happened that kept my father moving nervously and impatiently throughout his youth until he met Nan Doyle from Lock Street in Ringsend who agreed to marry him because, she told me later through baffled tears, he used to make her laugh.

⁘

It is twenty years on and I have come from New York in cowboy boots, flares, sideburns and hair to my shoulders to a theatre in Ayr in Scotland to talk with my father. Ayr is a seaside resort but it's winter now and outside the grey sea is smashing the memory of summer illusions to smithereens.

I come into his room and sit down beside him as he makes up. I ask him how he is and he says he's a bit depressed. I ask how the show is going and he says not great. He is the support act for an Irish tenor and a girl who had a record hit, but "maybe the mix is wrong" he tells me, "or the timing". He looks at me in the mirror.

'It's very nice of you to come backstage'. He seems dazed. 'Who are you? Do I know you?'

I tell him who I am.

'Jesus, I'm sorry. Did your mother tell you... I'm a little depressed'. He begins to cry.

He is not a little depressed; he is clinically depressed. He is intrigued with the word for his depression: 'endogenous'. He says it many times. I find myself telling him that Joyce couldn't understand how such a beautiful word as 'glaucoma' could be destroying his eyes.

'You know while you were away they had a competition in one of the papers for the best parody of "Finnegans Wake" by James Joyce. Well, you know me and parodies. I found the book in your room and I sent one in'.

'How did you go?' I ask him.

Wrong! He'd won but my ear had missed 'I found the book in your room' and that this was a cue for us to heal old wounds. He couldn't like Stan Keaton or Lenny Bruce and at some point Joyce got bundled in with these other 'semi-pros'. Not to be talked about.

'It was very good' he back-feeds himself. 'Of course the whole thing is parody but he is great with words. "Halt on eat words" is very good for "Hilton Edwards". That's the way Hilton used to talk. Wonderful timing, MacLíammóir – but you have more time in plays. They're both gone now of course'. He begins to place the red dots in the corners of his eyes.

'I'm next, I think'.

I look at him, startled.

'I'm on' he explains. 'I'd better go down'.

I follow him down to the side of the stage. Everything of life has been drained from this occasion. Everything is hollow. Sounds are hollow as the music lags and the drab conductor keeps his eyes down, turning the sheet music mechanically. Without laughter the litany of my father's parody woes sound raw. Parody depends on a shared, known mythology, but here there is only the cold unforgiving reality of desperation, going out from him and playing itself back into the white circle of light that imprints and illuminates his isolation.

I follow him to the dressing room. I have to tell him that this is upsetting my mother; that he's got to try and get a grip on this.

'I know. I know'. He breaks down again. 'But what *is* this? What's happening to me?'

'You're going to be alright, head. Don't worry'. I tell him.

His perfect ear catches the fear and falsity of the line. What is happening to him is chemical and language disintegrates in the torpor of its sullen toil.

I bluster the line: 'Where's your fuckin' anger, man?'

We both listen as the once potent word hangs in the silence, signifying nothing. There is no centre to this and words won't hold. The red dots of vanishing points instead of bringing me close drive me back several hundred feet to look down upon us. We are one in this pool of genetic endogeny and I feel myself suddenly drawn to its source through the carmine vanishing points in his eyes. It is terrifying and as I tighten the pressure on my clasped hands I notice that I am a mirror image of himself. We seem as fictions; parodies of men.

I begin to collage bits and pieces of anecdotes he had told me about himself. Reminding him. Trying to build a structure into memory.

When Charlie Chaplin came backstage to him at the Metropolitan Edgware Road and they talked about music hall; how, on tour, he beat the Hungarian gymnast at arm wrestling and the man's wife woke him up at three in the morning asking him to let her husband win because he couldn't sleep and how he let him win because the man was the frog in the transformation scene of the panto, but also because he knew that humiliation was paralysing for a pro and that his own upholsterer's strength was not like 'a speciality act', not the very centre of a man's existence as 'a pro'. And then the time he got the gallery in The Olympia to quiet down after the English double act left them in uproar, insulting them because in answer to the innuendo in the straight line 'what can you get in Dublin for a penny?' a young women's voice rang out the perfectly pitched 'An Erinox' and how the roar of support split the two cultures and the English woman panicked and gave the crowd the finger and how he had to go out and get quiet and explain that she didn't know what an Erinox was and didn't mean anything against Dublin and how he turned it around and brought the anger off the cushion to line up the laughter to fall into the pockets and.....

This house of cards collapses and I take him home.

❦

'You know I've cured about four people since I've been here' he tells me.

We are in St. Brendan's where, to judge by the smiles and waves he gets from staff and patients, he is a clear favourite. He is torn between the anguish of his endogenous depression and his pro's desire to get traction. He is still in business.

'I visit the wards first thing in the morning and my opening line is "good morning campers". After that I do the business with the tablets pretending to mix them up and describing what will happen to each one when they get the wrong medication. I tell the one about the 70 year old couple who took the monkey gland pills and the next year they had a baby'. He looks at me.

'Was it a boy or a girl'? (I try to finish high).

'I don't know'. (Pause, low). 'They couldn't get it down off the chandelier to find out'.

I try one: 'another 70 year old couple got married recently; they spent the honeymoon getting out of the car'.

He explains in detail why this joke 'wouldn't do for Dublin'. He still has no hesitation in speaking for the entire city in these matters. And he does know something about a time in Dublin and he wrote it and sang it and showed it to itself. Now he is planning a panto for Christmas, he points out the patients he has written parts for. We talk about everything except my mother who died earlier in the year. It is too late now for either of us to speak of not upsetting her; we have both made a complete bollox of that. For him now, with her gone, the rest is mechanical, academic. Finally everything is game ball, lined up and it's just a matter of clearing the table.

A mental image of my father lines up with my other art heroes; those who were blest and marked. Real pros; hard acts to follow. And my mother – even better than that.

Noel Sheridan – April 1 1993.

Cecil Sheridan with his son Noel, Dublin, 1958

Select Bibliography

Agate, James	Immoment Toys	London, 1945
Sir Jonah, Barrington	Personal Sketches	
Bailey, Harry (Ed. O'Shea Tom)	Encore	Dublin 1990
Bennett, Douglas	Encyclopaedia of Dublin	Dublin 1991
Barker, Felix	The House That Stoll Built	London,1957
Cagney, James	Cagney by Cagney	New York, 1976
Chambers, Anne	La Sheridan, Adorable Diva	Dublin, 1989
Cronin, Anthony	No Laughing Matter	London, 1989
de Burca, Seamus	The Queen's Royal Theatre	Dublin, 1983
Delfont, Bernard, Sir	East End, West End	London 1990
East, John M.	Max Miller	London, 1977
Fitz-Simons, Christopher	The Boys	Dublin 1994
Flanagan, Bud	My Crazy Life	London,1961
Frow, Gerald	Oh, Yes It Is	London, 1985
Goodie, Shelia	Annie Horniman	London,1990
Green, Benny (ED.)	The Last Empires	London, 1986
Guinness, Alec	Blessings In Disguise	London, 1985
Joyce, James	Dubliners (Reprint)	Dublin 1992
McCann, Sean	The Story of the Abbey Theatre	London, 1967
Macqueen Pope, W.J.	Theatre Royal, Drury Lane	London, 1945
Molloy, Fitzgerald J.	Peg Woffington (2 vols.)	London, 1884
Morecambe, Gary; Sterling, Martin,	Behind the Sunshine	London, 1994
Read, Jack	Empires, Hippodromes and Palaces	London, 1985
Rix, Brian	Tour de Farce	London, 1992
Ryan, Philip B.	Jimmy O'Dea	Dublin 1990
Ryan, Philip B.	Noel Purcell	Dublin 1992
Sawyer, Paul	The New Theatre, Lincoln's Inn Fields	Society for Theatre Research, London 1979
Stein, Charles W. (ED.)	American Vaudeville	New York, 1984
Taub, Michael,	Jack Doyle — Fighting for Love	London, 1990
Wilmut, Roger	Kindly Leave the Stage	London, 1985
Williams, Bransby	An Actor's Story	London, 1909
Watters, Eugene & Murtagh, Matthew	Infinite Varieties	Dublin 1975

and Philip Chevron's original collection of theatrical memorabilia (London and New York) presented to the author in December, 1995.

Index

Numbers in bold refer to illustrations
Italic text refers to Shows and films

232

234

235

Index of Songs

Index of Theatres and Cinemas

Numbers in bold refer to illustrations